Although Kleist had little direct contact with the theatre of his day, and even claimed on occasion not to have written his plays for the current stage, it is nevertheless clear that he possessed a great sense of the theatre and did want to have his plays performed. When and where they were performed, by whom and with what success, is unfortunately not something that has been considered to any significant extent. There is a large body of scholarly writing about Kleist's plays, but it is based almost entirely on the texts as read, not on the plays as performed, even though the scholarly interest in his works reflects, in part at least, Kleist's fluctuating fortune in the theatre. Based, as far as possible, on contemporary descriptions and reviews of the most important productions of Kleist's plays from the earliest days to 1987, *Kleist on Stage, 1804–1987* provides a succinct historical account of interpretations of these plays as performed, an account that dispells any doubt about their unsuitability for public performance and provides those unable to see them performed with insights that will enhance their reading.

WILLIAM C. REEVE is a professor of German at Queen's University.

# Kleist on Stage, 1804–1987

WILLIAM C. REEVE

McGill-Queen's University Press
Montreal & Kingston • London • Buffalo

© McGill-Queen's University Press 1993
ISBN 0-7735-0941-0

Legal deposit first quarter 1993
Bibliothèque nationale du Québec

Printed in Canada on acid-free paper

This book has been published with the help of a grant
from the Canadian Federation for the Humanities,
using funds provided by the Social Sciences and
Humanities Research Council of Canada. Funding has
also been received from the School of Graduate
Studies and Research and the Faculty of Arts and
Science, Queen's University.

**Canadian Cataloguing in Publication Data**

Reeve, William C., 1943–
  Kleist on stage: 1804–1987
  Text in English and German.
  Includes bibliographical references and index.
  ISBN 0-7735-0941-0
  1. Kleist, Heinrich von, 1777–1811 – Stage history.
  2. Kleist, Heinrich von, 1777–1811 – Dramatic
  production. 3. Theater – Europe, German-speaking –
  History. I. Title.

PT2379.Z5R45 1993   792.9'5'0943   C92-090376-2

Typeset in Palatino 10/12
by Caractéra production graphique inc., Quebec City

*For my Doktorvater*
*Herbert Deinert*

# Contents

# Acknowledgments

Many people have contributed to the completion of this stage history but I am especially grateful to Mrs Margaret Boesch for her patience and suggestions, to Mrs Brigitte McConnell and Mrs Julia Steven-haagen for the typing of the final section, to Professor D.L. Basti-anutti and Professor M. Pinho for their translation of Italian reviews, to Michael Bauer for his careful proofreading, to Herr Hartmut Rambaldo and the Schiller-Nationalmuseum/Deutsches Literaturarchiv for their efficient research services and to my wife for her never-failing support and counsel.

Others to whom I am also thankful include the German Embassy (Ottawa), Frau Bettina Walche (Volkstheater, Vienna), Professor Saul Elkin (University of Buffalo), Ms Lynne Walker (Royal Exchange Theatre, Manchester), Professor Jürgen Flimm (Thalia Theater, Hamburg), Frau Jutta Bendt (Schiller-Nationalmuseum), Frau Elisabeth Gaulhofer (Staatliche Schauspielbühnen, Berlin), Ms Karen Bell (Queen's University), Hofrat Univ. Doz. Dr Oskar Pausch (Österreichisches TheaterMuseum) and Frau Sabine Herder (Institut für Theater- Film- und Fernsehwissenschaft).

The chapter on *Die Hermannsschlacht* and the conclusion include approximately two pages from an article, "The Lion That Squeaked?: Kleist's *Hermannsschlacht* on Stage," *Seminar* 23 (1987). The author wishes to thank the editor of *Seminar* for permission to reprint these passages.

A grant awarded by the Advisory Research Committee, Division II of the School of Graduate Studies and Research, Queen's University, enabled me to collect much of the material needed to write the monograph and also defrayed the cost of preparing the manuscript.

Finally I should also like to acknowledge a grant in aid of publication generously provided by the Faculty of Arts and Science and the School of Graduate Studies and Research, Queen's University.

*Der zerbrochene Krug*. Film version, 1937. Director, Gustav Ucicky; Adam, Emil Jannings. Compliments of Deutsches Institut für Filmkunde

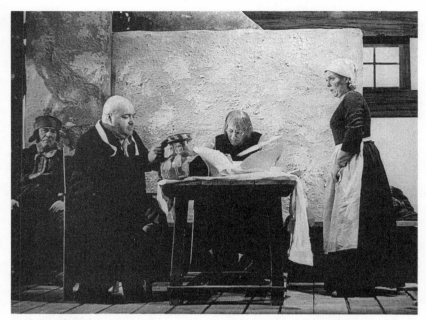

*Der zerbrochene Krug*. Volkstheater, Vienna, Austria, 10 December 1971. Director, Bernd Fischerauer; Adam, Helmut Qualtinger; Licht, Walter Langer; Veit Tumpel, Oskar Wegrostek; Frau Marthe Rull, Hilde Sochor. Compliments of Volkstheater, Vienna

*Das Käthchen von Heilbronn*. Schauspiel Köln, 6 October 1979. Director, Jürgen Flimm;
Käthchen, Katharina Thalbach. Compliments of Professor Jürgen Flimm

*The Fall of the Amazons*. The Center for Theater Research, Buffalo, NY, 26 April 1979. Director, Saul Elkin; Penthesilea, Lorna Hill; Achilles, David Lamb. Compliments of Irene Haupt and Saul Elkin

*The Prince of Homburg*. the Royal Exchange Theatre, Manchester, England, 16 September 1976. Director, Caspar Wrede; The Elector, James Maxwell; Princess Natalie, Judy Bowker. Compliments of Brian Linney and the Royal Exchange Theatre Company

*Amphitryon*. Das Schauspielhaus, Cologne, March 1982. Director, Jürgen Flimm. Finale.
Compliments of Theatermuseum der Universität zu Köln

*Der zerbrochene Krug.* Schlosspark-Theater, Berlin, 23 January 1980. Director, Hans Lietzau; Adam, Helmut Wildt; Walter, Bernhard Minetti. Compliments of Frau Ilse Buhs

"Kleists Traum vom Prinzen von Homburg," Schaubühne am Halleschen Ufer, Berlin, 4 November 1972. Director, Peter Stein; Forefront: Kottwitz, Otto Sander; Homburg, Bruno Ganz; Hohenzollern, Werner Rehm. Background: Electress, Katharina Tüschen; Elector, Peter Lühr; Natalie, Jutta Lampe. Compliments of Frau Ilse Buhs

*Das Käthchen von Heilbronn*. Staatsschauspiel, Stuttgart, November 1975. Director, Claus Peymann; Kunigunde, Kirsten Dene; Wetter vom Strahl, Martin Lüttge. Compliments of Frau Abisag Tüllman

*Die Familie Schroffenstein*. Schauspielhaus, Frankfurt a.M., April 1985. Director, Hans-Dieter Jendreyko. Compliments of Frau Abisag Tüllmann

*Die Hermannsschlacht*. Schauspiel Bochum, November 1982. Director, Claus Peymann. Compliments of Frau Abisag Tüllman

*Kleist on Stage, 1804–1987*

# Introduction

Having sought to promote in my students an appreciation of and love for the plays of Heinrich von Kleist, I have found myself guilty of ignoring the fact that he wrote his dramas primarily with an aim to having them performed on a stage. Even though he declared in a letter to Goethe, "[*Penthesilea*] ist übrigens ebensowenig für die Bühne geschrieben, als jenes frühere Drama: der Zerbrochene Krug," he nevertheless adopted an obsequious tone in his efforts to have his comedy put before the public: "und ich kann es nur Ew. Exzellenz gutem Willen zuschreiben, mich aufzumuntern, wenn dies letztere gleichwohl in Weimar gegeben wird."[1] Of course, a dramatist realizes that his/her plays will in all likelihood be read more than staged, but reading can never do full justice to that one dimension that sets the dramatic apart from the lyric or the epic – a *visual* reenactment which the German language in its inimitable transparency has captured in the word *Schau-spiel*. Although Kleist had no direct rapport with the theatrical currents of his age, he still possessed a remarkable, inherent sense of the stage. Take, for example, the optical impact of the first scene in *Prinz Friedrich von Homburg*: the visible tension between high and low, light and darkness, group and individual, waking and sleeping, or giving and taking, and the underlying implications of these contrasts, surely one of the most dramatically effective expository sequences the German theatre has to offer.

When I attempted in 1980 to fill in the quite substantial gaps in my knowledge of Kleist's plays on stage, I soon made two surprising discoveries: the lack of a comprehensive reference work in German, let alone in English, outlining the history of Kleist's dramas and the failure to recognize the role the theatre has played in his acceptance as one of the greatest German dramatists, and in the growing respect for his writing amongst academics. Responsible for this development have been directors, actors, and even set-designers. Posterity owes a substantial debt of gratitude in particular to the Meininger whose spectacles, especially their staging of *Das Käthchen von Heilbronn*, helped to keep Kleist's name alive during the nineteenth century. Jean Vilar's now celebrated 1951 production of *Le Prince de Hombourg* at the Festival d'Avignon contributed significantly to a renaissance in Kleist research after the Second World War and, more recently, Claus Peymann's 1982 Bochum version of *Die Hermannsschlacht* has gone a long way towards reintegrating this controversial play into "das dichterische Werk Kleists."[2] In Hans Neuenfels's *Penthesilea* staging (Berlin, 1981), the actress Katharina Thalbach, with her street-wise portrayal of Prothoe, gave a new dimension to our understanding of this most insightful of Kleist's confidants, while subtle differentiations in tone and gesture by actors playing Walter or Licht have added to our appreciation of *Der zerbrochene Krug*.

Before proceeding any further, I believe it only fair to warn the reader of my own limitations and prejudices as I perceive them. Since I have been trained primarily as a *Germanist*, I cannot lay claim to being a drama historian, and therefore I have endeavoured to write a predominantly *descriptive* account that will serve to increase colleagues' and students' awareness of that equally valid world of live performance beyond the walls of the ivory tower. I have always sought to let the reviewers and the productions speak for themselves, but inevitably my own biases come to the surface and thus should be disclosed in advance. In my judgment, the director has complete freedom with the play, provided that he/she generally respects the text. Kleist himself, in a letter to Heinrich von Collin, recognized the need to delete some lines: "Das Käthchen von Heilbronn, das, wie ich selbst einsehe, notwendig verkürzt werden muß, konnte unter keine Hände fallen, denen ich dies Geschäft lieber anvertraute, als den Ihrigen" (2: 818). However, directors should avoid gimmicks for the mere sake of gimmicks and have faith in Kleist's challenging but beautiful verse and in his talent as a writer for the theatre. His dramas have proven to be eminently stageworthy with the possible exception of *Penthesilea*. If one bears in mind its long, undramatic narratives, its success when performed or recited by a single actress, director G.F. Hering may well be correct in his assertion: "Die gültige Aufführung der *Penthesilea* spielt auf der Bühne unserer Phantasie."[3] Having dealt with Kleist now for more than twenty years in the classroom and in the confines of my own "Phantasie," I have developed some very strongly and dearly held notions about his plays, and for this reason no staging could live up to my ideal expectations.

I have made extensive use of several dissertations written between 1920 and 1932 as a convenient major source for this early period, especially for the nineteenth century. These theses, such as Kurt Lowien's "Die Bühnengeschichte von Kleists *Penthesilea*" (1923), Egon-Erich Albrecht's "Heinrich von Kleists *Prinz Friedrich von Homburg* auf der deutschen Bühne" (1921), or H. Ziegelski's "Kleist im Spiegel der Theater-Kritik des 19. Jahrhunderts bis zu den Aufführungen der Meininger" (1932), and W. Kühn's book, *Kleist und das deutsche Theater* (1912), deal extensively with the various adaptations of Kleist's texts, such as the Holbein versions, and the extent to which they differed from the original i.e., from the "Erstdruck" or from the "Buchausgabe." These studies contain useful descriptions of the productions themselves, quote reviews at great length, and thus give some indication of the director's reading, the quality of the acting, and the reception of the performance by the audience. For stagings since 1945, I am grateful to the Schiller-Nationalmuseum/Deutsches Literaturarchiv, Marbach a.N., for having supplied me with a very extensive collection of theatrical reviews, a collection which, of course, concentrates on the German-speaking countries but does include some items from elsewhere. My own university library's microfilms of the *New York Times* and *The Times* of London have been another valuable source, as have numerous articles and chapters that have appeared in journals and books. The *Kleist-Jahrbuch* has on occasion contained a theatre-oriented article; however, the clash between the academic critic and the theatre director becomes particularly obvious in this forum.

Since I have had the pleasure of seeing only two Kleist productions, I relied almost exclusively and indiscriminately upon the evaluations of the professional newspaper critics or local reviewers and what has emerged might be more appropriately described as a history of stage reviews. (I have also included critical responses to radio, television and recorded performances.) Because of this limitation, several problems have arisen, the most conspicuous being contradictory notices. One commentator may claim in his/her assessment of a *Prinz Friedrich von Homburg* staging, "Eine Sprechtechnik von so außerordentlicher Klarheit und Nuanciertheit, wie man das in Deutschland seit Jahrzehnten nicht mehr erlebt hat,"[4] while another, describing the very same production, may declare, "Kaum war, der schlechten Artikulation wegen, dem Gesprochenen zu folgen, der Sinn flog am Gehör vorüber, von Schönheit ... keine Rede."[5] How does one account for such a wide divergence of views? Because Kleist has become a "classic" of the stage, people, myself included, tend to have very strong opinions as to how his dramas should be presented, opinions that can easily lead to inflexibility. One of the most common criticisms levelled at almost every controversial interpretation has been the director's failure to honour the author's intent, a claim that in one instance resulted in a court case: a patron demanded a refund on the grounds that what had been billed as a play by Kleist was in fact an adaptation loosely based on a play by Kleist.[6] Who can really determine the aim of a playwright as notoriously difficult and ambiguous as Kleist? To the best of my knowledge, he never explicitly outlined his intent[7] in writing a particular work. Moreover, an author does not always necessarily achieve his/her avowed goal[8] and may indeed turn out to be the worst possible interpreter of his/her own creation. Two other elements further complicate the issue – the actors and the audience. Most theatre critics attend and evaluate the *première*, and it is a well-known fact that "opening-night jitters" can adversely affect a production which may, however, run more smoothly once the players have overcome their initial fears and can relax more in their respective parts. Audiences can also differ from night to night, from supportive or indifferent to hostile, and since actors play to an audience, an unsympathetic one can have a negative influence upon a performance. As a final problem, one can easily discern an annoying tendency on the part of some critics to attempt to impress their readers with their erudition by indulging in theoretical or philosophical digressions that have little or nothing to do with the performance they are supposed to review. The prospective theatre-goer would have some difficulty in extracting from such reviews sufficient descriptive information on which to base the decision to pay the price of admission.

I apologize in advance to anyone whose production has been omitted, but in my defence I would simply plead that it would be impossible to cover every staging without writing a history in several volumes. For example, *Der zerbrochene Krug* was the most popular play on German-speaking stages during the 1977/78 theatrical season with a total of seventeen different productions and 408 performances. My procedure has been to concentrate on the critical reactions to those major productions that attracted more than usual press coverage up to and including the year 1987. In a few instances I have described less important interpretations such as an Indian or a Canadian adaptation of *Der zerbrochene Krug* in the local tongue. Such translations bear important witness to Kleist's increasing reputation outside Germany, Austria, and Switzerland.

As a final note I should point out that I have chosen to exclude *Robert Guiskard* from this discussion. This fragment, consisting of only ten scenes, has rarely been staged and then only as an appendix or prologue to some other work. Despite its dramatic excellence, it is simply too short to fill a whole evening and yet, to judge from a recent tandem production in Bochum's Schauspielhaus, *Robert Guiskard* still commands sufficient interest and relevance to warrant performance:

"Preußische Gesänge": Das Bochumer Ensemble veranstaltet zum 8. Mai [1985] mehr als nur die obligatorische Lesung; es bringt eine eigene Inszenierung heraus. Der Titel vereinigt Kleists fast nie gespieltes "Guiskard"-Fragment und Heiner Müllers Text "Russische Eröffnung." Es entsteht – in der Regie Alfred Kirchners ... – ein Theaterabend, der in faszinierender Weise teil hat an der Diskussion um diesen Jahrestag.[9]

## CHAPTER ONE

# Die Familie Schroffenstein

*Die Familie Schroffenstein*, published anonymously in 1803 by Heinrich Geßner in Switzerland, ironically achieved more acclaim in the author's lifetime from critics, including Jean Paul, Ludwig Uhland, and Ludwig Tieck, than any of Kleist's later masterpieces. Having refused to put his name to his first play, Kleist referred to it as "eine elende Scharteke"[1] and never made any attempt to have it produced. Despite this repudiation and lack of interest on his part, a distorted version of the drama was *premièred* in the Nationaltheater in Graz on 9 January 1804 in a staging about which there appears to be little information and which took place without the permission or even the knowledge of its author. This inauspicious first performance won the support of the local press, for on 14 January the *Grätzer Zeitung* reported: "In Shakespeares hohem Kothurn [laced half-boot worn by Greek and Roman tragic actors] tritt mit diesem Werke ein neuer Dichter Deutschlands aus der Dunkelheit hervor." *Die Familie Schroffenstein* then lapsed into total oblivion, until editor Ludwig Tieck issued a challenge in his preface to Kleist's *Gesammelte Schriften*: "Bei der jetzigen Armut unserer Bühne wäre es ein verdienstliches Werk, wenn ein Dichter, der das Theater kennt, dieses Schauspiel für die Aufführung bearbeiten wollte. Leicht ist diese Arbeit gewiß nicht, aber einer geschickten Hand doch nicht unmöglich."[2] Encouraged by his tremendous success with an adaptation of *Das Käthchen von Heilbronn*, Franz Ignaz Holbein, the later director of both the Hamburg Hoftheater and the Vienna Burgtheater, accepted Tieck's invitation, and by his transformation of Kleist's tragedy into a popular knightly play he at least rendered it stageworthy for an era which had considered it totally unperformable.

Holbein, freely conceding his primary concern with box-office receipts, laid no claim to any merit as a writer, and in the preface to his adaptation he wrote: "Sehr bescheiden ist der Platz, den ich in der Reihe der dramatischen Dichter mir selbst anweise. Aber was sich für die Darstellung eignet, was Effekt macht, auf das große Publikum wirkt, das weiß ich gründlich sicher und nur selten werde ich darin irre."[3] When he later boasted that the conclusion of the fourth act and almost half of the adaptation both in structure and in language were of his creation, and that he contributed more to the success of the play than Kleist, his humility had obviously succumbed to his vanity. He further exposed his total disregard for the author's intent by changing the title to *Die Waffenbrüder, Gemälde der Vorzeit in 5 Abteilungen*. Holbein kept to Kleist's plot for the first four acts, cutting and revising any lines that might arouse the ire of the censor or offend public taste. To this end, the warring cousins of the original became mere feuding comrades in arms, the illegitimate Johann a noble servant, and the severed finger a blond lock of hair. He deleted Johann's description of his rescue at the hands of the bathing Agnes and completely destroyed the final love scene. Indeed, he even went as far as to rewrite the whole of the last act in the tradition of the knightly drama in order to ensure a positive reception. The family feud now concluded with a conciliatory marriage, a serious misrepresentation which both contradicted the tone of the rest of the work and ignored Kleist's tragic view of life. As one critic remarked: "Das ganze verfehlte nicht nur den beabsichtigten Effekt, sondern gleicht vor allem nur mehr einem schönen Torso ohne Kopf."[4]

The inappropriateness of Holbein's optimistic finale manifested itself in the public's reaction to the adaptation at its official *première* on 29 October 1822 in Leipzig's Stadttheater. This production made use of an earlier Holbein version in which he preserved the family relationship of the original and made few changes in acts one to four. The manager of this theatre, Küstner, recorded that the first four acts enjoyed a positive response; however, the happy ending not only served to weaken this positive impression, but was largely responsible for the audience's rejection of the staging. "Durch eine neue gelungene Bearbeitung des 5. Aktes mit einem tragischen Ausgang, welchen die Anlage des Stückes erfordert," Küstner observed, "würde das Repertoire einen bedeutenden Gewinn machen."[5] Although Küstner was committed to the classical acting style of the Weimar stage, he still strove to avoid excessive declamation and empty gestures, while insisting upon good ensemble acting. Hence the limited recognition this production received could be largely attributed to the unified, well-integrated efforts of the whole cast, coupled with the excellent individual performance of Eduard Stein as Ottokar.

Between the years 1814 and 1832, Vienna's Königliches Hofburgtheater was turned into the leading German-speaking theatre by its director-manager Joseph Schreyvogel who, committed to the Weimar approach, endeavoured to create an harmonious cooperation between the style of an author and the demands of the stage. Since Kleist's *Familie Schroffenstein*, with its more realistic tone, ran counter to the ideal form of classical beauty, it is not surprising that Schreyvogel opted to produce Holbein's *Die Waffenbrüder*, the romanticized perversion of Kleist's work, calculated to appeal to public taste. The *première* took place on 13 September 1823. The popular success of this staging (thirty-two repeat performances), second only to that achieved by *Das Käthchen von Heilbronn*, may be ascribed in part to the participation of the most outstanding cast possible for the period.[6] There were, however, two weak links. Just as Nicolaus Heurteur proved incapable of revealing the depths of Sylvester's character, so Maximilian Korn, noted for light, unassuming parts such as the *bon vivant*, failed to convey the heroic, problematic nature of a seventeen-year old youth. Heinrich Anschütz, owing allegiance to both the realistic Hamburg and the idealistic Weimar schools, gave a strong psychological portrait of Rupert, which tended to downplay the sheer villainy assigned to this role by Holbein. But above all, the Hofburg theatre could boast of two exceptional actresses, Sophie Müller and the celebrated Sophie Schröder. Whereas Tieck felt that the latter had become too exaggerated and affected, Holbein maintained that "die große Schröder die letzte Szene des 4. Aktes zu einem ihrer größten Triumphe [erhob]" and further declared: "[Eine] Schröder kann wohl viel, sehr viel für den Dichter tun."[7] The critics lavished praise on Sophie Müller's ability to bring across to the audience the childlike innocence, charm, and sweetness of Agnes: "Das Ganze war mit dem entschiedensten Beifall aufgenommen und seitdem schon einige Male bei gedrängt vollem Haus wiederholt" (*Der Sammler*, 2 October 1823).

This Viennese triumph encouraged others to produce Kleist's drama in one of Holbein's adaptations, specifically in Braunschweig (4 November 1824), Hannover (21 September 1828) (where the actor playing Ottokar was wildly applauded since, by jumping from the tower, he crushed his arm and leg), and most significantly in Berlin's Königliche Schauspiele on 18 August 1824. This last staging, which saw three performances in a combination of the Iffland and Weimar theatrical styles, deserves some consideration because of the distinguished interpretations by Friedrich Wilhelm Lemm of Rupert and Luise von Holtei of Agnes. Renowned for his ability to penetrate to the essence of each part, Lemm evidently overwhelmed his audience. The same could be said of Holtei, one of the leading actresses of her age: "In der Darstellung naiver und sentimentaler Rollen suchte Frau von Holtei vergeblich ihresgleichen. Sie war die unvergeßliche Darstellerin des Käthchens."[8]

The next significant production directed by Friedrich Ludwig Schmidt took place in Hamburg's Stadttheater on 2 August 1836. At the beginning of the nineteenth century, Hamburg had come to be recognized as the uncontested seat of a new theatrical outlook developed under Friedrich Ludwig Schröder and continued by his successor Friedrich Schmidt, the co-director of the Hamburg Nationaltheater. This new approach, which must be seen in contrast to that practised in Weimar, required a stage language devoid of rhetoric and pathos and a more realistic mode of performance; it strove for great precision, agility, ensemble acting, and a discriminating use of gesture. The key word was "naturalness." Although Schmidt availed himself of the Holbein version, he did so with greater respect for the original and used the Hamburg style, which clearly accommodated *Die Familie Schroffenstein* more readily than the idealizing Weimar manner. The main drawback seems to have been an almost total lack of cooperation, as each participant performed his or her part without any regard to the overall effect. In fact, the whole staging, offered in the framework of a guest performance by Sophie Schröder as Eustache, tended to glorify the actress rather than the play. In assessing her achievement, one critic praised "jene Wahrheit und Naturtreue auch in den heftigsten Gemütsaufregungen."[9] Theodor Döring, *the* Adam interpreter of the nineteenth century, also celebrated one of his greatest triumphs in Hamburg in a portrayal of Sylvester which reportedly went beyond the mere mould of the heroic father to Kleist's tragic seeker after truth, while Christine Enghaus, later to become Friedrich Hebbel's wife and a distinguished tragic heroine, provided an emotional rendering of Agnes which supported and complemented Schröder's Eustache. Whereas these individual efforts were fully rewarded at the conclusion of the evening, the audience showed little sympathy for the production itself. "[Ich] hatte die Wirkung dieses Dramas immer bezweifelt," remarked Schmidt, "und es deshalb nie zu geben gewagt. Der Erfolg bestätigte meine Aussicht. Die Schroffensteiner sprachen nicht an, mit dem abgeschnittenen Finger würden sie ohne Frage gänzlich gefallen sein. Wir konnten die Aufführung nur einmal wiederholen und das geschah vor leerem Haus."[10]

The first person who attempted to recover Kleist's tragedy from Holbein's distortion was Karl Immermann. Although he sought in his version to increase the theatrical effects and to reduce the play to a more concise form, he unfortunately failed to appreciate Kleist's text, an oversight underlined by his numerous cuts, which did serious damage to psychological motivation, especially in the case of Rupert. Other deletions, several out of deference to censorship, included the role of Sylvius, the prison scene, and some of the most moving aspects of the love interludes. In the last act he eliminated the exchange of clothing and the intrusion of Johann and Sylvius in the dénouement, and he closed the play with a universally applicable moral statement spoken by Sylvester; otherwise, he respected the original, a real advance on Holbein's concocted optimistic conclusion. Immermann first tried out his adaptation in his own production for Düsseldorf on 12 February 1837. Despite the laudable aim of uniting the best features of both the Hamburg and Weimar stage traditions and the inspired performance of Wilhelm Salomon Reger, who played Rupert almost exclusively from the point of view of the intriguer, the experiment turned out to be a complete failure and was not repeated.

Eager to provide one of his leading actresses, Auguste Crelinger-Stich, with a tragic mother role, Karl Theodor von Küstner, the general director of Berlin's Königliches Schauspielhaus, procured Immermann's version, altered it slightly, and gave it to his leading director Stawinsky, an outspoken adherent of artistic realism, to put on stage. The casting, with a few exceptions, was well done: "Herr [Moritz] Rott hat mit dem Grafen Rupert eine verhängnisvolle Aufgabe, denn es bedarf der Nachforschung, um an dieser Gestalt noch etwas Menschliches zu entdecken. Herr Rott hütete sich aber glücklich vor zu starker Schwärzung, unbeschadet der dämonischen Gestalt."[11] While Karl Franz apparently delivered a consistent interpretation of Sylvester, Crelinger-Stich never approached the passionate side of Eustache's character. The Ottokar of Joseph Wagner, a man who in stature, temperament, and voice seemed ideal as Kleist's young lover, supplied the real highlight of the performance. Despite the fact that the critics generally enthused about this production (17 March 1849) and its first-rate cast – "Was die Darstellung betrifft, so entspricht sie jeder gerechten Erwartung"[12] – it was nevertheless only a qualified success.

Heinrich Laube, the managing director and reformer of Vienna's Hofburgtheater, also tried to revise *Die Familie Schroffenstein*, but strangely enough, he kept more or less to the Holbein version in the first four acts, except for the preservation of the original love scene and the severed finger. In the last act, ignoring the dramatist's tragic design, he rewrote the plot so that it terminated with the conciliatory engagement of the two children, a rather obvious attempt to appeal to public taste for a heart-lifting, moralistic conclusion. The production, opening on 2 May 1855, spared no effort to realize every possible theatrical or rhetorical effect. Laube also took pains to find for his principals those roles which best suited their talent and hence, not surprisingly, most of the applause was accorded to the truly outstanding portrayals of Marie Seebach as Agnes, Joseph Wagner as Ottokar (according to Laube, "der erste tragische Heldenliebhaber der deutschen Bühne"),[13] the seventy-year old Anschütz in the patriarchal role of Sylvester, Karl Franz as a convincing Rupert, and Julie Rettich, whose Eustache reportedly emphasized the intellectual rather than the irrational side of her personality. In keeping with Laube's principle that the sets should never be allowed to detract from the main concern (i.e., the acting), the décor, shunning any attempt at historical accuracy, had only suggestive force. Notwithstanding the star cast, the staging saw only five performances before being withdrawn, a relative failure for which Laube's totally inadequate and inappropriate adaptation had to bear most of the blame.

The fate of *Die Familie Schroffenstein* continued to be linked to the popularity of various adaptations, such as that of Albert Dulks, which experienced only one poorly received performance in Stuttgart's Königliches Hoftheater on 8 October 1862. Gottfried Strommel, reworking the play on the basis of Tieck's advice, left the first three acts basically untouched, but wrote two new acts designed to conform not to the tone and aim of the author, but to the then prevailing taste for naturalistically oriented theatre. This version was presented on 21 January 1888 in Düsseldorf's Stadttheater – "Die Darstellung war trotz redlichsten Bemühens der Schauspieler, die offenbar ihr Bestes taten, nur von ziemlich bescheidenem künstlerischem Wert"[14] – and at the Königliche Schauspiele in Wiesbaden on 17 October 1888 with very limited results. While the local press rejected the latter staging, visiting critics proved more generous, praising the competent ensemble acting. Director Max Köchy, who also played Rupert almost exclusively as the villain, prepared the production carefully to ensure a unified approach, but Strommel's inadequate adaptation seems to have thwarted this effort. On 18 October 1916, Düsseldorf's Stadttheater again offered *Die Familie Schroffenstein* in a revised adaptation by Strommel, but it met with even less understanding and was repeated only once. In short, throughout the whole of the nineteenth century, *The Family Schroffenstein* gained recognition and some degree of success solely in the guise of Holbein's misrepresentation.

At the approach of the hundredth anniversary of Kleist's death, Eduard Tempeltey attempted to win the dramatist's youthful play for the stage as part of a proposed five-evening cycle of his works (*Amphitryon* and *Penthesilea* he still considered unsuitable). More concerned with ethics than with Kleist's fatalistic view of life, he created a concluding operatic apotheosis where the tragic muse appeared and mercifully dropped a discreet veil over the final horror which an actor merely declaimed as an epilogue. This unsatisfactory solution, which did justice neither to the play's dramatic nor to its thematic purpose, was first presented on 18 October 1910 in the Großherzogliches Hoftheater in Schwerin, where the highpoint seems to have been Albert Wolf's "glänzende Spielleitung"[15] in the court-theatre mode. However, in the same year, out of deference to Tempeltey, Duke Georg von Meiningen personally requested that Max Grube, the manager of Meiningen's Hoftheater, perform the new version as well, but in a form which preserved more of Kleist's text, such as the double murder and its discovery by Sylvius – the very details which the adapter had sought to avoid by his epilogue. Tempeltey later blamed the failure of the staging on the retention of the realistic ending. When the production opened on 22 November 1910 in memory of Kleist's death, the golden age of the Meininger had already passed and their preference for the picturesque had become old-fashioned and totally opposed to the symbolic simplicity of the emerging expressionistic style: "Mit ganz besonderem Aufwand an Kostümen, war auch gestern wieder das Trauerspiel in Szene gesetzt worden. [It saw one performance only.] Die Regie hatte alles aufgeboten, ein einheitliches Spiel und glanzvolle Massenszenen herauszuarbeiten. Aus dem Brücknerschen Atelier war wieder eine effektvolle Dekoration hervorgegangen, die bei der äußerst geschickten Beleuchtung die größte Natürlichkeit vortäuschte" (*Meininger Tageblatt*, 23 November 1919). Famous for their technical excellence, the Meininger did not change their sets behind a dropped curtain, but on the darkened stage, "mit einer Sicherheit, Geräuschlosigkeit und Schnelligkeit, ... die Bewunderung regte."[16] Helen Thimig, at the beginning of her career, won the sympathy of the audience with her delightfully girlish performance as Agnes, but her male counterpart, Fritz Delius as Ottokar, induced laughter in one serious scene. In a sense this opera-like, historic, panoramic production served more as a memorial to the Meininger tradition which, by the end of the nineteenth century, had made a significant contribution to the appreciation of such works as *Das Käthchen von Heilbronn* and *Die Hermannsschlacht*.

While Eugen Kilian was director of the Hoftheater zu Karlsruhe, he elected to revise *Die Familie Schroffenstein*, using as his basis the earlier manuscript version, *Die Familie Ghonorez*. The latter, having survived in Kleist's hand, is the only completed version which we can safely assume to be totally the author's own work while the same claim cannot be made for *Die Familie Schroffenstein*, the first printed version, since the manuscript has been lost and may include Ludwig Wieland's and Heinrich Geßner's influence. Kilian, who ultimately adapted the play twice, retained more of the original than any of his predecessors. Toning down the more passionate utterances, he kept the complete love scene and most of the finale, although the exchange of clothes was only hinted at. As soon as the double murder occurred, the drama came to a rapid conclusion with Barnabe's disclosure of the true state of affairs. This first Kilian version, *premièred* in Karlsruhe on 17 October 1902 under the direction of the adapter, proved to be a notable triumph. Joseph Mark made a strong impact upon the audience with his unsentimentalized portrait of Sylvester, but the critics censured Wilhelm Wassermann for his unconvincing interpretation of Rupert. Kilian's second adaptation, written when he was the senior director of Munich's Hoftheater for the initial offering of a Kleist cycle in 1911, captured for the first time the true sense of the drama. Kilian himself claimed: "Das Vorurteil, das bis dahin gegen dieses Jugendwerk des Dichters bestanden hatte, wurde durch den unbestrittenen Erfolg der Münchner Aufführung auf das Erfreulichste widerlegt und insbesondere die verhängnisvolle Klippe, die der gefährliche Schlußakt bietet, mit vielem Erfolg umschifft."[17] Richard Elchinger further observed: "[Es] hat sich sogar gezeigt, daß die beiden letzten Akte, denen man bisher bei den wenigen Aufführungen, die das Stück seit dem Jahre 1803 [sic] erlebte, immer Gewalt angetan, ohne wesentliche Striche zu bestehen vermögen und logisch aus den drei ersten hervorwachsen."[18] The *Münchner Zeitung* (25 September 1911) called this staging (22 September) "eine der Besten unter den vielen guten, die wir Herrn Dr. Kilian bis jetzt zu verdanken haben." Julius Klein's sets, commended for their beauty, were efficiently changed with the house in darkness – the Meininger technique which served to shorten the evening. The production also took full advantage of lighting to underline the dramatic mood: "In der Liebesszene III.1 blieb es dunkel bis Agnes das Wasser getrunken hatte, um dann bis zum Ausgang der Szene heller und heller zu werden."[19] The critics conferred lavish praise on the actors, feeling that each had been suitably cast, but especially complimented Albert Steinrück on his energetic delineation of a cruel but nonetheless human Rupert.

After Strommel failed to gain public support for his second reworking of *Die Familie Schroffenstein* in 1916, the play disappeared from the stage until J. Gielen came to Dresden, anxious to resurrect it in the context of a program to perform the youthful dramas of great authors. Gielen's adaptation, dictated by the practical demands of the theatre, avoided any arbitrary additions or cuts (he for the first time kept the complete divestment scene), and concentrated on the tragic element. But by presenting the outcome as determined exclusively by character, he apparently skirted the fate motif, the strength of Kilian's interpretation. Gielen's version, first performed on 2 October 1924 in Dresden's Schauspielhaus under the adapter's own supervision, scored a notable victory with nine more performances in the same year. In keeping with the reputation of the Schauspielhaus for technical mastery, the staging provided a high degree of both artistic and theatrical excellence, as the gloomy sets and the lighting combined to produce a tragic atmosphere calculated to play on the emotions of the spectators, especially in the very impressive opening scene. Lothar Mehnert "schuf eine Gestalt [Rupert] ganz von Mißtrauen, von Dämonen geritten, hart, dunkel, unnahbar der Frau, dem Sohn. Urbild einer ausgestorbenen Rasse vor der Sintflut, die der Feudalismus wegschwemmte. Dem glaubt man das Hineinstürmen in ein Schicksal, das Niedertrampeln der Unschuldigen."[20] Also, Rupert's habit of whistling really got on the audience's nerves. Lilly Kann's Eustache furnished an appropriate contrast figure to Mehnert's Rupert, while Bruno Decarli gave an heroic, totally believable portrayal of Sylvester, which the *Dresdner Neuste Nachrichten* called "[die] stärkste, rührendste Gestalt, die Decarli je geschaffen hat." The one major weakness of the production lay in the uninspiring, lifeless portrayal of the young lovers by two older actors, Antonia Dietrich as Agnes and Willi Kleinoschegg as Ottokar.

Only those plays which could be viewed as a glorification of the Germanic spirit were performed extensively during the Third Reich, and hence *Die Familie Schroffenstein* had to wait until some time after the Second World War and the growing popularity of the theatre of the absurd for the next major production. With the tendency to view Kleist as a precursor of this movement, his first drama came to have imposed upon it a new, contemporary point of view which chose to play down the youthful rebellion against the blind rule of fate. This attitude can be seen from the "unterkühlten Inszenierung"[21] of the Landestheater in Darmstadt in March, 1962, which, in an experimental vein, gave *Die Familie Ghonorez* complete with Spanish names. Director Hans Bauer transformed the play into a "Denkdrama ... , in dem das Denken selber seinen Sinn verloren hat. Nur die Attitüde des Denkens ist noch da."[22] The unifying approach Bauer derived from the all encompassing theme of mistrust: "Es [das Mißtrauen] zerstört hier die Sprache, löst den Rhythmus der Dialoge auf, als wollten die Sätze nicht mehr gesprochen sein; brechende oder gepreßte Stimmen, Bedenken hinter jedem Satz, Mißtrauen, ihn zu sagen, weil das Wort Wirklichkeit schafft." He played the five acts without a break, a procedure which lent the staging an irresistible forward movement, and without the aid of a curtain, so that the

actors themselves frequently carried on and off stage the few unavoidable props. No attempt was made to suggest any local colour:
on either side of the stage rose two giant, roughly carved totem
poles, and a gauze curtain, illuminated by coloured spots, formed
the background. During the revenge-filled scenes of the grown-up
world black predominated, while a green-gold colour illuminated the
young lovers in their nature setting. Needless to say, the sober adult
world eventually obliterated the hopeful, light-filled idyll of youthful
dreams. In short, the director's conception, reinforced by acting,
lighting, and sets (designed by Teo Otto) conveyed the impression
of helpless creatures lost in a dark room, seeking contact in one long
futile interrogation of each other. The absurdist influence can be
further documented by Günther Rühle's assessment of the acting:
"Der Rodrigo (Ottokar) Anfried Krämers pflegt in dieser nacht-
schwarzen Welt die Pose larmoyanter Güte, als suche er auf diese
Weise sein Wissen um die chaotische Einrichtung der Welt zu über-
decken. Eine Menschenpuppe voll von Traurigkeit. In ihm geschieht
nichts, der Tod scheint ihm nur eine andere Form, das Leben zu
verlieren. Der versöhnliche Antonio Arwed Fleischers hat die Fremd-
heit Beckettscher Clowns." Generally, the critics applauded this
modern interpretation. "Die Aufführung gehört gewiß zu den besten
dieser Spielzeit in Darmstadt."[23]

Two stagings attained some notoriety in the West German press
in the seventies. The first of these, mounted by Göttingen's Junges
Theater in September 1974 took to heart "ein Charley-Tante Effekt,
über den Kleist selbst, beim Vorlesen, mit seinen Berner Freunden
in 'stürmisches' Gelächter ausgebrochen ist,"[24] a reference to the
exchange of clothes in the last act. With its abundance of drastic
situations, *Die Familie Schroffenstein* readily lends itself to comedy,
since the more serious parts constantly run the risk of becoming
ludicrous. Hence, one would assume that some entertainment could
have been derived in Göttingen from a parody: "Aber die Langeweile
kehrt denn doch nach einer kurzen Zeit des Eingewöhnens ein, man
lachte nur noch über Gags ... "[25] "Eine kunstvoll inszenierte Parodie
hätte daraus einen Mordsspaß machen können. Die Göttinger jedoch
bieten nichts als eine Art albernen Studentenjux."[26] What in this latter
travesty amounted to a sought-after effect, humour, became a very
real danger in Guido Huonder's production for Dortmund in April
1977: "Er pendelte zwischen dem Trauerspiel und seiner Parodie
wechselweise hin und her."[27] Following Hans Bauer's example,
Huonder elected to rely on *Die Familie Ghonorez*, with its "schmerz-
hafte[n] Ineins von frühromantischem Schicksalsdrama und
nachKantianischer Erkenntnistragödie."[28] In the critic Eo Plunien's

opinion, the director took the drama much too seriously, and this only succeeded in frequently producing the totally opposite reaction in his audience. He had a real horse and two barking dalmatians appear on stage, let the grandfather be played by a girl and the witch by a man, and gave old Ghonorez a wig so that he could really pull out his hair. In this interpretation the witch and the grandfather embodied the ruling forces of the dramatic world. Even before the play began, the witch closed off the proscenium from the audience with a red string, and at the conclusion, once she had made the grandfather see again, she rolled up the thread of fate and threw it into the auditorium. This experiment met with a mixed reaction, being totally repudiated by Eo Plunien of *Die Welt*, but enthusiastically endorsed by the reviewer in the *Frankfurter Rundschau*.

Rainer Behrend directed the first postwar Berlin production of *Die Familie Schroffenstein* with mixed but on the whole unfavourable results in March 1982. In the assessment of Hellmut Kotschenreuther (*Der Tagesspiegel*, 9 March 1982), the director's greatest accomplishment was the very decision to stage the work for the Tribüne. Set designer Reiner Terweg and Behrend transferred the action in time and place from the Spanish or Swabian Middle Ages to "ein imaginiertes frühes 19. Jahrhundert zwischen Poesie und Schauerromantik" in Kleist's own Prussia. Once again the perennial problem surfaced in the reviews: "Behrend hat sich nicht entscheiden können, ob er nun die Kruditäten der Vorlage betonen sollte ... oder ob man Kleist nicht doch als Vorlage ernster nehmen müßte ... ."[29] To compound the difficulty, the director apparently made such severe cuts in the text that the spectators were at a loss to follow the plot – a complex one under the best of circumstances, and with the exception of the lovers, played by Torsten Sense and Katja Nottke, the characters were thus denied the opportunity to develop into well-rounded, recognizable personalities. The controversial final scene became a dream sequence in slow motion in which the protagonists appeared as sleepwalkers miming their relationships to one another. This experiment culminated in "das zu Jürgen Kniepers Musik schockartig ausgeblendete Schlußbild mit streng geordnetem Leichen-Tableau," to cite Kotschenreuther. Such an innovative but arbitrary experiment found favour with Kotschenreuther as an example of how "die vorangegangenen Aufzüge für ein heutiges Publikum zu erschließen waren," but Karena Niehoff (*Süddeutsche Zeitung*, 27/28 March 1982) maintained that this "Traumspiel-Pantomime" "verlegen und leicht komisch [wirkte]." In anticipation of developments only two to three years later, Roland H. Wiegenstein, while repudiating Behrend's interpretation for its lack of a unified approach and its abuse of

Kleist's language, still used his review to defend the play's contemporary relevance and to demand a new staging which, after thorough study, casting, and coaching, would prove equal to the demands made by Kleist's first tragedy.[30]

One has to concede the appropriateness of producing *Die Familie Schroffenstein* in March 1983 to commemorate the city of Thun's 600th anniversary, for it was here in 1802 that Kleist completed the play "und hier war es 1322 auch zu einem Brudermord gekommen, der mit einem Erbschaftsstreit wie jenem in der *Familie Ghonorez* zu tun hatte."[31] This school production offered by the students of class 11A of the Staatliches Seminar, relocated the plot in Thun with slides projecting well-known sights, such as the local castle, as fitting backdrops to the story. In the same year Hans Neuenfels also wanted to mount the drama for Berlin's Schiller-Theater, but since this plan failed to materialize, he decided to resort to a filmed version, a ZDF (Second German Television Network) production in collaboration with the ORF (Austrian Broadcasting Network), first aired on 29 May 1984 as part of the series "Die aktuelle Inszenierung." Referring to the tragedy as Kleist's "klarstes und unmittelbarstes Schauspiel" and calling his film "Die Familie oder Schroffenstein"[32], a reflection of his social-psychological bias, Neuenfels emphasized the nightmare quality of life when human beings always assume the worst of others. Considerable blood flowed throughout, emotions tended towards the extreme, and the interior shots, being predominantly gloomy, clashed with the exuberantly colourful nature scenes. "Es erfordert Geduld und Bereitschaft des Zuschauers," warned Wilfried Mommert (*Ludwigsburger Kreiszeitung*, 27 March 1984), "sich auf diesen sich keiner Norm unterwerfenden Film einzulassen." The same year also yielded a promising production by Dieter Reible for Wuppertal, enthusiastically reviewed by Jochen Schmidt for the *Frankfurter Allgemeine Zeitung* (1 July 1984). The poetic love scenes, brought to life by Mechthild Reinders (Agnes) and Gregor Höppner (Ottokar), evidently conjured up a memorable love idyll, a utopian island located in the orchestra pit to which a single plank provided access (set designed by Claudia Doderer).

When Hans Neuenfels read an essay before the annual meeting of the Kleist-Gesellschaft in 1984, the same year in which his film appeared, he designated Kleist's first play as "auch sein realistischstes."[33] In April of the following year, Neuenfels's influence may be detected in the first of two productions of *Die Familie Schroffenstein* to receive extensive press coverage, i.e., in Hans-Dieter Jendreyko's interpretation for Frankfurt's Schauspielhaus, where "ein vorsichtiger historischer Realismus"[34] resulted in an action-packed medieval

*Ritterschauspiel*. What struck several commentators was the surprising realization that despite the historical setting the staging nevertheless lent itself to disturbingly modern associations with the absurdity of the arms race or with the mistrust behind the nuclear balance of terror: "Die Frankfurter Inszenierung interpretiert nun gerade das Gewaltsame eines auf das Prinzip sinnloser Vernichtung gegründeten Weltentwurfs als das uns Naheliegende und Entsprechende."[35] Overall, the critics liked this Frankfurt version and commended the ensemble acting, singling out Susanna Kraus's credible portrayal of Agnes, especially in the final scene, and the effective utilization of the extensive stage by designer Götz Loepel. A massive grey-stone cliff on either side and a painted horizon with red lightning both framed the space and created an ominous atmosphere. From the gridiron hung wooden poles, arranged to intimate a church, a forest, or even the cave of the conclusion. Each time the action became threatening or led to actual friction, a loudspeaker emitted appropriately suggestive electronic music. Despite reservations – the slow-motion ending caused some laughter and negative critical response – a general consensus emerged that the director and his collaborators had demonstrated convincingly, "wie sich das unzeitgemäße Stück gegenwärtig machen und aufregend spielen läßt" (Günther Schloß).

The second offering in the same month of April differed both in concept and in practice from the Frankfurt version. Whereas the latter depended heavily upon realism, Valentin Jeker focused his interpretation for the Hessisches Staatstheater in Kassel on a psychological investigation into human relationships, especially between husband and wife, which in the view of one critic, Eckard Franke, was indebted to the "Geist der Romantik mit dessen vornehmstem Stilmittel, der Ironie."[36] Jendreyko opted for medieval knights dressed in period armour; Jeker outfitted his cast in early nineteenth-century costumes from the "Salons des verbürgerlichten Adels."[37] In the first scene to feature the Warwand branch of the family, the audience saw what seemed to be a domestic idyll: Sylvester was playing his cello, Gertrude was knitting. "Jäh läßt das Mädchen [Agnes] seinen Löffel sinken und führt ihn klirrend durch die Tasse."[38] This veiled, weak protest, however, only briefly interrupted the concert since the conventional façade quickly reasserted itself. The essential falseness of this image was highlighted by the director later in the evening: in the very same room the decapitated body of Rupert's herald hung from the chandelier. To convey further Sylvester's betrayal of civilized values (music) for the sake of survival, Agnes reproduced her father's account of the feud with the aid of tin soldiers and a book covered with a black cloth: "Der Krieg findet auf dem (Buch)-Rücken der

Kultur statt" (Kühn). At one point a midget in knightly armour leaped from the tomb of Rupert's youngest son and then stationed himself in the background, "als schrecklich-komische Miniatur eines Todesengels" (Kühn). But despite such questionable additions, Jeker achieved a major accomplishment by circumnavigating the reef on which many good intentions had foundered – the implausible conclusion. While Agnes and Ottokar rejoiced in their love, the parents already loomed in the background, tapping their way with the long white canes of the blind. When they finally began to see, their future lay dead at their feet: "Vor dem Schluß mit Bruderkuß bittet Jeker die Vettern Schroffenstein zum Ringkampf. Häßliches Licht beleuchtet die Versöhnungsszene. Hier glaubt Valentin Jeker Kleist nicht."[39]

The 1980s saw, if not appreciation of, at least a pronounced attention to the traditionally least performed of Kleist's plays, *Die Familie Schroffenstein*. Since the modern spectator must contend with the threat of terror and that sense of individual helplessness which is symptomatic of the twentieth century, it should come as no surprise that in a drama which portrays its protagonists as impotent playthings of both an inner and an external fate, directors have discovered some affinity with the current situation. If one bears in mind the four generally well-received major productions of *Die Familie Schroffenstein* in just two years, 1984–85, one has to concur with Günther Schloß's judgment: "Nach den neuen Erfahrungen mit dem frühen Kleiststück steht außer Zweifel: das wiedererwachte Interesse unserer Bühnen für die elende 'Scharteke' hat Raison."[40] Notwithstanding this more encouraging evaluation, *Die Familie Schroffenstein* will no doubt continue to challenge directors as to what approach they should adopt in order to do justice to, or to come to terms with, its dramatic extremes, especially its perilous and problematic dénouement. Eo Plunien, in an article for *Die Welt* (14 April 1977), succinctly outlined the difficulty: "Zum Schluß stellt sich dann auch noch heraus – und ein Blinder muß es erkennen, ein irrsinniger Bastard es aussprechen –, daß alles nur ein Versehen war. ... Wie ist so etwas zu spielen? Als ernstgemeinte Schicksalstragödie, als schauerliches Possenspiel oder schwankhafte Moritat?"

## CHAPTER TWO

# Der zerbrochene Krug

Writing to Kleist's promoter Adam Müller, Goethe, the manager-director of the Weimar Hoftheater, commented in reference to a manuscript submitted for his approval:

Der zerbrochene Krug hat außerordentliche Verdienste, und die ganze Darstellung dringt sich mit gewaltsamer Gegenwart auf. Nur schade daß das Stück auch wieder dem unsichtbaren Theater angehört. ... Könnte [der Verfasser] mit eben dem Naturell und Geschick eine wirklich dramatische Aufgabe lösen und eine Handlung vor unseren Augen und Sinnen sich entfalten lassen, wie er hier eine vergangene sich nach und nach enthüllen läßt, so würde es für das deutsche Theater ein großes Geschenk sein.[1]

Although Goethe, committed at this period of his life to a neo-classical tradition that advocated the progressive development of a dramatic action, failed to appreciate the comedy's analytical structure, the roots of which may be said to go back to *Oedipus Rex*, he nevertheless agreed to stage Kleist's work and always claimed to have gone to great lengths to make the production a success, as illustrated by a letter addressed to Johann Daniel Falk in 1810: "Sie wissen, welche Mühe und Proben ich es mir kosten ließ, seinen [Kleists] 'Wasserkrug' aufs hiesige Theater zu bringen. Daß es dennoch nicht glückte, lag einzig in dem Umstande, daß es dem übrigens geistreichen und humoristischen Stoffe an einer rasch durchgeführten Handlung fehlt."[2] Goethe spent a considerable amount of the "Mühe" referred to, making the drama conform to his preconceived notion of the classical comedy, and in this sense he was the first adapter. One of his alterations was the arbitrary division of the drama into three acts with a curtain at the end of each, a change which obviously impeded the natural tempo of the work. One may also assume that he attempted to accommodate the play to the Weimar theatrical style. Its acknowledged goals of ideal beauty, solemnity in the portrayal of human personality, aristocratic distinction in gesture, and a rhetorical manner of speech, resulted in an excessive, rigid stylization that would conflict with the more realistic style of Kleist's language and delineation of characters.

Preceded by a performance of the popular opera *Der Gefangene* by Della Maria, the *première* of *Der zerbrochene Krug* occurred on 2 March 1808 without the presence of the author. Until recently critics have taken for granted that the first significant performance of a Kleistian play was an unqualified failure. "Ein fürchterliches Lustspiel," commented Fräulein von Knebel eight days after the event, "ein unauslöschlicher, unangenehmer Eindruck ... so etwas langweiliges and abgeschmacktes hätte ich nicht für möglich gehalten."[3] Other reports, drawn primarily from the diaries and letters of Goethe, Luise Wieland, Stephan Schütze, or Friedrich Wilhelm Riemer, also make reference to a "höchst ungünstigen Aufnahme," a comedy which "gänzlich durchfiel" and was greeted by whistling and hissing at the conclusion. The *Zeitung für die elegante Welt* (4 April 1808) claimed: "Diesem Kruge ging's übel. Das Publikum nahm in seinem Unwillen eine so laute Satisfaktion, dergleichen es hier noch keine genommen hat, und statuierte allen Krügen dieser Art zur Warnung, ein auffallendes Exempel an demselben." The actor Anton Genast blamed the failure on the inappropriately drawn-out speeches of Heinrich Becker's Adam. However, Helmut Sembdner's research into the circumstances surrounding the *première* has called into question most of these commonly held views.[4] The *Zeitung für die elegante Welt* speaks of the last act as being too long-winded and Sembdner has argued convincingly that the Weimar Hoftheater used what is now categorized as the long variant text. The "Buchausgabe" of 1811 (the manuscript has been lost) reduced the 514 lines of the original, longer version to a mere 56 but included it as a "Variant" in the appendix. To support his contention, Sembdner quotes at length from Leipzig's *Allgemeine Deutsche Theater Zeitung* of 11 March 1808:

[Aber] hilf Himmel, hilf! nun müssen wir noch den zweyten und den (das ganze Stück verdarb dritthalb Stunden) eine Stunde währenden dritten Akt, alles ein einziges Verhör, mit anhören. Dem Erzähler kommt es wohl zu, und wird bey ihm interessant, aber der dramatische Dichter darf die entdeckte Wahrheit nicht so unendlich weit vom endlichen Bekenntniß entfernen, daß der Verfasser kein Dramatiker ist, beweißt seine Unkunde jeder dramatischen Regel. Ich höre, daß es ein Herr von Kleist sey. ... – Hr. *Becker* war als Dorfrichter Adam vortrefflich, seine Mahlerey sehr passend. Demois.

*Elsermann*, die eigentliche plagende Erzählerin, Jungfer Eve, hatte sich recht gut kostumiert. Richtig ergriff Hr. *Unzelmann* den Ton des Schreibers Licht, Mad. *Wolff* war Frau Marthe Null [!], Gerichtsverwalter Herr *Oels*, Frau Brigitte Demois. *Silie*, der Bauer Ruprecht Hr. *Wolff*.

This review also contains a different version of the spectators' reaction. "Dem Publikum gereicht es zur Ehre, daß es, am Ende des Stückes (was ich nie hier erlebte) wirklich pochte." Whatever the cause, the comedy was immediately removed from the program and as Achim von Arnim later noted: "Der schlechte Erfolg dieser Aufführung hatte etwas Herbes in Kleist zurückgelassen."[5] This led to a rupture in his relationship to Goethe, rumours of a duel, and the vindictively mocking allusion in *Phöbus* to Goethe's delayed marriage to Christiane Vulpius.

Three productions followed, all of which adhered more or less to the tradition of the popular Viennese farce. The first, directed by Karl Carl and offered in Munich's Königliches Theater am Isartor on 27 November 1816, enjoyed considerable favour with the public. According to the *Münchener Theater-Journal*, "Das Lustspiel 'Der zerbrochene Krug' dankt dem lebendigen Spiele des Herrn [Johann Gottfried] Wohlbrücks, Dorfrichter Adam, und der Mad. [Margarethe] Karl, Evchen, die freundliche Aufnahme, die sich so laut aussprach."[6] This same success was repeated in the Breslauer Nationaltheater (14 April 1818) where the performances of Heinrich Ludwig Schmelka (Adam) and his wife (Magdalena Schmelka as Frau Marthe) rescued the evening from an otherwise drawn-out, tiring performance. Schmelka's success apparently encouraged him to bring the Breslau version to Berlin's Königstädtisches Theater (18 January 1825), and already in these early popularized stagings the essential feature upon which the public acceptance or the rejection of the drama often depended could easily be discerned – the crucial role of judge Adam. In an article written by Willibald Alexis for the *Vossische Zeitung* (22 January 1825), we read: "Herr Schmelkas Spiel riß selbst die, welche den *zerbrochenen Krug* langweilig finden wollten, ... mit sich fort, und wenn das hier und dort vernommene Husten absichtlich gewesen sein sollte, werden auch diese Störer ... zur besseren Einsicht gelangen."

As Gustav Buchtenkirch has noted, "[der] Stil der Hamburger Bühne enthält ... starke Annäherungswerte an den speziellen Kleistischen Stil im *Zerbrochenen Krug*."[7] When Friedrich Schmidt decided to produce the comedy, he soon concluded that it could not be introduced to Hamburg as it stood. He therefore reluctantly took it upon himself to adapt Kleist's masterpiece in order to make it more stageworthy by the standards of his day, but to his credit he recognized that his version greatly weakened the poetic qualities of the original: "Sollt' der Erfolg gelingen, so galt es, das Interesse und die Grenzen eines Aktes mit Sicherheit abzumessen, daher waren Kürzungen unvermeidlich. Aber auch das Zusetzen ist bei einem genialen Werke nicht minder schwierig. Diese Klippe ist gleichfalls umschifft, denn nur einige Verbindungsstrophen, nebst der Schlußrede gehören mir an."[8] In other words, Schmidt kept to Kleist's text as closely as possible and made allowances only for technical problems and the prudishness of his public. The play, opening on 28 September 1820 with Schmidt himself in the lead role, met with an enthusiastic response. The characters were carefully and vividly portrayed and the sharing of a line amongst three or four actors painstakingly perfected by Schmidt. Above all, in order to avoid the criticism "boring" so often levelled at the work, the plot moved forward swiftly, so much so, in fact, that the reviewer Friedrich Gottlieb Zimmermann faulted the performance for proceeding too quickly. Although the play remained a favourite with the Hamburg public, it was not performed that frequently, since there was greater interest in melodrama and farce. Still, Schmidt helped to create interest in the figure of Adam, and his adaptation was to have considerable influence upon other stages. For example, from 4 August 1822 until 18 September 1913, *Der zerbrochene Krug* appeared 147 times before the Berlin public in Schmidt's version.

The crucial nature of Adam's function became increasingly conspicuous. Indeed, one may also measure the success of the play in terms of the popularity of the actor interpreting the country judge. The Berlin production of 4 August 1822 found little favour, because Albert Leopold Gern drew out his part too much and was considered too loud and vulgar, while the "ausgezeichnet[e] Spiel des Herrn Meck"[9] saved a staging in Frankfurt a.M. (18 August 1832). The person who received the widest acclaim and who even went on tour with the role proved to be Theodor Döring. Portraying Adam for Berlin's Königliches Schauspielhaus on 15 April 1844, he was characterized as a "Meister, der seines Gleichen sucht."[10] Döring reportedly earned lavish praise with his skill in suggesting not only the brutality of the local despot, but also his fear at being unmasked by Walter, two mental dispositions effectively concretized in his tremendous agility contrasted with the disability imposed by his club foot. The most outstanding theatre directors of the age, such as Heinrich Laube and Franz von Dingelstedt, extolled his histrionic achievement. For example, Laube described Döring's Adam as sharp-witted, cynical, impudent, vital, in short a complete exploitation of every comic aspect of the role. Feodor Wehl wrote: "Der Moment, wo er mit Pathos ausruft: 'Nun denn, Gerechtigkeit, nimm deinen Lauf!' und nun aufs Ergötzlichste anfängt, loszuhinken, war von einer schlagenden Wirkung."[11] As a result of Döring's success, *Der zerbrochene Krug* gained a permanent place in the general theatre repertoire and the part of Adam came to be regarded as an excellent vehicle for a talented actor, but unfortunately Döring's concept tended to dominate the play's interpretation. Cities such as Königsberg, Hannover, Leipzig, Weimar, and even St Petersburg vied for his guest appearances. On 27 July 1844, in the framework of Munich's Gesamtgastspiele and under the direction of Dingelstedt, he played the judge in the presence of the King of Prussia who had especially selected the play from a list submitted for his approval. In the same year, the actor Franz Hoppe presented a more fanciful, comic Adam to the Berlin theatre-goers, one which they greeted with approbation, but the critic of the *Vossische Zeitung* (11 June 1844) still felt that Hoppe had turned to account a toned-down, less harsh Döring model: "So blieb *Der zerbrochene Krug* überall aufs engste mit der Darstellungskraft des Adamspielers verbunden, und dort, wo dieser mitreißend genug wirkte, spendete das Publikum, durch keine kunstästhetischen Erwägungen gehemmt, begeisterten Beifall."[12]

In Vienna, the manager-director of the Burgtheater, Heinrich Laube, had to conduct a persistent campaign to have this north-German work accepted with its, by local standards, crudely realistic comic effects. Treating it as a classical play and basing his version primarily on Schmidt's adaptation, he sought to achieve a compromise since, as a result of several guest performances from the north, the Viennese had some familiarity with the "natural" Hamburg approach. In a review of the production for the *Wiener Allgemeine Theaterzeitung* (5 March 1850), Adolf Bäuerle remarked, "Der zerbrochene Krug setzte unser gutes Publikum in einige Verlegenheit. Es wußte nicht recht, ob es sich langweilen dürfe, ohne vom hohen kritischen Äropag [the highest court in ancient Greece] die allergnädigste Erlaubnis dazu zu haben. ... Hr La Roche [Adam] war sehr wirksam und sparte nichts an komischer Kraft, vielleicht könnte man hier und da seine Verschwendung bedauern dürfen." According to the records, it was not until the third performance that the comedy could be classified as a success, a conquest of public opinion due in no small measure to Karl Ritter von La Roche's inspired interpretation of Adam. Giving a controlled, well-rounded portrayal of the village judge, La Roche eventually earned the reputation of being "the Adam of the south," although he was never to achieve the recognition accorded to "the Adam of the north," Döring. Laube's production also avoided the danger of allowing the play to degenerate into a mere showpiece for the portrayer of Adam. A stage arrangement by which the judge did not sit at a table raised above the other participants, but at ground level, suggested this attempt to achieve balanced ensemble acting.[13]

When Döring came back to Berlin in April 1856 for a new staging of *Der zerbrochene Krug*, he repeated his great triumph as Adam which the reviewer of the *Deutsche Theater Zeitung* (5 April 1856) designated as a "Kunstschöpfung" of decided value, and he was even to return once more to his most widely applauded role for yet another Berlin production in 1874. The majority of the commentaries written at that time testify to the fact that Kleist's comedy had now been fully acknowledged as a masterpiece of the German stage. Interestingly enough, one of the critics, of no small fame himself, Theodor Fontane, expressed serious reservations about the play, seeing it primarily as a "Lesestück." On the positive side, he admired the powerful characterizations, the strict logic of its dramatic sequence, and the simple, straightforward nature of the plot. On the other hand, he could never come to terms with what he called this "Schmuddelwelt."[14] The judge, with his brutal, lying, cunning ways, was a "Greuel" to him and the drama in general lacked, in his view, charm or beauty, and its performance always left him uncomfortable. However, another commentator of note, Otto Brahm, reviewing the production at Berlin's Königliches Schauspielhaus in 1892, enthused about Kleist's ability "mit greifbar realem Leben sein Werk [zu erfüllen]," and his gift in creating "die scharf geschaute Mannigfaltigkeit der Fragen,"[15] capable of delighting an audience. Brahm's respect for the comedy manifests itself indirectly in his assessment of the male lead: "Nicht so überragend wie in Kleists Gedicht, aber doch drollig genug als ein närrisches Original stand dieser ertappte Adam in Herrn Krauses Darstellung da; und was ihm an genialer Eigenart fehlt, deckte ein gut gestimmtes Ensemble glücklich zu."[16]

By the end of the nineteenth century, *Der zerbrochene Krug* was a standard feature in the program of all the major Berlin theatres and thus, not surprisingly, enjoyed some of its greatest triumphs in that city. Adolf L'Arronge directed the comedy in 1883 for the Deutsches Theater; a Schiller-Theater production (28 January 1895) had a run of fifty-two performances; Victor Barnowsky used it to open the Kleines Theater on 15 September 1905; and Emil Rameau provided the Neues Volkstheater (8 January 1912) with a very lively, independent version which saw forty performances in one season. This warm welcome in Berlin has been explained in terms of a tendency to view this work as an excellent example of *Heimatkunst*, and this particular point of view obviously influenced Gerhard Hauptmann's staging for Berlin's Künstlertheater on 2 October 1913. As a former adherent of naturalism in drama, Hauptmann possessed a deep understanding for the setting of Kleist's play and real feeling for its style. In fact, his own great comedy, *Der Biberpelz* (1893), owes much of its inspiration and tone to *Der zerbrochene Krug*. Although Hauptmann kept very closely to the original text and procured the services of some excellent actors, Julius Bab remarked about the production – still very successful by the standards of the day with thirty-five performances in 1913 alone – that it was "sehr amüsant in den Einzelheiten des Milieus, aber ... nicht sehr stark in der Ausarbeitung des dramatischen Tempos."[17]

*Der zerbrochene Krug*, the first Kleist drama to be translated into French (1884 by Alfred de Lostalot), was also the first to be performed in France, on 20 February 1904 in the Théâtre Victor Hugo in Paris. Unfortunately, J. Gravier and H. Vernot took it upon themselves to adapt the drama for the French stage, and in so doing, they evidently failed to respect the dramatist's intent. They shortened the comedy by almost one half, cutting Adam's prophetic dream (scene 3), the genealogy of the jug, and the wine-and-cheese interlude. Since Licht came across as an intriguer anxious to usurp Adam's position, he victoriously assumed Adam's seat in the final scene. The adaptation also tampered seriously with characterizations: Adam became less comic and Eve was transformed into a mere observer. But as Frank C. Richardson makes clear, the conclusion suffered the most. While the reconciled Eve and Ruprecht kissed and Frau Marthe again raised the issue of her broken jug, Walter pointed to the lovers, saying: "Elle [la cruche] n'a jamais été cassée, Dame Marthe." "The altered ending also [replaced] the psychologically accurate and superbly stage-wise lines of Kleist with the rather silly, factitious closing lines of a French farce."[18] Running for a period of six weeks, the production was largely ignored by the press except for Emile Faguet's positive critique for the *Journal des débats*, which concluded: "Il est incontestable que *la Cruche cassée* est un petit chef-d'oeuvre."[19]

Reviewing Reinhard Bruck's staging of *Der zerbrochene Krug* for Berlin's Königliches Schauspielhaus of 19 September 1918, Siegfried Jacobsohn noted, "daß die Komödie ... an manchen Stellen zum Schwank vergröbert wurde. Aber das ist der natürliche, also verzeihliche Rückschlag gegen die steife Hoftheaterkonvention, die sich jahrzehntelang, seit Dörings Tod, nicht getraut hat, ein 'klassisches' Werk, einen Akt in 'Versen' mit den Augen von heute zu betrachten und mit den Lippen von heute zu sprechen."[20] The passing reference to Döring, the prototypical Adam of the nineteenth century, proved to be especially appropriate, perceptive, and prophetic, for the success of this at times slapstick, at times down-to-earth production can be attributed primarily to Emil Jannings's naturalistic delineation of the same part. "Aber auf den oft entweihten Brettern lag Jannings, und sie wurden zu Erde, zu fetter, fruchtbarer, sprießender, krumiger Erde, in der ein heidnischer Waldmensch mit beiden stämmigen Beinen wurzelte." Because Jannings's primitive, sensual approach came to dominate almost all other interpretations of this crucial role in the first half of the twentieth century, it is worth quoting Jacobsohn's description at greater length:

Die Bühne trieft von dem Saft, der Jannings aus allen Poren spritzt. Die Spitzbubenaugen im feist-ordinären Schlemmergesicht befehlen, drohen, betteln und zittern reihum mit jagender Schnelligkeit. Spielend, in doppeltem Sinne spielend erreicht ein Künstler, der sich jauchzend der neuen Freiheit freut, ohne sie jemals zu mißbrauchen – erreicht er, worauf der Zauber, die Göttlichkeit großer Komödie beruht: daß der Schuft losgesprochen, daß er zum Mitmenschen, daß er in seiner kreatürlichen Nacktheit, aus Fülle den animalischen Lastern besonders widerstandslos unterworfen, schlechterdings liebenswürdig wird. Eine unsinnige Einrichtung des Theaters? Nein: nicht, wenn solche Gaukler solchen Dichtern zu ihrem Recht an die Nachwelt verhelfen.

In time, Jannings gained such fame as the village judge that in 1937 a film version was made, directed by Gustav Ucicky, which tended to emphasize the Dutch milieu. In the opening scene, the camera focussed upon a large canopy bed. At first, one heard only crude animal-like sounds emanating from the concealed giant; then there was the first visual image, his big rear end. This pantomime introduction immediately set the tone for the remainder of this much heralded film which further promoted the standardization of Jannings's good-natured but evil Adam. For example, in Heinz Hilpert's production for the Deutsches Schauspielhaus in Hamburg, which even went on tour to Moscow, Hermann Schomberg also played Adam as the primitive animal and, to quote Klaus Wagner of the *Frankfurter Allgemeine Zeitung* (5 March 1960), proved "nicht minder vital als einst Emil Jannings."

Although Adam came to dominate most performances of *Der zerbrochene Krug*, some directors did recognize the importance of the minor roles. Reminiscing about a staging with Emil Jannings, Else Heims, and Paul Dahlke, Heinz Hilpert remarked:

Es ist mir unvergeßlich und war für mich als Regisseur beglückend, wie sehr diese kleine Rolle der Magd durch die markante Arbeit der [Gisela von] Collande das Stück, seine Atmosphäre und seinen Ablauf mitbestimmte. Aber das Einprägsamste auf diesem Gebiet war ein früh verstorbener Schauspieler, der den Büttel spielte. Der Büttel tritt fünf- oder sechsmal auf und wird jedesmal wieder weggeschickt, ohne daß er ein Wort zu sagen hat. Die Art, wie dieser Mann, er hieß Herbert Prigrann, immer wieder kam, den Auftrag erwartete, von allen vergessen wurde und sich in einem geeigneten Moment wieder hinausschlich, war überwältigend und riß das Publikum zu Ovationen hin.[21]

In the 1950s, the ever-increasing favour enjoyed by *Der zerbrochene Krug* helped to foster a greater international awareness of Kleist as a dramatist of worldwide significance. The spring of 1953 saw the English *première* of the work as a radio play. The success of this experiment no doubt encouraged the airing of the drama on television in a translation by Lawrence Wilson, a production hailed by the critics as one of the best televised dramas of the year. The Kleist renaissance reached a peak in France during the 1954/55 season. On 21 March 1955, in a staging for the Théâtre Grammont in Paris, director René Dupuy opted to treat the comedy as a farce, while at the same time preserving an awareness of "an often thinly veiled note of tragedy as well as a kind of sadism that [Jean-Paul] Fauré [a French critic reviewing the performance] judges to be very German."[22] Despite the serious overtones, including a tendency to regard the work as a satire on the Dutch legal system, Dupuy's own portrayal of the lead role gave the personality of Adam "a certain debonaire charm"[23] which prevented the tragic element from being taken too seriously. Whereas this production achieved general recognition and earned praise for its acting, the same cannot be said for Roger Planchon's production for the 1954–55 season of the Théâtre de la Comédie in Lyon-Villeurbanne that utilized a new French adaptation by the noted avant-garde dramatist, Arthur Adamov. Accorded some approbation in Lyon and later in Brussels in 1958, the Adamov version was poorly received in Paris, but this did not discourage director Hubert Grignoux from resurrecting it again in the 1959–60 season for the Centre dramatique de l'Est in Strasbourg.

"Translators have found Heinrich von Kleist's plays intractable, and outside Germany even *The Broken Jug*, by his countrymen acclaimed one of their finest comedies, remains unknown to theatre audiences. The Kurfürstendamm Theater Company, presenting it at Sadler's Wells as part of a week's programme, energetically create the impression that by an accident of language the rest of the world is being deprived of something very good." With these words the theatre critic for *The Times* (20 June 1957) commences his enthusiastic review, one which goes to great lengths to acquaint the English-speaking public with the dramatic merits of "the most hilarious comedy ever to have sprung from a mind deeply pessimistic and morbidly introspective." The staging, directed by Oscar Fritz Schuh, appears to have emphasized the lighter side of the play, while not losing sight of the profound sense of universal guilt. Therese Giehse and Ida Krottendorf gave a spirited interpretation of their respective roles as Frau Marthe and Eve; the scene where Frau Brigitte (Hanne Hiob) produces the lost wig made an unforgettable impression; but the complementary acting of the two central male protagonists was the outstanding feature of the evening. "Mr. Ernst Schröder continues to combine the innocence of a Pickwick with the wiliness of a Falstaff and to throw in for good measure occasional lapses into a Dogberry-like asininity. Altogether he gives a delightfully large and energetic performance which is nicely set off by the whimsically smiling and keenly watchful visiting magistrate of Mr. Hans Jungbauer." The second offering of the Kurfürstendamm Theater Company, Lessing's tragedy *Philotas* met with a less favourable response.

In the 1950s, German productions continued to follow the tradition established by Jannings, as can be readily ascertained in Erich-Fritz Brücklmeier's production for Stuttgart's Staatstheater (November 1957): "Im Bette wälzt sich der Falstaff von Huisum, der nicht zum erstenmal seinen Adamsfall getan hat, 'unlieblich' anzuschauen, und zeigt, wie weiland Emil Jannings im Film, dem Publikum zunächst seinen Riesenhintern" (*Stuttgarter Zeitung*, 18 November 1957.) According to Walter Koch of the *Südwest Kreiszeitung*, Brücklmeier elected to present the comedy almost exclusively as a Dutch village farce, complete with cheap theatrical effects calculated to appeal to the audience. Koch deplored such additions as Adam's chain of office made of sausages or his "dekorativ geschwärzte Unterhosen" because they could in no way be justified from the text. Frau Marthe walked across the stage like a figure from a comic opera, and the maids ran into one another in an obviously contrived fashion. This lack of faith in the inherently comic element of the work resulted in "ein Bruch, der durch das ganze Stück ging. Figuren wie die Jungfer Eve [Liselotte Rau], der Gerichtsrat Walter [Ludwig Anschütz] oder die Muhme Brigitte [Elisabeth Flickenschildt] paßten nicht zur schwankmäßigen Aufmachung der anderen Gestalten." This also applied to Hans Mahnke, the village judge, whom Koch considered basically miscast in this part. In contrast, the critic of the *Stuttgarter*

*Zeitung* (18 November 1951) could not have been more glowing in his praise of this same production which in his opinion did justice to the mimic, dialectical nature of Kleist's dialogues, especially in Mahnke's portrayal of Adam: "Es ist eine der großartigsten Rollengestalten, die uns Hans Mahnke in seiner gewiß reichen, wandlungsfähigen Laufbahn beschert hat. ... [Er] trägt die ganze Aufführung, als ob sie seinetwegen gemacht sei." Although both reviews are frequently in sharp contradiction, they concur in acknowledging the vociferous reception on the part of the audience, a positive public reaction further confirmed by Hermann Missenharter's concluding assessment: "Erich-Fritz Brücklmeier, der Regisseur, hat noch nie werkgerechter inszeniert als an diesem Abend, der reinstes Vergnügen schlackenlos darbot und auch entsprechend bedankt wurde."[24]

In 1956, Michael Lengham of the Ontario Stratford Festival commissioned Donald Harron, noted for his creation of Charlie Farquharson, to rewrite Kleist's comedy for the Canadian stage. "In Mr. Harron's adaptation, *The Broken Jug* is a sort of *Inspector General* about official skulduggery in a small settlement in what is now western Ontario in 1813, during the war between Canada and the United States."[25] This version and *Two Gentlemen of Verona* were produced in 1958 for a six-week international tour by the Festival Company of Canada to London (Ontario), Toronto, Montreal, and finally to the Phoenix Theatre, New York, where Brooks Atkinson characterized it as "low pressure entertainment." Apparently attracted to the burlesque aspects of the play, Harron avoided any reference to the more serious background, the less than optimistic recognition of Adamman's *condition humaine*. The set designed by Tanya Moiseiwitsch, an "open-work pot-pourri of doors, windows, steps, alcoves and foolish entrances," aided and abetted the acting, the sole goal of which was to promote laughter. This becomes especially apparent in Atkinson's description of the male lead, the equivalent of judge Adam: "Douglas Campbell, an old hand with a low-gag, is in his most cheerful mood. Playing the part of a frontier charlatan who brazens out his iniquities, Mr. Campbell wears a bandage on his head, which is the official uniform of the farceur, and stumps around the stage on one bandaged foot, which is also part of the traditional uniform, and in general, behaves outrageously in a ludicrous style. He is one of our most reliable drolls." It is somewhat regrettable that *Der zerbrochene Krug* had to make its American début in this burlesque version, which only remotely resembles the German original, but it is also quite understandable, given the amazingly complex, fractured nature of Kleist's verse with its wealth of untranslatable puns and comic subtleties. The tendency to transform the comedy into a ludicrous genre play to the detriment of the language play is a temptation which many directors even in Germany cannot resist, for example, Curt Bock in his 1959 open-air staging in the courtyard of Freiburg's city hall which, according to one critic, "das Drastisch-Schwankhafte so stark [betonte], daß der tragische Akzent dieses Lustspiels kaum zur Geltung kam."[26]

"The notion that the University German Club [Oxford] was unenterprising in marking the 150th anniversary of Kleist's death with a performance of his only play that is at all well known in English does not hold water. *The Broken Jug* as it comes out in German under the direction of a specialist in Kleist, Mr. Denys Dyer, is not the play that those who have read the original text but never before heard it spoken have come to expect."[27] The production referred to here (at the Oxford Playhouse) and generally found unacceptable by *The Times's* special correspondent, serves to point out by its failings some of the pitfalls faced by any director anxious to produce Kleist's comedy. The German nineteenth-century dramatist Friedrich Hebbel once observed: "Seit Falstaff ist im Komischen keine Figur geschaffen worden, die dem Dorfrichter Adam auch nur die Schuhriemen auflösen dürfte."[28] Although the work does contain its fair share of droll effects, it still remains a very perceptive character comedy, a fact which the reviewer somehow overlooked: "It appears indeed, that the middle distance and the background of Kleist's canvas hold most of what is original, interesting and unique in it. The foreground, which is Adam's territory, is no-man's-land. Kleist when he passed that way, Molière's way, left no mark on it." The production, totally lacking in suspense, bogged down not so much because of Rolf Scheibler's interpretation of Adam but, in the reviewer's opinion, on account of an inherent structural weakness within the work itself. "But what else can the actors do – what can Emil Jannings have done in the film version made in 1937 – when the play as it emerges depends less on Adam than on Frau Marthe ... and the visiting privy councillor?" The point is surely that Jannings and before him Döring, despite a tendency to single out a certain aspect of character, an actor's prerogative, did create such a powerful "foreground" impression that it left its mark upon more than half a century. In fact, the danger of stressing "the background" was clearly exposed in the wooden-clog version of the Düsseldorf Schauspielhaus: "Was Karl Vibach [Director] dort auf die Bretter brachte, war beileibe kein Kleist, eher schon Hoftheater und antiquiert bis zur Folklore der niederländischen Holzschuhe."[29] Indeed, the wooden shoes managed to drown out the crucial element, the language.

Attention to "[den] dialektische[n] Prozeß der Wahrheitsfindung" expressed "mit echt Kleist'scher Sprachpedanterie in fünffüßigen Jamben" and to the psychological depths, "in welchen sich nicht nur die Rollen verdichtet haben, sondern auch die tragische Figur des Dichters sichtbar geworden ist,"[30] can be rewarded by a spirited public reaction, as shown by Günter Rennert's much applauded production of *Der zerbrochene Krug* for the Württembergisches Staatstheater in Stuttgart (February 1968). Rennert's sensitive interpretation, appropriately supported by Rochus Gliese's costumes and set whose realistic details suggested the sights and smells of a human stall, managed to sustain a dramatic movement "ohne Zäsuren, ohne Akte, pausenlos ohne Aufenthalt,"[31] a tempo fully supported by the excellent cast. The critics were generous in their praise of Hans-Helmut Dickow, whose Adam offered another dimension to the traditional image established by Jannings by presenting the judge in a much more sympathetic light: "Kein feister, kahlköpfiger, dem Greisenalter naher Lüstling, sondern ein schmuddeliger, verschlagener, dummdreister, selbst in der peinlichsten Lage noch in Gefasel und Schwindel ausweichender kleiner Schuft."[32] Elisabeth Schwarz played an Eve who could have been "eine Schwester der Alkmene,"[33] Ludwig Anschütz a Walter who actually developed during the trial, and Karin Schlemmer a Frau Marthe whose description of the jug was a "Meisterstück." "Komödiantisches Theater also mit psychologischem Hintergrund, mit zu Ende gedachten und gespielten Rollen, mit einem Hinweis auf die tragische Situation des unglücklichen Dichters, die auch in dieser Komödie zu erkennen ist." However, to concentrate solely upon a more literary interpretation, in which "[der] Regisseur ... auf sorgfältige Sprachbehandlung größtes Gewicht [legt]"[34] while neglecting action and mime, can also have its pitfalls, as demonstrated in Zürich's Schauspielhaus in February 1969. Director Gerhard F. Hering's intellectual approach was reinforced by Ruodi Barth's sparse décor, suggestive not of a Dutch interior, but of an unembellished, spacious barn of justice. The scarcity of props coupled with a maximum stage depth permitted the juxtaposing of various acting groups dressed in predominantly grey-brown costumes. René Deltgen's Adam was "bloß ein schwacher Mensch im Sinne eines Jedermann," bereft of the excessive vitality and lasciviousness frequently linked to the rôle. Unfortunately, and not surprisingly, this understated staging tended to lag in its tempo, especially during the second half which frequently lacked the inner suspense necessary to hold the audience: "Man wird der Aufführung zugute halten, daß sie ... – gerade um des Maßes willen – auch nie in Gefahr gerät, sich dem

Schwank zu nähern. Der Besucher ist vor allem aufgerufen, die schöne Klärung von Kleists Text mitzugenießen."

According to the theatrical "best-seller list," *Der zerbrochene Krug* was the second most performed and *the* most attended play of the 1971–72 season, attracting more than 250,000 spectators. Cities such as Hamburg, Böblingen, Bregenz, Lindau, Ravensburg, Munich, Bremen, Zürich, and Vienna all hosted a major production, a choice frequently rewarded by a full house. Helmut Qualtinger as Adam enjoyed the greatest popular success, first of all in Hamburg's Thalia-Theater in February 1971, and later that same year in a new staging for the Volkstheater in Vienna. His interpretation, striving for a more radical, more animalistic anti-hero, – "[den] häßlichst[en] Adam, den es je gab"[35] found little favour, however, with the critics. Hering's veneration for the poetic language (Zürich 1969) was here completely discarded: the overall conversational tone pointed to prose, an impression further reinforced by Qualtinger's tendency to scream all his lines without deference to rhythm, so that one had no inkling that Kleist had written his comedy in verse. But above all, both Joachim Kaiser of the *Süddeutsche Zeitung* and the critic for the *Frankfurter Allgemeine Zeitung* censured the egocentricity of the lead actor whose flamboyant antics intimidated his fellow-actors to the point of rendering effective ensemble-acting impossible. "Qualtinger brüllt und tobt fast in einem fort. Er vergröbert jeden Effekt, suspendiert alle Logik und betätigt sich ingrimmig schnaufend als Pointentöter. ... Der in Hamburg 'Zerbrochene Krug' wird quälend und peinlich, zum Gericht über einen tyrannischen Selbstinszenator."[36] Although Gotthard Böhm of *Die Presse* (13 December 1971) reached basically the same conclusion in reviewing Qualtinger's contribution to the performance in Vienna's Volkstheater, the audiences in both cities appear to have expressed their ardent approval of this overstated portrayal of a distorted creature.

The year 1971 also witnessed the first performance of *Der zerbrochene Krug* as a chamber opera for the Kellertheater in Leipzig (German Democratic Republic). This work, composed by Fritz Geissler, represents "eine der spielbarsten und zugleich modernsten Bühnenkompositionen"[37] to come out of the GDR and received such a favourable reaction that it was presented as the concluding staging at the East Berlin Theatrical Festival in the fall of 1972. While setting the work to music, Geissler was fully aware of the difficulties posed by Kleistian verse, but nevertheless sought "den Sprachduktus genau zu erfassen und ihn der melodischen Erfindung zugrunde zu legen." In his endeavour to suggest certain textual statements of the dramatist, he gave each person a distinctive motif, so that, for example, "der 'teuflische' Tritanus" was reserved for those vocal parts allotted to the judge. At all times the composer showed great respect for the text, which he merely sought to interpret or highlight through his music and, as a further sign of self-effacement, he promoted "die Einbeziehung alcatorischer Kompositionsprinzipien, durch welche die Sänger und Instrumentalisten zu improvisatorischen Beiträgen ermuntert werden sollten." The dramatic aspects of the comedy attained full realization through the sustained efforts of the East-Berlin director, Horst Bonnet, who also kept close to the text, trained his actors with an eye to a well balanced performance, and thus did justice to the play as well as to the music: "Wie die elf Personen, die sich auf der Bühne um eine gerechte und akzeptable Interpretation des Kleist-Lustspieles bemühten, ermöglichten auch die elf Instrumentalisten ... unter der Leitung von Heinz Rögner einen positiven Gesamteindruck." This chamber opera experienced its West German *première* in December 1974 in Solingen-Wuppertal, but in the opinion of the critic, Horst Koegler, of the *Rheinischer Merkur* (13 December 1974), it was indeed fortunate that the East-Berlin authorities did not permit Geissler to attend the performance. Ignoring the composer's fidelity to the realistic tone and intent of Kleist's play, director Kurt Horres, assisted by Jürgen Dreier's fantastic sets, sought to transform the opera into a surrealistic work complete with electronic music uncalled for by the score.

Although *Der zerbrochene Krug* had already demonstrated its versatility with Donald Harron's adaptation to a nineteenth-century North American environment, it earned recognition even farther afield in Calcutta, India, through a Bengali translation by physicist Nihar Batthacharyya, who transplanted the play into a Bengali milieu. Adam, in Bengali, Monu, becomes the leader of the village council, the Panchayat, an organization originating with Mahatma Gandhi. It is one of the functions of the Panchayat to settle village disputes, and out of respect for the great teacher, Monu-Adam wears a Gandhi cap instead of a wig. Ruprecht (Rupa) struck Monu, not with a door handle – which Indian huts lack – but with the iron weight of a scale, and Frau Marthe's jug, brought to her as a present by her husband from Calcutta, possessed the magic power of fertility. When the husband took a young second wife, Frau Marthe, barren at the age of forty-five, prayed to the jug for a child and promptly gave birth to her first son. Unfortunately, the potent talisman blessed her rival with twins three times, but it finally heard her supplications, since the young woman died while giving birth a fourth time. The details of the Dutch setting have been skilfully made to conform to the social realities of a small, contemporary Indian village: "Die Szene bleibt in allen Auftritten, unverändert, alles spielt sich unter freiem Himmel ab, beschattet von einem alten Banyan-Baum, unter dem Gerichtsfälle seit alter Zeit abgewickelt werden."[38] First performed in the context of a German theatre week in collaboration with the Goethe Institute, the production went on tour, where "Kleist ... sich sozusagen verdient um die Hebung der Amtsmoral in Indien [macht]." Some four years later, to commemorate the Kleist year, the Indian theatrical company Yatrik staged *Der zerbrochene Krug* in New Delhi, again with the support of the Goethe Institute and once more with noteworthy success.

As a further indication of the comedy's flexibility the ZDF presented a televised version of the play, especially adapted and abbreviated for this medium by Franz Peter Wirth, and first aired in April 1974. Without really departing from the author's text or design, this production offered an excellent example of how an imaginative approach can give a new dimension to a traditional classic. In the original, when Adam is supposed to show his club foot to Walter, he does indeed do so, but the district supervisor then proceeds to act as if the incriminating limb were in fact whole. Most directors have assumed that either Walter was inattentive in this instance or that Kleist simply made a mistake. Wirth opted to take Kleist at his word and thus assumed: "Der Gerichtsrat Walter und der Schreiber Licht stecken von Anfang an unter einer Decke, der Gerichtsrat, weil er die Affäre vertuschen und so klein wie möglich spielen möchte."[39] Since Walter [Ernst Schröder] was actually portrayed as Adam's accomplice, the drama became a general exposé of corruption extending beyond the judge to those sitting in judgment over him, and consequently the unmasked villain did not run off in the final scene but remained, so to speak, in the picture. Perhaps taking his cue from Gerhard F. Hering's 1963 Darmstadt production, which portrayed Adam not as a gourmand but as a gourmet, Wirth, in direct contrast to the interpretations of Adam as a vulgar beast by Emil Jannings or Helmut Qualtinger, strove to depict Adam as a frustrated scholar: "Wolfgang Reichmann spielt diese Variante ganz einleuchtend, wirklich ein etwas verluderter Intellektueller auf dem platten Lande. Reichmann ist von allen Adams ... durchaus der modernste, verständlichste."[40] The third positive aspect of this production was the skill with which Wirth used the television screen to its best advantage. The camera was set up in such a way that "die genau bedachten Effekte doch zum Zuge kamen."[41] Friedrich Luft appropriately summarized the importance of this televised event: "Kleist wird in dieser Form und Besetzung neu abgeklopft. Franz

Peter Wirth hat formal eine Möglichkeit gefunden, wie, was strikt fürs Theater gemacht war, auf den Schirm kommt, ohne gemindert, geändert oder gar strapaziert zu werden. ... Man ist dem alten Vorgang auf neue Weise nahe."

As was to be expected, the Kleist year 1977, the two-hundredth anniversary of the writer's birth, brought numerous efforts to stage Kleist's very popular work, but two productions received especially extensive coverage in the media. The first of these was at the Jagsthausen Festival in the courtyard of the local castle. Both Dieter Schnabel of the *Schwäbische Zeitung* and Wilhelm Ringelband of the *Badische Neueste Nachrichten* criticized Ulrich Erfurth's interpretation, feeling that it did not do justice to the intellectual, witty subtleties of the comedy. Most of the laughter was occasioned not by the drama itself, but by the director's artificial creation of a comic situation. In the opening scene, for example, Adam ran about for some time in the courtyard dressed only in long underwear. Both commentators also deplored the inadequate or inappropriate casting. Wolfgang Völz, a famous television star who played the minor role of Licht, resorted to almost any means to induce laughter and thus managed to upstage Adam and become the focal point of the performance: "Vital und komödiantisch, fast kabarettistisch im Spiel, dominierte dieser Schauspieler [Völz] vom ersten Auftritt an."[42] The combination of Herbert Fleischmann's Adam – "gescheit und kühl"[43] – and Wolfgang Schenck's colourless Walter could not outweigh the vigour and determination, the playing to the audience, of the ambitious court secretary. The notoriety which the second controversial 1977 production aroused was due largely to what one critic called a "Gag."[44] Once the curtain was raised and the audience had the opportunity to take in the naturalistic setting, Licht appeared, performed a few minor duties and sat down at a table. Because one of the drawers refused to budge, he crept under the table with a knife to open it. "Raschelnd bewegt sich eine Klopapierrolle, geisterhaft am langen Streifen gezogen, durch den Raum, auf eine rückwärtige Tür [W.C.] zu. Während Licht sich unter dem Tisch hervorarbeitet, geht die Tür auf und eine faunische Gestalt hastet humpelnd in den Saal: Der Richter Adam [Norbert Schwientek] im Adamskostüm, ängstlich geduckt, mit flackerndem Blick."[45] In this Basle interpretation, a cross between a peasant farce and a highly stylized classic, the toilet paper, the WC, and a naked Adam not only served as sensational gimicks, but were also intended to underscore from the outset director Nicolas Brieger's concept of Adam as a symbol of humanity, a defenceless, suffering victim of "ein fast mythologisches Spiel von Zerstörung und Selbstzerstörung." When, for example, Adam caught sight of the judge's chair, he was overcome by cramps and convulsions, a visual representation of the aversion he felt for his office. Walter came across less as a benevolent *deus ex machina* than as the cold, merciless executioner of a machine-like principle that destroys not only the judged but the judging. While fully exploiting the humour, this version evidently also succeeded in suggesting the underlying tragic dimension which so preoccupied Kleist: "[Nicht] nur Frau Marthes Krug bleibt in Briegers Inszenierung am Ende zerbrochen, sondern mit ihm der Schein der heilen Welt, an den sich die Beteiligten vor Prozeßbeginn noch klammern konnten."

The 200th anniversary of Kleist's birth contributed greatly to a resurgence of interest in his comedy, and since 1977 it has remained a favourite with the public. In the 1977/78 theatrical season, *Der zerbrochene Krug* was the most popular play on German-speaking stages, enjoying a total of seventeen productions and 408 performances seen by more than 150,000 theatre-goers.[46] The productions included one in French at the Centre Culturel de Chelles, in which Pierre Meyran assumed the double responsibility of director and chief actor, playing Adam with "les grâces ubuesques d'un ours, pourchassé par un essaim d'abeilles" (*Les Nouvelles Littéraires*, 9 February 1978), and Istvan Bödy's version for Karlsruhe's Staatstheater which won recognition for the attempt to convey "den Schock über die Selbstentfremdung des Menschen."[47] The two stagings which received the most extensive press coverage, those of Wolfgang Lichtenstein for Tübingen's Landestheater and Werner Düggelin for the Schauspielhaus in Zürich, illustrated the often diametrically opposed approaches used by directors in mounting *Der zerbrochene Krug*. Lichtenstein elected to offer a "Neubearbeitung" of the play based on the variant version. When the curtain rose, Licht made his way through the ranks of the waiting parties, entered the wretched and disorderly courtroom and proceeded to remove funds from the cash-box, while in the background Adam could be heard getting dressed to the accompaniment of his own groans. The major change, however, was in the conclusion. The alleged deception of shipping Ruprecht off to die in the East Indies proved to have substance, a conspiracy which Walter keenly desired to conceal. Adam (Hans Helmut Staub) finally overthrew the table and the judgment chair, tipped the court documents and his wig onto the ground, and then exited proudly and defiantly with his head held high, a far cry from the crushed, embarrassed, speedy flight of the customary ending. Some critics detected in Lichtenstein's adaptation a conscious reflection of current controversies in the Federal Republic of Germany: "Das Tübinger Ensemble hat einen *Zerbrochenen Krug* gespielt, der nicht nur die Willkür und die Ungerechtigkeit eines Obrigkeitsstaates preußischer Prägung um 1800 ... bloßlegt. Es hat auch eine klassische Vorlage so bearbeitet, daß politische Parallelen zur Gegenwart deutlich hervortreten."[48] Indeed Wolfgang Spielvogel, writing for *Unsere Zeit* (12 October 1978), attempted to make a case for seeing in the play's realism, the implied social criticism and the theatrical approach of the actors, a link to a celebrated Kleist detractor, Bertolt Brecht. In contrast, the evening began in Zürich with a cry of pain from Adam, in an immaculately clean and tidy room intended to stress deceptive appearances, as he tried to pull his shoe over his injured foot – "Dann kommt der Text, ungestrichen und nicht bearbeitet, ohne Pause, bis nach zwei Stunden das Gelächter von Gerichtsrat Walter über Frau Marthe (Rosel Schaefer), die wegen eines zerbrochenen Krugs bis nach Utrecht gehen will, die Aufführung schließt."[49] Other than the scream at the beginning and the laugh at the end, Düggelin kept to the text, avoided any allusion to topical issues, and concentrated upon a faithful rendition of Kleist's language. "Und das Zürcher Publikum honoriert vollauf dieses Auswiegen des sprachlichen Karats in jedem Wort und jedem Dialog."[50] This interpretation also retained the traditional source of audience appeal with Hans Dieter Zeidler's spirited portrayal of the village judge: "Ja, so hat man den Adam aus dem Film mit Emil Jannings in Erinnerung: urwüchsig, beleibt, den mächtigen kahlen Schädel von zwei schweren Schlägen gezeichnet. Ein solcher Polterer reißt alle Aufmerksamkeit an sich, macht alle Fragen nach den tieferen Schichten des Stücks überflüssig und schert sich auch nicht um Zeitbezüge."[51] Both the Tübingen and the Zürich productions gave guest performances, the former in Tettnang and the latter at the Schwetzinger Festspiele (May 1979), where it was the only nonmusical contribution to that annual festival.

As reported in the *Bayern Kurier* (5 January 1980), *Der zerbrochene Krug* again surpassed all classical and modern plays to secure the top ranking in the 1978/79 season: "Mit 421 Aufführungen in der Bundesrepublik Deutschland, Österreich und der Schweiz lag es unangefochten an der Spitze aller Aufführungen." The first of these productions to attract considerable critical attention, Alfred Kirchner's version for the Stuttgart Staatstheater in February 1979, sought to realize the tragedy underlying the comedy and reflected in its author's life. In an interview, Kirchner expressed the view, "daß dieses Lustspiel viel ernster, bitterer und trauriger ist, als es meistens dargestellt wird."[52] The director broached the topic of Adam as a tragic victim in the opening sequence, where the judge first appeared as a sort of helpless mummy caught up in the expansive curtains running from the back of the stage. Jan Peter Tripp reinforced this sense of helplessness and isolation by designing an open structure on piles positioned in a sea of shrubs, with several gangways, a door that hung in the air leading nowhere, and numerous beams to which the court records were attached in cellophane bags – all of which reminded Heinrich Domes (*Schwäbisches Tagblatt*, 27 February 1979) of a "Henkersgerüst." In his reading of Adam, Gert Voss, "der Spindeldürre" (Domes), downplayed the excessive vitality and vulgar sensuality normally associated with the role, and attempted to give a more intellectual dimension to the judge's character. By implication, his individual fate served to point out the fallible nature of justice in general, essentially Lichtenstein's message in Tübingen. (Several reviewers also mention parallels to the then current political situation.) Kirchner's production received a lukewarm reception from the critics, who objected to the arbitrariness of the set, the interruption of the speeches and action by a series of drawn-out pauses, and – contrary to the director's avowed intent – the ascendancy of the comical over the tragic: "Die intellektuellen, mehr witzigen als komischen Feinheiten kamen in Alfred Kirchners originalitätssüchtiger Interpretation des Lustspiels *Der zerbrochene Krug* etwas zu kurz."[53]

In an effort to cast new light on the comedy, Dietrich Haughs, like other directors before him, included parts of Kleist's longer first version in his staging for Munich's Cuvilliéstheater but otherwise respected the text, made no cuts or adaptations, and gained "ein[en] voll[en] Publikumserfolg"[54] for his rather conventional interpretation with its commendable attention to the drama's poetic language: "Aus der Genauigkeit der Sprachbehandlung, von der Sinnbetonung bis zur Diktion, erhalten [Kleists Figuren] Kontur."[55] Joachim Kaiser regretted Haughs's failure to take advantage of the more complex portrait of Eve implied in the original version, while Rolf Lehnhardt (*Schwäbische Zeitung*, 11 April 1979) faulted actor Hans Korte for having neglected "die Triebleben-Komponente" that usually arouses sympathy for Adam as a victim of nature.

The third production of 1979 to attract more than usual press coverage *premièred* in the context of Hans Richter's Heppenheim Festival. The stage scenery created by Friedrich Goebels stood in the courtyard of the Heppenheim Winzerkeller, an arrangement which enabled the spectators to sit on benches at tables under an awning and to imbibe the local wine during the performance. "Da entsteht sie von selbst," noted Monika Lanzendörfer (*Mannheimer Morgen*, 3 August 1979), "eine erwartungsgespannte Festzelt-Atmosphäre, die sich während der Eröffnungsvorstellung des *Zerbrochenen Kruges* in knalligen Lachsalven und im überschäumenden Applaus entlud." This jovial outdoor ambiance, no doubt abetted by the wine, was enhanced by the choice of the male lead, Burgtheater actor Fritz Muliar. After his notable success as Schweik in Vienna, he again reaped "donnernden Beifall" (Lanzendörfer) as Adam: "Fritz Muliar besitzt das Kreatürliche, das der Adam haben muß. Auch hat er das Bauernschlaue und Lauernde, um immer blitzartig aus der Falle auszubrechen, bevor sie zuschnappt. Jovialität aus Berechnung, Gefährlichkeit, wenn Eve unter Druck gesetzt wird."[56] Christa Lantz even went as far as to compare Muliar's to Jannings's Adam, maintaining that the former's "leichtere, charmantere Erfassung der Figur zunehmend an Reiz [gewinnt]" (*Rhein-Neckar-Zeitung*, 3 August 1979). Yet another feature contributing to the enthusiastic reception was Joachim Hess's capable directing of the drama. Hess acquired substantial notoriety in 1959 when he prepared for Studio Hamburg Kleist's *Der zerbrochene Krug* as the first "Klassiker-Live-Sendung," a courageous undertaking given the difficulties of televised live performances (where anything can go wrong, and usually does) and the dominance of the film starring Emil Jannings. Despite these potential problems, "Es wurde," to cite Wilhelm Ringelband, "ein Bombenerfolg," one that helped to release the play from what many had perceived to be the incomparability of the Jannings version. With understandable reluctance, Hess returned to the comedy twenty years later, ignoring his earlier decision: "Den *zerbrochenen Krug* wollte ich nie mehr inszenieren."[57] Lantz raised the only major complaint against this second triumph: the actors playing the minor parts lost in significance in light of the outstanding performances of Eva Pflug (Frau Martha), Hans Richter (Licht) and the star of the show, Muliar.

Of the several other 1979 productions one additional example warrants inclusion, that of Harald Clemen for Düsseldorf's Schauspielhaus. The reviewer (J. Sch.) for the *Frankfurter Allgemeine Zeitung* (6 November 1979) criticized the staging for its overall flat interpretation of Kleist's original version and for inadequate portrayals of Adam and Eve: "Alois Strempels Adam ... verliert seine komplexe Menschlichkeit weitgehend. ... Doch das meiste Gewicht hat das Mädchen Eve in der Darstellung von Gudrun Gabriel verloren." However, a colleague in Hungary proved more generous in his/her evaluation of the Schauspielhaus's guest performances in the framework of the "Kulturwoche der BRD in Budapest": "Es war keine leichte Aufgabe, das Stück auf Grundlage des Kleistschen Originalmanuskriptes auf die Bühne zu bringen, doch Clemen meisterte diese Aufgabe in einer seinem 'Haus' völlig würdigen Weise. Freilich hatte es auch mit ganz ausgezeichneten Schauspielern zu tun, so verkörperte Alois Stempel den Richter Adam und Gudrun Gabriel das Evchen."[58] The actors spoke German, but the Hungarian reviewer remarked, "Freilich wurde und wird [*Der zerbrochene Krug*] auch von ungarischen Theatern oft gespielt – in der heimischen Sprache natürlich." Only three years later, after opening at the Ruhrfestspiele in Recklinghausen, Wolf Sesemann's social-critical interpretation, in which the letter conscripting Ruprecht for duty in the colonies turns out to be genuine, went on a tour to Hungary. The *Budapester Rundschau* (4 July 1983) reported that Tatabánya and Budapest welcomed it with enthusiasm and high praise – another sign of Hungarian appreciation of Kleist's comedy.

While *Der zerbrochene Krug* forfeited its position as the most performed play in the German-speaking world during the 1979–80 season to Michael Pertwee's comedy *Sextett*, it nevertheless had 413 performances and maintained its top ranking with theatre-goers, attracting close to 200,000 spectators. One particular production in the Gießen Stadttheater gained notoriety by going to extremes. After a preparatory period of cooperation between theatre people, university students in Germanistik, and the Kleist-specialist Dirk Grathoff, director Henri Hohenemser and designer Dieter Bode presented "'Lebende Bilder' nach Gemälden eines alten Niederländers."[59] Coherence was seriously jeopardized by an attention to detail that entailed even accurate reproduction of sounds – barking dogs, wooden shoes resounding on a wooden floor, and clucking chickens that remained on stage throughout the evening. In direct contrast, the most celebrated production of 1980 eschewed the naturalistic, genre-painting style: "Die Bühne von Andreas Reinhardt ist offen und kahl, seitlich von weißem Gemäuer begrenzt, nur mit Stühlen und Tischen spärlich bestückt. Kein 'Milieu', keine ländliche Folklore, kein wärmender Mief."[60] Hans Lietzau, who had inaugurated his Berlin tenure as theatre director with a *Prinz Friedrich von Homburg* that was eventually eclipsed by Peter Stein's version, elected to end his eight-year stay in Berlin with a new staging of *Der zerbrochene Krug* for the Schloßpark-Theater, and this time his efforts met with a more positive response, as reported in all the major West German newspapers. The reviewers, however, were equally in agreement that most of the credit should go to the inspired interpretation of one person. "Insgesamt bliebe uns der Regisseur Lietzau allerdings die zündende Idee schuldig," observed Sibylle Wirsing (*Frankfurter Allgemeine Zeitung*, 26 January 1980), "wenn die Erleuchtung nicht selbstverständlich durch [Bernhard] Minetti gegeben wäre. Mit seinem Auftritt entbrennt das Spektakel, das eingangs nur nach besten Kräften konventionell war, in frostiger Glut." Minetti did not play Adam as one might expect – critics have usually regarded the casting of the judge as crucial to the success of the comedy – but rather his antagonist: "In Lietzaus Inszenierung fällt überraschend groß die Rolle des Amtsrats Walter aus. Ja, weil Bernhard Minetti ihn spielt, mit seiner eigensinnig bohrenden hohen Stimme, seinem inquisitorisch vorgerecktem Kopf, seinen hellen Augen, die auf Durchblick geschärft sind. Er stattet den ausgebildeten juristischen Kopf mit den Effekten kühler Amüsiertheit aus."[61] Minetti's Walter came across as a visitor from another world, the cultivated urbanite clothed in silk and furs and sporting as a sign of sophistication "an langer Schnur ein[en] schwarz[en] Seidensamtmuff" (Weber). Confident in the wisdom and dignity age bestows (Minetti celebrated his 75th birthday only two days after the *première*), this district justice showed signs of thoroughly enjoying the cat-and-mouse game played at Adam's expense. At one point he cunningly seemed to fraternize with his victim over a glass of wine, to be taken in by Adam's attempted bribes and diversions, but "[j]etzt wird er [Walter] nach der Erfrischung behutsam den Start einleiten, die strenge Kommission sein, die nicht mehr durch die Figur sieht ..." (Wirsing). Because Minetti's ironic *tour de force* became the "Zentrum der Aufführung"[62] – not only for the critics, but also for the audience: "Langer stürmischer Beifall zum Schluß. Er galt Minetti"[63] – Helmut Wildt's portrayal of Adam as a wretched, small-time crook, arousing sympathy more than revulsion or indignation, paled in dramatic significance: "Daß Minetti keinen adäquaten Partner hat, ist die Scharte des Abends" (Wirsing).[64] The general public received this production so positively that Munich hosted a guest performance where, to quote Joachim Kaiser (*Süddeutsche Zeitung*, 31 May/1 June 1980), "Lietzau ein Inszenierungs-Gedicht bot, das an seine größten Münchner Momente anschloß"; and the national television network ARD (Allgemeine Rundfunkanstalten Deutschlands) broadcast it throughout West Germany in September of the same year: "Eine ganze Reihe ausgezeichneter Schauspieler ... sorgte dafür, daß dieser 'Bestseller' der Weltliteratur auch bei denen ankommt, die sich lieber von modernen Späßen unterhalten lassen."[65]

What could be generously described as a modest accomplishment, *The Broken Pitcher* in Jon Swan's English translation, opened at the Martinique Theater in New York City on 7 October 1981. The director, Carl Weber, once a member of the Berliner Ensemble, had already acquired a reputation for mounting German stage classics, but in this instance, according to the *New York Times*'s reviewer (8 October 1981), his staging seriously lacked in "comic virtuosity." The critic blamed the play itself as much as the performance, finding the parallels between Adam and either his biblical namesake or Oedipus "forced," and deploring the predictable nature of the plot, "an endless series of excuses, subterfuges and delays as Adam tries to shift the blame." George Ede failed to demonstrate the requisite humorous verve to fill Adam's focal role, even though the implied rivalry between the judge and his clerk (Larry Pine) provided some initial amusement. The growing European popularity of *Der zerbrochene Krug* would seem to contradict the review's concluding judgment: "[The] play operates under an unveiled cloud of heaviness" and points rather to problematic casting and directing.

Similar complaints arose against Jürgen Bosse's poorly received two-hour version for Das kleine Haus des Nationaltheaters in Mannheim. Gerhard Stadelmaier (*Stuttgarter Zeitung*, 24 October 1981) singled out a lack of suspense, since "alle [so tun], als sei nichts im Spiel als ein wenig Herumsteherei," while the *Mannheimer Morgen* (K.H., 24/25 October 1981) noted a propensity to eliminate or minimize contrasts in order to convey a homogeneity unbecoming to the comedy: the "Kollektiv-Unternehmen" of ensemble acting predominated over the "individualistische Ausstrahlung" of great personalities. But Kleist's language proved to be the main stumbling block, partly the fault of the actors – "Schlechte Sprecher" (Stadelmaier) – and partly the result of a large, empty stage from whose considerable depth the performers had to recite their lines: "Das Ergebnis: schon in der siebten Reihe waren ganze Passagen des Textes nicht mehr zu verstehen" (K.H.).

In a new twist to the comedy, but one which nonetheless respected the author's text, the Gruppe 80 presented in September 1982 the "Alptraum des Dorfrichters"[66] in the Treffpunkt Petersplatz in Vienna. Intrigued by the dreamlike, somnambulistic atmosphere in many of Kleist's works and taking his cue from Adam's self-condemning dream at the beginning of the third scene, director Helmut Wiesner transformed the play into a single, continuous nightmare sustained by Robert Kneitschel's distorted, expressionistic stage set: "So realisiert sich für den seltsam schlaftrunkenen Adam, vom ersten Erwachen an, der böse Traum in der Wirklichkeit."[67] Consequently, Alfred Schedl's depiction of Adam suggested not so much the cunning, robust country judge as the fearful loner who realizes deep down that he has lost. Commentators deplored Schedl's "miserabl[e] Sprechtechnik" (Butterweck), but Kathrein, in a strong endorsement, even managed to turn this vice into a virtue: "Wenn dieser Schauspieler schlecht artikuliert, die Konsonanten verschmiert und die Dialektfärbung nicht verbergen kann, so schmerzt das bei Kleists großartiger Sprache, gleichzeitig holt diese Ungelenkigkeit jedoch neue Valeurs aus dem Text, die der Dichtung durchaus gerecht werden." Although the reviewers recorded some inconsistencies in theatrical style and awkward moments where suspense faltered, they had only praise for the dialogues between Adam and Licht (Ottwald John) and the drinking scene with Adam and Walter (Dieter Hofinger): " [So] komisch, berührend und den Gehalt des Werkes vermittelnd hat man Kleists geniale Komödie in Wien schon lange nicht gesehen" (Kathrein).

As if to gainsay the "drastisch[e] Komik" of Klaus Heydenreich's staging of *Der zerbrochene Krug* in Stuttgart (February 1983) – "Stöhnend, rülpsend und keuchend wie der Dorfrichter Adam, ... so wälzt sich die Inszenierung in Kleists herrlichem Text schniefend und schnaubend herum"[68] – Ernst Wendt endeavoured in his production for Hamburg's Schauspielhaus to free the comedy "aus den tradierten Zwängen der lauten Komik"[69] in the most widely covered and controversial interpretation of 1983. As Simon Neubauer aptly summarized it: "So ernst, so zurückgenommen in der Aktion, so 'unkomödiantisch' im Ausdruck hat man des Dorfrichters Fall wohl noch nie gesehen." This attempt to remove the play from the usual conventions of the comedy began with the alienating set contrived by Roger von Moellendorf – a gigantic room in depressing, sober grey tones with a bare minimum of props, prompting Mechthild Lange to comment: "der Raum läßt eher an Kafka denken denn an ein holländisches Genrebild" (*Frankfurter Rundschau*, 19 March 1983). When the curtain was raised, the audience did not observe a snoring Adam in bed but rather a vulnerable Adam clothed in white, seated on the floor binding his injured foot and gazing at himself in a mirror. He barely noticed the entrance of his secretary dressed in black, smoking a cigar. As soon as Licht climbed on a chair to open a window, light suddenly streamed down upon the wretched, helpless figure below. In the subsequent dialogue Adam recounts his prophetic dream, and several reviewers gained the impression that for him the nightmare never ended, but persisted in his conscious world as well. Wendt was intent upon discovering and bringing to the fore the tragic potential of the drama's characters, especially that of the village judge whose presentation suggested someone on the verge of a mental breakdown: "Dieser Adam [Peter Roggisch] ist ein kranker Mann, ein Verstörter, dessen gerade noch bemeisterter Wahn jederzeit ins Offene brechen konnte."[70] He seemed to be a person who has already given up, who openly coerces his witnesses in his superior's immediate presence, as if inviting disaster, and who lacks the cunning and the energy to extricate himself from his predicament. As had almost become the rule rather than the exception by this time, Wendt used Kleist's longer version, in which Eve outlines her version of the nocturnal visit, but by stressing the part of her narrative where she reports, "Läßt er [Adam] am Tisch jetzt auf den Stuhl sich nieder, / Und faßt mich so, bei beiden Händen, seht, / Und sieht mich an ... / Zwei abgemessene Minuten starr mich an" (2214–8), he opened up another perspective: "Wendts Inszenierung, eher tiefsinnig als sinnenfroh, entdeckt noch ein ganz anderes Stück darin: ein Traumspiel vom *verliebten* Richter."[71] Adam thus joined the ranks of those lovelorn Kleistian protagonists who, in a somnambulistic state of mind, come into conflict with the real world. But in his disturbing relationship to reality, he was not alone: "Nicht bloß der Krug, die ganze Welt, schreibt Wendt im Programmheft, ist in diesem deutschen Lustspiel 'zerscherbt'" (Heinrichs), and hence Walter (Hans-Peter Korff), far from being a *deus ex machina*, was merely a tired, ill-humoured civil servant who found himself overtaxed and who, like Adam, assumed an attitude of resignation. When Eve finally unmasked the real culprit, Adam opened up his arms towards her with a smile on his face, walked towards the edge of the stage as if to confide in the audience, but remained silent and exited. According to Heinrichs, theory and practice did not achieve a happy union in this production. Still, on the whole, the critics appreciated Wendt's innovative approach, notwithstanding its lukewarm reception by the audience.

In 1961 the Maxim Gorki Theater in East Berlin presented *Der zerbrochene Krug* as a realistic portrait of the times. In October 1983 the Volksbühne in the same city sponsored a production, again with a strong realistic bias, under the joint direction of Helmut Straßburger and Ernstgeorg Hering. The critic of the East German *Neues Deutschland* (12 October 1983) had some praise for the staging, pointing out the "nontraditional" interpretation of Frau Marthe's role, which was played "nicht mit draller plebejischer Vitalität, sondern als kleinbürgerlich-spießige Moralhüterin." However, Andreas Roßmann, in a devastatingly negative review for the West German *Weser Kurier* (14 January 1984), objected to the arbitrary allusion to Kleist's Prussia to the detriment of the work's universal, timeless appeal. A gigantic pile of potatoes arose between the miserable pieces of furniture and the "Allgemeine Gerichtsordnung für die Preußischen Staaten" was reproduced in the program. "Kleists Grab, das die Rückseite des Programmhefts abbildet, liegt bekanntlich am Kleinen Wannsee, heute West-Berlin. Nun können es auch die Ost-Berliner besichtigen: in der Volksbühne am Luxemburger-Platz."

The productions of 1984 included Bernard Sobel's nonfarcical treatment of the comedy, "chuchotements sur la neige,"[72] for the Théâtre de Gennevilliers in Paris (January) and Holger Berg's successful realization of *Der zerbrochene Krug* on the small stage of the Kammerspiel in Frankfurt a.M. (July), which, because of the limited space available, drew the spectators into the courtroom. But the two stagings to pique more than average interest were Wolfgang Gropper's Bavarian version for Munich's Volkstheater and Dieter Hilsdorf's sombre interpretation for Ulm's Stadttheater, the latter reminiscent of Wendt's Hamburg experiment. The Munich dramatist Leopold Ahlsen wrote what amounted to an adaptation of the comedy, translating Kleist's text into the Bavarian dialect and removing the action to an imaginary little town, Huisenhofa (near Dachau), in 1832, the year in which Ludwig I's son Otto went to fight in Greece. Adam thus threatened to send Ruprecht to certain death not in the East Indies, but in Greece. The adaptation was first aired as a "bayerisches Hörspiel" before Gropper put it on stage. In both mediums, Gustl Bayrhammer played Adam to the zealous approbation of the audience, and despite some critical reservations: – "Und man fragt sich natürlich, ob es sinnvoll war, Kleists hochartifizielle Sprache in ein schwieriges Bayrisch zu übersetzen"[73] – the noisy, energetic theatrical version was an unqualified "success" at its *première*.

Hilsdorf's attempt to take the comedy seriously began in the very first scene, when he had Eve (Ellen Schulz) narrate the whole incident as it appears in the original conclusion to the play. This transposition obliged the audience to be more concerned – in the Brechtian manner – with the process than with the outcome: "'Der Richter Adam hat den Krug zerbrochen!' ruft das Mädchen Eve ins Publikum und nimmt mit diesem ersten Satz nebst weiterem Dialogwerk vorweg, was der Dichter ihr und anderen Prozeßbeteiligten erst ganz am Ende in den Mund gelegt hat."[74] It also had the effect of transferring the major interest away from Wolfgang Jaroschka's portrayal of Adam to the lovers who, despite their feelings for one another, must often remain speechless, frustrated, and essentially alone. One commentator, Martina Prante of the *Schwäbische Zeitung* (29 March 1984), came away with the notion that Hilsdorf wished to raise some doubt as to whether or not Eve was in fact innocent of encouraging Adam's advances. "Das Happy-End," Thomas Thieringer typically noted (*Süddeutsche Zeitung*, 3 April 1984), "verspricht keine schönen Zeiten. Dafür sind Eve und Ruprecht [Michael Schlegelberger] schon zu sehr vom Leben gezeichnet." A Berlin audience also heartily applauded this reading of "das liebe alte Stück" (*Schwäbisches Tageblatt*, 15 February 1985) during a guest performance in February 1985.

In the year 1985 two productions attracted critical attention and both of them took place in Switzerland. The Teater Grischun mounted a translation in the Rhaeto-Romanic or Romansh language of southeastern Switzerland by Ursicin G.B. Derungs, with some deletions and revisions of scenes. District judge Walter spoke German, and any dialogue involving this outsider was conducted in the same tongue, while the characters otherwise spoke Rhaeto-Romanic among themselves. Director Marco Gieriet sought to convert the comedy into "Volkstheater" by emphasizing in the words of the reviewer for the *Neue Zürcher Zeitung* (28 June 1985) "eine bewegte, turbulente Szenerie," and to promote the preservation of a threatened minority language. The staging achieved wider exposure when it enjoyed an enthusiastic reception during a guest appearance in Zürich's Theater am Neumarkt. Whereas this adaptation adhered to a well established pattern on the part of smaller theatres of accommodating Kleist's text to local interests, with an emphasis on comical entertainment, director Peter Borchardt, in the second Swiss production, which opened in February in Bern's Stadttheater, followed another trend, one practised by the larger, well established theatres, of allowing the comedy's universal, timeless aspect to inform his interpretation: "Lachen als Mittel der Erkenntnis und Selbstfindung, als Befreiung von dem Zwang, unsere Fehler und Unzulänglichkeiten zu verdrängen und zu vertuschen. Als 'Möglichkeit des Überlebens' auch; eine Möglichkeit, die Peter Borchardt in unserer an grauenvollen Perspektiven des Schreckens reichen Zeit ebenso bedeutungsvoll erscheint wie Erkenntnisprozesse im Kleinen in der persönlichen Begegnung mit Menschen."[75] As a consequence of the director's darker perception, the performance was reportedly reserved and text-oriented. Laughter never ran the risk of drowning out the underlying philosophical view of life, although, as the critic for *Der Bund* stressed, "die reiche Situationskomik des Stücks weiss Borchardt gut auszunützen." This Bern staging garnered positive reviews and public approval, no doubt attributable in part to the first-rate casting: special accolades went to Hans-Heinz Moser who as Adam did not forget "die stilleren Töne, die blossen Andeutungen, die verschmitzten kleinen Gesten."[76]

In 1986 two further adaptations of Kleist's comedy, both faulted for their slow pace – "Lacing the mad with ant-paced satire";[77] "[Kleist] wird langsamer gespielt"[78] – attracted critical response. In the first instance Philip Hedley presented for the Stratford East Theatre (London) Henry Livings's version,[79] in which the action of the play was shifted to the English Pennines at roughly the same historical period as in the original, and became a social critique of the rural working class's lot during the Napoleonic era. Adam became Adam Kenworthy JP and Walter a rather pompous, ineffectual visiting MP Don Crann, playing the judge as a "grotesque buffoon," indulged in excessive digressions; at one point he even invited the prompter to step forward for a bow. Secondary parts, exploited extensively for comic effect, kept audience interest alive. Noteworthy in this regard was John Halstead's drunken constable who, asleep below a portrait of the "mad" George III, would revive briefly at the opportune moment to roar "Silence in court." In the estimation of Martin Cropper, the staging lacked direction and failed to put across the satire: "Philip Hedley's static production gives the bizarre impression of a Shakespearean subplot gone mad."

In the second adaptation of the same year, no doubt encouraged by Gropper's popular success in Munich, Klaus Sonnenschein, availing himself of Sabine Thiesler's text of *Der zerbrochene Krug* "ins Berlinische jesetzt,"[80] produced the comedy for West Berlin's Tribüne with himself in the main role, to the general delight of the audience: "Die einen im Publikum genießen die popularische Transformation deutlich, die anderen staunen, was man mit unseren Altklassikern alles machen kann."[81] Much of the humour, however, could be attributed not to the drama, but rather to the local Prussian flavour, which the spectator could more readily relate to and appreciate, while the serious undercurrent championed by Ernst Wendt evidently did not receive its due.

This criticism could not be levelled at the production which obtained by far the most extensive press coverage in 1986. It is surely a fitting indication of *Der zerbrochene Krug*'s enduring importance and popularity that Dieter Dorn staged it for the small Landestheater to open the Salzburg Festival in July, an event marred by much controversy, including Herbert von Karajan's reprise of *Carmen*[82] and the presence of the Austrian chancellor Kurt Waldheim – "mit Beifall, aber auch mit Pfiffen empfangen."[83] In an interview with Karin Kathrein, Dorn attempted to justify his interpretation of the play, suitably supported by Jürgen Rose's desolate sets in tones of grey and brown, as a black comedy, or as Dorn put it, "ein Stück Totentanz." "Ich habe nicht versucht, irgendwelche Aspekte besserwisserisch herauszuschneiden, sondern mich bemüht, es ganz in seinen Versen und Vorgängen zu belassen ... . Aus der Grundsituation, Recht zu erforschen, entwickelt sich ein groteskes, irrwitziges Sprachstück über die Gesellschaft, über den Verlust des Vertrauens in die Obrigkeit wie in den Nächsten, über die Liebe, den Menschen und den Tod."[84] Rejecting the temptation to resort to gags or situation comedy, "holte Dorn alle Komik nur aus dem Kleist-Wort,"[85] a feature praised by most commentators, but not without some reservation: "So überzeugend Dieter Dorn diese Konflikte [Vertrauen, Mißtrauen, die unbedingte Liebe] und ihren Gehalt sichtbar zu machen versteht, so geht die Sensibilität, mit der er den Text auslotet, doch mitunter auf Kosten der Dramatik."[86] Adam, interpreted by a slim Rolf Boysen, far from being the hedonistic village tyrant, is a lonely, tormented, overworked country magistrate seeking consolation and escape in wine and love. The production took pains to suggest a genuine affection on the part of the old bachelor for his late friend's daughter. One of the major themes of the staging referred to by the majority of reviewers was the loss of faith, not only in human institutions such as the law or the central authority (Walter), but also in the intimate human relationships involving the loved one, father, or mother. Kathrein singled out the particularly memorable moment where Eve (Sibylle Canonica), her back turned to the audience, described to her fiancé her understanding of an authentic, loving relationship based on trust. Dorn chose to conclude his two-and-a-half-hour, uninterrupted production with the longer version in which Eve speaks out against the social system and its abuse of power. As a visually dramatized case in point, C. Bernd Sucher described Walter's (Claus Eberth) purported conciliatory gesture: "Walters Kuß, so derb und feist Eve auf den Mund gepreßt, daß diese verstört ist über die Vergewaltigung, zu der Verlobter Ruprecht [Axel Milberg] auch noch enthusiastisch seine Erlaubnis gegeben hat, er bleibt ungeahndet."[87] This interpretation, in which "dem Zuschauer bei Kleists Lustspiel das Lachen vergehen sollte,"[88] seems to have achieved its objective, for in the words of Kathrein, "Es wurde weniger gelacht als am Ende applaudiert" (*Die Presse*, 28 July 1986). In October of the same year, Dorn brought his staging back home to Munich to open the season for the Kammerspiele where it was sold out for several evenings in advance.

This tendency to produce *Der zerbrochene Krug* as "desillusionierte Komödie"[89] continued with the last major staging of 1986 in the Stadttheater of Basle. Director Mark Zurmühle endeavoured to show, "dass der 'Zerbrochene Krug' das denkbar unartigste, straffste Stück Alptraum ist, über das man lachen kann,"[90] an interpretation once again no doubt indebted to Wiesner or Wendt. A bed placed on a ramp between the rows of spectators in the orchestra section symbolically dominated the action and served as a constant reminder of the nightmare quality of the production set in black (designed by Erich Fischer). In the prologue, Adam (Jo Kärn), a little man, sits up in bed staring off into space, as if still caught in the grip of a terrifying vision. Above him appears the figure of Eve reciting the incriminating verses from the twelfth scene in the original version: "Und faßt mich so, bei beiden Händen, seht / Und sieht mich an. ... / Zwei abgemessene Minuten starr mich an" (2215–17), words repeated later in the evening as part of a scandalous exposure. "Ein Lustspiel," wrote

Christoph Schneider, "wo einem die Lust um die Ohren geschlagen wird und die unordentlichen Wünsche inkriminiert sind. Daran hat dann der Zuschauer Lust, Adam träumt schwer davon."

Despite *Der zerbrochene Krug*'s inauspicious *première* at the Weimar Hoftheater in 1808, its present position as the most accessible and the most performed of all Kleist's dramas has confirmed the appropriateness of its being the first of his plays to experience a major production. Its popularity may be explained in part by the dearth of native German comedies in the German theatrical repertoire, but surely also in part by its dramatic excellence and audience appeal which, transcending international boundaries, have resulted in adaptations in France, England, North America, and even India. As with many great comedies, *Der zerbrochene Krug* lends itself readily to both a comic and a tragic interpretation, and not surprisingly, its stage history reflects an oscillation between these two poles. Throughout most of the nineteenth and the first half of the twentieth century, productions have been inclined to emphasize the humorous aspect, a strategy guaranteed to ensure a box-office success, and the casting of an energetic, robust actor with the talent to exploit the comic potential of Adam's character has been instrumental in achieving this success. One has only to consider Theodor Döring's and Emil Jannings's domination of the part in their respective centuries to appreciate the extent to which a skilled comic actor can leave his mark upon a drama. But in the 1970s the pendulum began to swing towards the underlying tragic potential which some directors found better expressed in the longer original version. As Eve's concluding speech came to be the focal point of the interpretation, Adam increasingly lost both in status and in stature, becoming a wretchedly small, thin, overburdened village functionary, a piteous victim of life in general, and often the dramatic interest shifted accordingly to either Walter or the lovers. In any case, the message that has emerged is a depressing one of human fallibility and isolation. While no one can deny the fundamental importance of these themes in Kleist's *Weltanschauung*, the preservation of some balance between the two extremes, when coupled with an appreciation of and respect for Kleist's poetic genius, has perhaps done more justice to the greatest comedy of the German language.

## CHAPTER THREE

# *Amphitryon*

Almost from the day of its publication, *Amphitryon* has suffered severely from its designation by Kleist himself as "Ein Lustspiel nach Molière" (245). Unwittingly, the dramatist played into the hands of ardent nationalists on both sides of the border who exploited the work as a vehicle to demonstrate alleged cultural superiority. In 1807 a commentator writing for the *Morgenblatt* proclaimed: "Die bekannte Fabel, ... die unter Molières Händen zu einer echt rationellen Hahnreischrift geworden, ist von Kleist mit solcher Keuschheit und Heiligkeit wiedergeboren, daß uns bis auf den heutigen Tag kein Werk bekannt ist, in welchem eine vielsinnige Mythe der Griechen auf so überraschende, übermenschliche und edle Weise gedeutet worden. ... Es ist eine Aussicht, die dem Römer fremd bleiben mußte, und zu deren Ahndung der Franzose sich nie erheben wird."[1] This chauvinistic attitude, symptomatic of the hostility and narrow-mindedness expressed also by other German newspapers, soon elicited responses in kind, such as that printed in the *Journal de Paris*: "Un poète allemand, nommé M. de Kleist, a fait imprimer à Dresden un *Amphitryon* qu'il veut bien donner comme une imitation de la pièce de Molière, qui porte le même nom. Un journaliste du même pays, moins modeste ou plus hardi que l'imitateur, croit que cette pièce est aussi supérieure à celle de Molière, que la nation allemande est supérieure à la nation française dans tous les genres dramatiques."[2] As this political rather than literary dispute was intensified over the years, a tendency arose to regard Kleist as the incarnation of the more serious, spiritual German approach to life as opposed to the wit and frivolity of French taste, a prejudice which has been corrected only in more recent times.[3] As Claude David has pointed out, "Und doch hat es, – Heine ausgenommen – kaum einen anderen deutschen Dichter gegeben, dessen ganzes Leben und Wirken so eng auf

Frankreich bezogen schien wie gerade Heinrich von Kleist."[4] In the heat of the controversy, critics lost sight of the crucial fact that German literature does indeed owe a debt of gratitude to Molière's comedy for having provided the incentive necessary to create a German masterpiece. The only loser in this battle turned out to be Kleist's *Amphitryon*.

Of all Kleist's plays, *Amphitryon* had to wait the longest for its *première*, which finally took place on 8 April 1899 in Berlin's Neues Theater as a special Sunday-afternoon performance mounted by the Verein für historisch-moderne Festspiele under the direction of its founder, Dr Wolfgang Kirchbach. With the aid of exceptional theatrical talent, the association aspired to bring to life unperformed works which, although written in or dealing with the past, still possessed a contemporary appeal. In keeping with this aim and in conformity with the prevailing naturalistic style, Kirchbach endeavoured to transform the comedy into a psychologically oriented treatment of a modern marital fidelity problem, while at the same time acknowledging: "das Ganze ist und bleibt Mythos, es ist Lustspiel. ... Frivolität der Anmut gehört in dieses Spiel."[5] This lighter approach helped to secure the favourable welcome which the production enjoyed, as can be inferred from the report of the *Berliner Tageblatt* (10 April 1899) which noted: "über die Clownsszenen [wurde] am meisten gelacht." But the efforts of the principals obviously also contributed to the success, since the audience applauded, often at great length, the serious exchanges between Alkmene and Jupiter, especially the fifth scene of the second act: "Frau Alwine Wieke (vom Schillertheater) als Alkmene, Herr Hofschauspieler [Max] Wegner aus Weimar als Amphitryon, Herr Hofschauspieler [Roderich] Arndt als Jupiter waren dank ihrem darstellerischen Können und dem regen Eifer, den sie ihren Aufgaben widmeten, in erster Linie die Träger des Bühnenerfolges, der dem Werk mit herzlicher Wärme zu Theil wurde."[6] It redounds to Kirchbach's credit that he had the courage to stage the comedy in the first place, that he managed to convey both the comic as well as the tragic implications, and that he thus paved the way for established playhouses to undertake their own version.

The positive response accorded the *première* encouraged the Schiller Theater to open a production on 30 January 1900 which saw thirteen performances in the first season and was to become a permanent feature of its repertoire. "In der Vorstellung des Schiller Theaters verkörperte Alwine Wiecke eine sehr sympathische, sinnige und keusche Alkmene. Albert Patry [who also directed] verlieh nach Kräften seinem Göttervater in der Gestalt des Thebanerfürsten

Majestät, Glanz und liebenswürdige Beredsamkeit, und Ferdinand Gregori wußte unser Interesse für die tragikomische Lage und Figur des Amphitryon bis zum Schlusse wach zu halten."[7] Both Kirchbach and Patry based their Berlin stagings on Kleist's original text with very few cuts. The same year witnessed another version, this time in the Berliner Theater, produced by Paul Lindau. Although he adhered to Kleist's text, he added Molière's prologue, in which Mercury implores the goddess of night to prolong her stay, and the conclusion, where Sosias's words give a satirical slant to the whole episode. Critics and audiences alike manifested their glowing approval of this interpretation, especially of the comic interludes in which Sosias figured so prominently and hence, as the *Vossische Zeitung* (4 March 1900) noted: "Das Burleske trat ein wenig einseitig hervor, während die mystische Tiefe, über der das Stück spielt, nicht recht sichtbar wurde."

Meanwhile, to the south, since the Bavarian capital refused to be outdone, the Literarische Gesellschaft München offered a special performance of *Amphitryon* in the Gärtnerplatztheater in December 1899. In direct parallel to the experience in Berlin, the comic portrayal of Sosias by Karl Heine won for the production a noteworthy triumph, but not one which could be directly attributed to the overall excellence of the drama. This became apparent on 3 March 1900 when the Hoftheater in Munich mounted both *Amphitryon* and *Der zerbrochene Krug* in one evening, the former presented in the adaptation written by Ludwig Ganghofer for the Gärtnerplatztheater, which reduced the original three acts to two, shortened the dialogue rather severely, and exhibited very little reverence for Kleist's language. Ganghofer also took it upon himself to rearrange the plot: Mercury now gave utterance to Amphitryon's request for a divine son. The failure of this distortion is attested to by the brevity of its stage life – a mere two performances in the Hoftheater and only one in the Gärtnerplatztheater. Even though Wilhelm Henzen made an even more severe revision for an ineffectual Leipzig production in 1903 with the intent of eliminating the inconsistencies between an antique mythical and a modern pantheistic Jupiter,[8] *Amphitryon*, despite the productions described so far, failed to achieve recognition as an eminently stageworthy drama.

An important breakthrough did, however, occur in that same year with the Austrian *première* in the court-theatre style: "Die Aufführungsmöglichkeit und Würdigkeit des Stückes erwies sich für das deutsche Publikum erst 1903 nach dem beispielgebenden Vorgang des Burgtheaters, nicht nach den verschiedenen Berliner Experimenten (1899). Freilich hat das Burgtheater nichts anderes getan, als aus all diesen Versuchen den durchgehenden Grundgedanken zu abstrahieren und ihm mit großen Mitteln eine beispielhafte und prägnante Verwirklichung zu verleihen. *Amphitryon, das Lustspiel, gemischt aus derbem Rüpelspaß und feinerer Verwechslungskomik.*"⁹ The manager of the Burgtheater, Paul Schlenther, strove primarily to underscore the comic content, but to the detriment of the philosophical, intellectual aspect. Evidently Alkmene's role lost much of its ideal orientation and was no longer the centre of attention. In fact, Hedwig Bleibtreu was obliged to play the part in an ironic light more in keeping with Hugo Thimig's Sosias, an exploitation of every conceivable burlesque element. Otto Tressler, responsible for Mercury, conveyed "ein sehr scharf karikierter Hugo Thimig, der das Publikum zu stürmischer Heiterkeit hinriß."¹⁰ The critics generally enthused about the performance but found fault with the play itself. Hermann Bahr, the theatre critic for the *Volkszeitung* (22 February 1903), called it "künstlerisch durchaus verpfuscht."¹¹ Nevertheless, the *première* marked the beginning of an enduring success in Vienna.

Despite the fairly warm acceptance of *Amphitryon* at the turn of the century, it disappeared from the Berlin stage until 1910, when again an association, the Literarische Gesellschaft, mounted an afternoon performance in the Deutsches Theater directed by Julius Bab (1 July 1910). Although the performance was technically and dramatically deficient, with amateurish sets and inadequate personnel to fill the minor roles, it elicited an encouraging response from the audience, and the Deutsches Theater even adopted the production and performed it nine times in 1915 (*première*, 5 September 1915) in the Theater in der Königgrätzer Straße with the same major cast and interpretation as that of 1910. Friedrich Kayssler who directed the 1915 version played Jupiter in both stagings and, according to the critics, was much too cerebral in his approach to the part: "Kayßler hatte die Majestät der Erscheinung und des Wortes. Wo es galt, der erhabene Donnerer zu sein, war er am Platz. Nicht so, wenn er sich in die Rolle des Liebenden schicken mußte."¹² Ludwig Hartau's Amphitryon came across as being too agitated – "[ein] leidenschaftliches, nervöses Temperament, eine wilde Männlichkeit rang nach Ausdruck" – while most of the reviewers faulted Helene Fehdmer for her inability to develop the full potential of Alkmene's personality. But Kayssler, like Bab before him, placed the main emphasis upon the farcical trio: Sosias (Guido Herzfeld), Charis (Margarethe Kupfer), and Mercury (Alexander Ekert). Obviously, the favourable reaction depended quite heavily upon the comic interplay between the servant figures, all of whom were carefully cast by a director famous for his expertise in the field of comedy. Part of the aversion of the theatre-

Malermodells Mitleid erregend nachahmender Jüngling" (*Prager Presse*, 11 November 1927), remained silent and then made his exit. Schwarz replaced the verbal exchange between Jupiter and Amphitryon with one between the latter and the assembled officers. With the exception of an exaggerated interpretation of Charis, the performance found favour with the local press. The *Prager Tageblatt* (10 November 1927) reported that Weindorf's "Jupiter eindrucksvoller [war], als sein Amphitryon. Die besten Augenblicke des Abends waren seine Dialoge mit Alkmene," played by Tilde Ondra as an "anmutig frauliches Wesen." Evaluating Schwarz's accomplishment, Rüdiger Dorr concluded: "[Die Prager Inszenierung] stellt ein ernst zu nehmendes Experiment dar, das zum Teil an den Unzulänglichkeiten einer ungenügend fundierten kleineren Bühne verunglückte, darüber hinaus jedoch ... eine durchaus genügende, Kleist entgegenkommende, ja, was den Regiewillen anbetrifft, sicher eine über den Durchschnitt stehende Aufführung, die auch beim Publikum Anklang fand."[18]

As soon as the National Socialists gained control of Germany's political life in 1933, there was a concerted effort to impose the party line upon the cultural life of the nation. The stage was exploited extensively and with some measure of success, especially in the rural open-air theatres or local playhouses, as can be attested to by the manipulation of *Die Hermannsschlacht* and *Prinz Friedrich von Homburg* for propaganda purposes. And yet the Nazis could not reduce all art to the lowest common denominator of their "Kraft durch Freude." "Es ist ein Witz der Theatergeschichte, wie man sich ihn glorioser kaum denken kann, daß der Widerstand gegen diese Zielsetzung sich just an jenen Bühnen zusammenballte, die das Regime zu seinen Repräsentations- und Renommiertheatern erkoren hatte – dem Staatstheater und dem Deutschen Theater."[19] Indeed, by skilfully turning to account the jealousy and rivalry between Hermann Göring and Josef Goebbels, Gustav Gründgens und Heinz Hilpert, although obliged to attend party functions, managed to continue the tradition of their Jewish predecessors, Leopold Jessner and Max Reinhardt: "Was damals in dem nobeln Schinkel-Bau am Gendarmenmarkt ... und in Reinhardts berühmtem Haus in der Schumannstraße geschah, war die Rettung des deutschen Theaters, wenn man pathetisch sein wollte, könnte man sogar sagen: seine Ehrenrettung."[20] Three *Amphitryon* productions have been regarded as an integral part of this vindication.

The first of these, directed by Lothar Müthel, one of Gründgens's gifted directors, took place on 7 April 1937 in Berlin's Staatstheater. Reviewing the production for the *Kölnische Zeitung*, K.H. Ruppel stressed the various options made available by the complexity of *Amphitryon*: "welche Forderungen stellt es an die Bühne! Soll man das Lustspiel geben oder das Mysterium? Soll man das Wort dramatisch gestalten oder musikalisch? Spielt man das Götterwagnis oder den Eheschwank?"[21] Since Müthel decided to ignore the more serious side in favour of the comedy, Jupiter, depicted by Paul Hartmann, became a divine *bon vivant* who found amusing diversion in the joke perpetuated on Alkmene and her husband. The merry tone of this escapade was enhanced by Rochus Gliese's sets depicting a frivolously stylized Greek house with a surrealistic flair. According to reviews, Günter Hadank bestowed a sense of human greatness on the role of Amphitryon, especially in the final scene; Will Dohm suggested the confusing mixture of cunning, cowardice, and enthusiasm which make up Sosias; and Hilde Weißner, while concentrating upon the spiritual aspect of Alkmene, still managed to project "den sinnlichen Zauberer, der einen Jupiter in Liebe erglühen läßt." Whereas Kleist once transformed a French social comedy into a partly metaphysical work, Müthel's staging tended to reverse the procedure. This same disposition to emphasize the comic element and thus guarantee a popular success can also be found in Richard Weichert's production for Berlin's Volksbühne on 23 November 1939, where Carl Kuhlmann's Sosias dominated the whole evening: "Er war der komische Solist der Aufführung, nicht der komische Partner eines tragischen Abenteuers."[22] The only actor capable of conveying the tragic potential behind the comedy was Ernst Wilhelm Borchert as Amphitryon. "Die Aufführung der Volksbühne [gab] das Bild eines sehr eleganten griechischen Ritters, der mit einer vornehmen Dame schwierige eherechtliche Gespräche führt, deren Sinn offenbar ist, die Dame gegen ihre Bedenken seinen Wünschen geneigt zu machen."

Ruppel felt that one of the main errors of Weichert's interpretation was the attempt by set designer Cesar Klein to combine Greek antiquity inappropriately with a contemporary setting. For example, the eagle which appears during Jupiter's concluding apotheosis had the form of the Prussian emblem and, in Ruppel's opinion, ill befitted Kleist's Greek landscape. But some three years later, in defence of a production of *Amphitryon* for Berlin's Deutsches Theater (10 March 1942), Heinz Hilpert proclaimed: "Dieses Werk, das sich der griechischen Mythologie bedient, ist trotzdem ein Werk märkisch-preußischen Geistes, wenn es auch in die Welt allgemeinmenschlicher Gesetze hineinreicht."[23] Jupiter wore ancient gold armour, but this was decorated with baroque shoulder-straps not unlike those depicted in portraits of the Great Elector; the Theban generals' costumes suggested direct descendants of late seventeenth-century officers; and Amphitryon's home devised by Caspar Neher looked strangely reminiscent of Schlüter's country home, Kamecke, in Berlin: "In dieser märkischen Umwelt entfaltet sich in der ganz auf dem Wort beruhenden Regie Hilperts die wunderbare Kontrapunktik des Lustspiels in ihrer ganzen thematischen Intensität und melodischen Fülle."[24] This respect for Kleist's poetic language grew out of the director's contention that *Amphitryon* remained "wirklich im tiefsten Sinn ein deutsches Lustspiel ... (mit dem Ausblick aufs Metaphysische)";[25] hence, the Prussian ambiance helped to convey the "Verwirrung des Gefühls" which Goethe once repudiated as inimical to his harmonious view of life, but which now captured the very essence of our modern existential plight. Hilpert regarded Alkmene as "[den] Mittelpunkt des Stückes,"[26] in whom the Kleistian glorification of absolute feeling enjoyed its most positive victory, and, according to Ruppel, Gisela von Collandes accomplished the demanding task of recreating a Prussian-Greek heroine: "Die schöne, gefühlsreiche Innerlichkeit dieser Schauspielerin strömt ganz in die schwere Rolle ein und erfüllt sie mit dem Zauber einer Frau, die eines Irdischen keusche Gattin und eines Gottes Liebe zugleich sein kann."[27] Jupiter, played by Ewald Balser, no longer resorted to irony or to mere frivolity to justify his unfortunate love adventure, but had to bear the consequences of his compromising, uncomfortable position and, despite the cosmetics of the conclusion, resigned himself to living with the consciousness of defeat.

A major problem facing a director who desires to mount *Amphitryon* is the need to find two actors capable of making the confusion of identities believable. In his staging for the Oldenburgisches Staatstheater in October 1956, Walter Thomas had the good fortune of acquiring the services of two such individuals, Robert Nägele, who apparently succeeded in preserving the balance between tragedy and comedy in his portrayal of Amphitryon, and Hans Schulze, who gave a dignified performance as Jupiter. Karin Behrmann's Alkmene complemented the two male leads with a rendition which was reserved and graceful but also sensual. The key note of this well-received production was one of moderation, a desire to do justice to both levels of the work: "Der Spielleiter Walter Thomas hält das vielschichtige, auf verschiedenen Ebenen ablaufende Spiel im Gleichgewicht."[28] Although the serious scenes surrounding Alkmene were effectively set off by the comic interludes centred on Sosias (Karl Otto Moderau), Thomas never permitted the humour to become uncontrolled nor the solemn aspects to become too heavy. The striving for equilibrium also dictated Wolf Gerlach's set, "eine helle klassizistische Szenerie mit romantischem Hintergrund," which a new lighting system turned to advantage. In the words of Norbert Hampel, it was an "Inszenierung mit rechten Maßen."

Franz Reichert's offering for Stuttgart's Schauspielhaus in April 1961 disclosed the risks inherent in an unbalanced *Amphitryon*, for he paid such close attention to Kleist's language, exploiting its full comic potential both in dialogue and implied gestures, that the "Humor ... sozusagen in einzelnen Jamben gereicht [wurde],"[29] and this tended to vulgarize the performance. On the positive side of the ledger, the audience could appreciate Kleist's mastery of the dramatic poetic idiom: "Angst, Frage, Ausruf, Erstaunen, Verwirrung werden durch die rhythmische Spannung der jambischen Verse aus tiefen seelischen Gründen geschleudert"; but, as Winfried Wild pointed out, language in the works of Kleist is the "Ausdruck der Lebensunsicherheit des Menschen, den das Schicksal vielseitig verwirrt und der sich verzweifelt an die Lauterkeit und Untrüglichkeit seines Gefühls klammert." Solveig Thomas provided a dignified, almost understated interpretation of the heroine, which, although it proved all the more moving when she raised her voice in sudden fear, failed to project that human greatness capable of bringing a god to his knees in admiration of his own creation. Unfortunately, Klaus Höhne's Mercury agreed neither in tone nor in stature with his supposed double, Max Mairich's Sosias, who monopolized most of the evening's laughter. By contrast, Heinz Baumann as the god and Max Eckerd as the mortal "glichen einander aufs Haar,"[30] the former pronouncing his lines with the intensity of the thunder god, while the latter exaggerated the comic aspect of his part to such an extent that it seemed almost incredible that Alkmene failed to notice the dissimilarity immediately. Despite these reservations on the part of the critics, the performance obtained a favourable public response.

The year 1961 furnished an abundance of *Amphitryon* productions, among them Edgar Walter's entertaining modern version for the Städtische Bühne in Heidelberg, and Walter Henn's staging for the Berliner Festwochen, in which he elected to ignore "Kleists tragische[n] General-Baß unter dem heiteren Concerto grosso."[31] Hans W. Lenneweit's highly colourful sets for the Berlin Festival contrasted sharply with the predominantly black, sparse décor conceived by Hansheinrich Palitzsch for Gustav Rudolf Sellner's interpretation in Darmstadt. Sellner tried to present the comedy as a dialectical process, but in so doing he created "[statt] des einen großen Dramas, das zwischen Tragödie und Lustspiel balanciert, eine Vielzahl von Miniaturdramen."[32] The director's rational bias also proved unequal to the task of coming to terms with the poetic verse, the perennial problem in any production of Kleist. Reporting on a novel theatrical experiment in Munich's Theater der Jugend in 1968, one which saw the *Amphitryon*s of Plautus, Molière, Giraudoux, and Hacks performed one after another, Alf Brustellin regarded the "respektierlich[e] Auslassung"[33] of Kleist's version as being determined primarily by the lack of the prerequisite language skill to tackle the German text.

"On the small stage of the Barbizon Theater last night [17 November 1970] the German language Brücke ensemble, opening its third American tour, made a 163-year old play glow ... an uncommonly skillful and compass-sure rendition of the Greek legend according to Heinrich von Kleist."[34] In all, the Brücke company gave eighteen performances in German of three comedies, including Kleist's *Amphitryon*. In order to make it easier for an American audience to follow the unofficial American *première*, an English synopsis was supplied. *New York Times* reviewer Howard Thompson expressed great enthusiasm not only for the simple and direct performance of the touring company, but for the play itself. He must have done his homework, for in addition to recognizing the farcical element of the cuckolded husband, he characterized the drama as "a very tough-fibered, even mystical comedy concerned with self-identity and the unassailability of pure love. That, at least, is what von Kleist and the perfectly elegant teamwork last night seemed to be driving at." Thompson had nothing but praise for the production, singling out the "superb sparse, honest direction" of Dieter Munck, Ursula Erber's "utterly convincing" portrayal of Alkmene, Christian Rode's "stupefied spouse, ... a welcome relief from the usual Amphitryon," and above all Erich Schellow's Jupiter, "suavely biting, manly and a bit of a fool." "With such a god on deck, and such a crew, the evening seemed too short."

One of the major difficulties presented by Kleist's works is that of dealing with a stage "classic," of actualizing a nineteenth-century play for a contemporary audience. One drastic solution has been to treat, for example, *Penthesilea* or Büchner's *Leonce und Lena*, as a circus act, but such an approach is often more revealing of the director than of the dramatist. The whole issue aroused considerable debate and controversy after Niels-Peter Rudolph's production of *Amphitryon* for the Staatsschauspiel in Stuttgart in November 1971. In an interview with Kurt Honolka of the *Stuttgarter Nachrichten* (4 November 1971), Rudolph maintained, "Kleist hat die meisten Bezugspunkte zu unserer Zeit und unserer Verständnismöglichkeit," and he therefore chose to leave the text "[v]öllig unverändert." Rudolph felt that, whereas some adaptations of certain classical works might be justified, it was the responsibility of the director to preserve the linguistically and scenically closed form of *Amphitryon*, and to present his/

her particular interpretation solely on the basis of the given material. Above all, Rudolph sought to reproduce Kleist's word-music and at the same time to challenge his audience to look objectively at the comedy's message: "In diesem Stück sollen Menschen aus ihren gewohnten Denkschemen gerissen werden. Dagegen wehren sie sich, sie beharren darauf, daß alles bleibt 'so freundlich wie es war', um mit Kleists Worten zu sprechen." To underscore the modernity of the drama and, as one critic had suggested, to make an ironic comment on German veneration of Greek antiquity,[35] the cast wore the nineteenth-century uniforms of Prussian officers (Heinz Hilpert used late seventeenth-century costumes for his Berlin version of 1942), and Karl Kneidl reduced his sets to "helle Quadrate, die bewegbar waren," and created an "Abstraktionswüste," which in the view of Joachim Kaiser would have been more appropriate in a "Fernsehballettproduktion."[36] Generally, the actors performed their roles adequately, but the comic pair of Hans-Peter Korff as Sosias and Rosel Zech as Charis earned special applause. While Hildegard Schmahl's Alkmene captured the proper tone in her first dialogue with Jupiter, a mixture of seriousness and joy, her final "Ach!" appeared to express sheer disappointment and she "[vergaß] leider nie, daß sie splitternackt war unter ihrer durchsichtigen Seidenhülle," so that her movements came across as uncertain: "Nun ist ein Busenhalter bestimmt nicht natürlicher als die Abwesenheit desselben, doch wenn das Fehlen dieses Kleidungsstücks als unnatürlich empfunden wird, dann wäre wiederum seine Benutzung natürlicher." Notwithstanding Rudolf's valiant attempt to maintain the proper balance between joy and pain, comedy and tragedy, there was unanimity among the critics that his production tended to degenerate into a farce, especially when in the final scene "Bühnenarbeiter ... Jupiter in die simple Flugmaschine [helfen], mit der er, ein wahrer Deus ex machina, in den Olymp entschwebt."[37] The evening concluded with only "freundlich[em] Beifall."[38] Ignoring this at best lukewarm reception, national television offered essentially the same version but with a different cast in 1975. The film medium enabled Rudolph to exploit special effects, so that the same actor, Helmut Griem, played both Amphitryon and Jupiter and Vadim Glowna, Sosias and Mercury. As Valentin Polcuch noted, this arrangement "stellt das Lustspiel in Frage, weil es die Auswegslosigkeit der Identitätsspaltung konkret ins Bild bringt."[39] Critical assessment remained decidedly divided, ranging from "was wäre über diese Inszenierung Konkreteres zu sagen, als daß der Schirm diese Dauer [two hours and twenty minutes] getrost und ohne Spannungen durchhielt. ... es war ein beherztes Spiel, ein Spiel am Rande des Erfahrbaren" to "Es gab

Gründe genug, nach fünf Minuten abzuschalten. Wer die ersten fünfzehn Minuten durchgestanden hat, den muß man beglückwünschen für seine Nerven, seinen Bildungshunger, seine optimistische Geduld."[40] Television repeated this same film version in March 1982 as the second offering in a series of programs designed to present and comment upon Kleist's main works.

Whereas Niels-Peter Rudolph endeavoured to come to terms with the first obstacle standing in the way of this rarely performed play – the language – Gerd Heinz in his 1973 production for Darmstadt refused to take into account the second obstacle – Kleist's serious attempt to deal with divine adultery as experienced by a woman for whom, at the conscious level at least, duty and inclination are one. Instead of contrasting the comic Sosias-Charis-Mercury grouping with the more solemn Amphitryon-Alkmene-Jupiter triangle, Heinz posited "eine Einheit ... eine Burleske der übertölpelten Männer, überhöht vom höchsten ironischen Kampf zwischen Jupiter und Alkmene, worin die Frau nicht übertölpelt, sondern wehmütig gesteigert wird."[41] The director therefore treated the drama primarily as a witty, divine joke. According to the notices, Angela Müthel gave a competent portrayal of Alkmene, especially in the interrogation scenes with Jupiter, but her interpretation seemed to lack conviction in the last scenes and her final "Ach!", expressing her dismay at losing the more desirable mate, occasioned a storm of laughter from the audience. Gerhard Garbers played Jupiter as a significant but nonetheless cunning playboy, while Walter Renneisen provided an outstanding account of Sosias with his "totale[n] Identität von Körper-Gesten- und Dialogbeherrschung." Rudolf Krämer-Badoni maintained that Heinz had discovered a new dimension in *Amphitryon*, but in reality he only returned to the popularized view (which had guaranteed success at the turn of the century) and rejected or downplayed the feature of this German *Amphitryon* which renders it unique *vis-à-vis* other treatments of the same theme.

One could easily see in Harry Buchwitz's *Amphitryon* for Zürich's Schauspielhaus in November 1975 the other dimensions which Heinz chose to ignore, for in the Zürich version there was a conscious effort to stress the note of human suffering and to intensify the question of individual identity: "Alkmenes Tragik: hier wird sie Ereignis."[42] The predominance of the theme of personal tragedy may well have been due to the exceptional acting of Sonja Sutter (Alkmene) who succeeded in intimating the many "fein verästelten psychologischen Nuancen im Spektrum von Hingabe und Glück, von Wirrnis und Verzweiflung," and who lent "der Gestalt des Dichters den Zauber ihrer Erscheinung und den Zauber einer wundervoll modulierenden und musizierenden Stimme." Wolfgang Stendar as Amphitryon fully complemented the female lead, revealing a carefully thought-out, thoroughly convincing delineation of a man caught between insight into the fateful turn of events and frustration, expressed in impassioned outbursts, at being powerless to rectify the situation: "Das Zusammenspiel etwa mit Alkmene in der 2. Szene des II. Aktes wurde zu einer unvergeßlichen Klimax, weil beiden [Alkmene und Amphitryon] das Unwahrscheinliche gelang, den delikatesten Balanceakt durchzuhalten: das tragische Dunkel mit zarten Funken einer Komödie der Irrungen zu durchlichten." The critics strongly censured Ezio Frigerio's scenery for its unsuitability: Sosias had to feel his way over an obstacle course laid out before Amphitryon's house, and the courtyard was surrounded by an ivy-covered wall out of which rose a gigantic stone figure, its face imploringly directed towards heaven. Wolfgang Schwarz's Jupiter emerged as too restrained and thus never approached the dignity and power of the Olympian deity: "Die inquisitorische Grausamkeit, sein bohrendes Fragen und die Folter seiner Dialektik teilten sich noch am ehesten mit." And finally, Hans-Dieter Zeidler's Sosias proved to be too much of a good thing. Although both in temperament and physical agility he seemed born to the role, his accomplishment overshadowed Hans Gerd Kübel's Mercury and threatened to "explode" the limits of the comedy. Indeed, to judge from the critical response, a general propensity towards disintegration, compromising the total effect, manifested itself as the action progressed in the second half.

The Kleist year 1977 brought many productions of his works, including thirteen in the German Democratic Republic. Stagings of *Amphitryon* in West Germany included an open-air performance in the marketplace of Schwäbisch Hall, directed by Kai Braak to inaugurate the summer festival, Peter Jost's interpretation for the castle theatre in Neulengbach – at the conclusion of which the gods made their exit via the castle window, a veritable "dei ex fenestra"[43] – Stephan Stroux's Brechtian approach in Kiel, designed to expose "die Ordnung der Gesetze ... in ihrem Scheinwesen,"[44] and another Gustav Rudolf Sellner version, this time for Basle's Stadttheater. This last production underlined once again the great difficulties posed by Kleist's comedy. Sellner transplanted the Greek myth into the context of Berlin and its uninspiring neoclassical architecture during the Napoleonic wars, a modernizing experiment already attempted with questionable success by Niels-Peter Rudolph for the Schauspielhaus in Stuttgart in 1971. Certain sections of Jörg Zimmermann's décor – "die Fassade des Durchgangs der verlängerten Wilhelmsstrasse unter den Linden in Berlin, als Palais des Amphitryons eingerichtet nach dem Wohnstil um 1800"[45] – could be raised so that the audience gained a perspective not only into the living room on the ground floor or the bedroom on the second level, but also beyond the house into the country landscape. This arrangement allegedly symbolized "den Durchblick durch Kleists Zeit auf den zeitlosen Stoff." Unfortunately, the rest of the production did not sustain this desirable aim. For example, Jupiter (Georg Martin Bode) and Amphitryon (Hansjörg Assmann) were inclined to speak in the same monotonous fashion and to employ identical gestures, with the result that, whether intentionally or not, "Stagnation ... sich einstellt." "Der Aufführung fehlt ... die dritte Dimension der interpretatorischen Bindung beider Zeitebenen durch seine, Sellners, eigene Person"; the text and the staging consequently seemed to go their own separate ways. Susanne Tremper's "kokette Naivität," the manner in which she uttered her Kleistian iambs, "als handle es sich dabei um die hübschen Belanglosigkeiten eines Broadway-Hits,"[46] did not come close to hinting at Alkmene's tragic dilemma, while her final "Ach!" sounded like a sigh of resignation.[47] And yet, one critic still felt that her performance constituted "[den] einzige[n] Lichtblick"[48] in this otherwise uninspired staging.

*Amphitryon* had to wait until 1979 for its Italian *première* under the direction of Gabriele Lavia, a student of Giorgio Strehler's school and probably the one person most responsible for introducing Kleist's plays to Italy. Lavia took his production based on an excellent translation by Luigi Lunari on tour to several cities where it was generally applauded. Performed in the open, the staging sought to create a dream ambiance by submerging in blue light a simple wooden structure representing the courtyard before the Theban commander's home. The palace doors bore mirrors so that "Der Spiegel ... die Handelnden ständig mit ihrem immer fragwürdiger werdenden Ich [konfrontierte]."[49] Above the set towered an immense eagle suggestive of the power wielded not only by Jupiter, but by another authority figure, Napoleon, for all the cast wore uniforms or dresses from the Napoleonic era, although their faces were made up like those of clowns. Although this last feature would seem to suggest a farce, the interpretation ultimately presented the players, including even the king of the gods, as tragic puppet victims caught up in a nightmare of confusing human emotions: "Gabriele Lavia hat seine Inszenierung konsequent wie eine psychoanalytische Abhandlung über die progressive Gefühlsverwirrung aufgebaut." For reviewer Monika von Zitzewitz, who attended a performance at the Villa Lippa in Milan, Ottavia Piccoli's tender portrayal of Alkmene and Lavia's depiction of the title figure both as a clown and as someone who loses faith in himself, warranted special mention among an outstanding cast. Apparently this first encounter with Kleist's version of the ancient myth amounted to a surprising revelation to Italian critics who suddenly discovered in Kleist "uno dei più moderni ed inquietanti [dramatists]" (one of the most modern and disturbing dramatists) and in his comedy evidence of a significant anticipation of many themes, such as "una vera e propria crisi di identità"[50] (a real identity crisis) or illusion versus reality, subjects commonly associated with the early twentieth-century Italian playwright Pirandello.

The Viennese touring company "Der grüne Wagen" took an *Amphitryon* production to several small cities such as Aalen, Lindau, Biberach, and Ludwigshafen with mixed results. The name Kleist largely explained the full houses to which the ensemble played, but the critical response remained divided. Writing for the *Schwäbische Zeitung* (12 March 1980), Gisela Linder could scarcely contain her enthusiasm for this interpretation in which "ein Ensemble ... den schwierigen Kleistschen Sprachrhythmus nicht nur meistert, sondern als Träger drängender Emotionalität erlebbar macht." In direct contradiction, the critic of the *Mannheimer Morgen* (29 April 1980) dismissed the production as "recht fade," beginning with the language: "An Kleists Versen, an seinen manchmal doch etwas gedrehten und geflochtenen Sprachlinien ward nicht gezupft. Wort für Wort kam der Text, brav gesprochen und brav gespielt, ohne Überraschungen, ohne ungewöhnliche Akzente, ohne auch nur den Schimmer einer eigenen Gedankenleistung." These two reviews are especially worthy of note, for the negative one comes across as a deliberate refutation of the positive one: "Der Berliner Kleist-Regisseur Boleslaw Barlog bietet eine maßvolle *Amphitryon*-Inszenierung, in der sich Komik und Tragik die Waage halten, die existentielle Not der vom Götterstreich Betroffenen gleichnishaft deutlich wird"; "Dabei hat Barlog wohl ganz übersehen, daß er den Kern dieser *Amphitryon*-Version nicht getroffen hat. Kleist ist eben kein Klassiker [Linder places him in this category], und ihm geht es viel eher um die schlafwandlerische Gefühlssicherheit Alkmenes." Although the two commentators attended a different performance in a different locale – Aalen and Ludwigshafen –, one gains the distinct and often amusing impression that they reviewed a different production as well: "Ulla Jacobsson vermag dieser Gestalt [Alkmene] jene Ausstrahlung zu geben, die sie über jeden Tadel erhaben macht, anrührend brachte sie die Verwirrtheit eines reinen Herzens ins Spiel"; "Ulla Jacobsson war als Alkmene unter dieser Regie nicht in der Lage, den Text zu interpretieren." Even if one takes into account discrepancies from one performance to the next, a good night versus a bad one, such a wide degree of disagreement reminds us that most people have preconceived ideas about how a "classic" should be performed. Respected works tend to elicit strong emotions and often an inflexible critical stance.

If opinion was divided on the "Der grüne Wagen" staging, there could be no doubt about the reaction to Thomas Reichert's *Amphitryon* presented in the Schloßpark-Theater in Berlin: "schlechtweg langweilig,"[51] "eine schmähliche Verhunzung des Dichters,"[52] "[e]in Fiasko, wie man lange keines hat miterleben müssen,"[53] "eine dröge und düstere Verunstaltung,"[54] "die künstlerische Freiheit der völligen Inkompetenz."[55] Commentators could not find a single redeemable feature in the whole production, citing a total lack of feeling for Kleist's language, incompetent or inappropriate casting, a set created by Nina Ritter reminding more than one person of a sterile waiting room in a modern-day clinic ("eine dekorative Abscheulichkeit"[56]), and most damning of all, a failure on the part of the director to appreciate the complexities and aesthetics of this comedy. In the first-act meeting between Alkmene (Martina Kräuel) and Jupiter (Alexander Wagner), the former entered as a housewife in her bathrobe followed by an older gentleman sporting a fencer's vest. Although the latter came to be identified as Jupiter, instead of projecting the forceful image of the Olympian deity, he conveyed the impression of an indifferent, worn-out, middle-aged mortal. Cheap effects were also in evidence as, for example, when Amphitryon thrust a miserable bunch of daisies under the nose of his wife upon his return.

I have included this stage disaster, because it is relatively rare to find so many critics united in their condemnation not only of the production, but even of the theatrical manager, Boy Gobert, responsible for its being offered: "Gobert hat es zugelassen, daß Thomas Reichert, ein mit diesem Stück offensichtlich überforderter Regisseur, ... mit einer krassen Fehl- und Unterbesetzung gearbeitet hat" (Günther Grack). Most telling of all, the ultimate court, the audience, voiced its disapproval in such strong terms that even the seasoned critic was taken aback: "Erinnern kann ich [Friedrich Luft] mich aus meinem langen Parkettleben nicht, einen Kleist (oder dessen Präsentation) vom Publikum bei offener Szene so gereizt, so höhnisch, so rachsüchtig und wütend angefeindet erlebt zu haben." This unfortunate production shows that no matter how radical one's interpretation of a Kleist play, whether it employ pontoons or mountains of ice, anachronistic costumes or no costumes at all, the director must nevertheless demonstrate some understanding for the underlying poetic spirit of the play, nebulous or indefinable as that may be.

The first of five major productions of *Amphitryon* in 1982 opened in the Maxim Gorki-Theater of East Berlin with limited success even in the eyes of the East-German reviewer Henryk Goldberg (*Neues*

*Deutschland*, 25 February 1982), who designated the effort diplomatically as "achtbar." Goldberg and Horst Wenderoth (*Neue Zürcher Zeitung*, 15 April 1982) both detected the major weakness in the youthful inexperience of the two principal male actors, Frank Lienert (Jupiter) and Udo Schenk (Amphitryon), from which resulted an "Inszenierung, die ihrer Zentralgestalt [i.e., Alkmene played by Swetlana Schönfeld] die Partner verweigert und von daher nicht so recht ins Laufen kommt" (Goldberg). However, a reviewer for the *Badische Neueste Nachrichten* (9 March 1982), signing him/herself as A.R., castigated the staging for its superficiality, its failure to explore the psychological depths or paradoxical nature of the work: "Ach, wie unbedarft und einfältig ist die Regie [Karl Gassauer]; ach, wie beliebig und bieder die Ausstattung [Dieter Berge]; ach, wie konventionell und flach die Darstellung."

The 1982 staging to have the widest exposure in the press and to be generally supported and even defended by the critics,[57] opened in Cologne's Schauspielhaus in March of the same year. As a prologue to the performance, the entering patrons witnessed on an improvised stage in the foyer Johann Daniel Falk's Viennese farce, *Das Ich und das Nicht-Ich oder Die lustige Hahnreyschaft*, based on the Amphitryon myth and written two years before Kleist's version. The set designed by Rolf Glitterberg for the evening's main event, aiming at utter simplicity, consisted primarily of two arc-lamps and a white gauze curtain in which a slit provided admittance to a dark interior tent, a forbidden, erotic realm accessible solely to the gods and Alkmene. The intentional lack of stage props obliged the actors and the spectators to concentrate more upon the major ingredient of the play, its language, and with gratifying results: "[Director Jürgen] Flimm beweist mit diesem ausgewogenen Ensemble ..., daß man sich Kleists Sprachgebilden überlassen und dem langweiligen Literaturtheater dennoch entgehen kann."[58] In his perceptive review Rolf Michaelis drew attention to the director's care with the blank verse, his skilful insertion of sudden pauses or surprising delays, and the effective utilization of symbolic gestures. When, for example, Jupiter torments Alkmene with his hypothetical scenarios, Flimm had the god lean over the prostrate woman, stroke the hair away from her neck and then plant a kiss upon it: "Das ist ein Bild nicht nur der Zärtlichkeit, sondern auch – und damit entspricht die Geste der doppelten Bedeutung, die Kleist seinen Worten von 'Liebe' gibt – der Unterwerfung, wie man sie von Tieren kennt, wo der Biß in den Nacken Rangunterschiede deutlich macht."[59] No one was particularly smitten with the acting, Michaelis maintaining, for example, that the chief protagonists "dringen selten in den innersten Kern dieses schwierigen

Stückes", and some contradiction is evident: "Ingrid Andree [Alkmene] ... gab die Rolle, wie sie nicht oft zu sehen ist: ganz Geschöpf, das dem Kompaß seines Gefühls folgt, vom Gott zwar düpiert, aber im Innersten nicht betrogen";[60] "Ingrid Andree ist ein schwer wiegender Schwachpunkt der Aufführung."[61] However, most reviewers had very high praise indeed for the "eigentlichen Helden der Aufführung":[62] "Daß trotzdem Köln mit diesem *Amphitryon* eine Theaterreise wert ist, steht außer Zweifel. Ein Hauptverdienst daran hat Wolf-Dietrich Sprenger. Einen solchen Sosias hat es seit vielen Jahren auf keiner deutschen Bühne gegeben. Kleist wird um kein Jota verkürzt, obwohl Sprachtheater sich hier immer wieder zur Pantomime hin öffnet" (Reitze). Sprenger turned his comic talent to account when he kissed the lantern representing his mistress and burned his lips or when, attempting to snatch his favourite sausage from his *alter ego* Mercury, he met his tormentor's lips in an unexpected kiss: "Aber Sosias reagiert nun keineswegs mit Abscheu, sondern vielmehr mit entspannter Beruhigung. ... Wie kann Tragik sich komischer offenbaren, als wenn der Gepeinigte an der Brust des Gegners Atem holt für neue Kränkung?" (Schmidt-Mühlisch). His performance so dominated the production and the critical response to it that he even inspired a *Spiegel* article entitled "*Amphitryon* als Glanzstück eines Komikers" (15 March 1982), in which Hellmuth Kurasek placed Sprenger's Sosias in the tradition of Schikaneder's Papageno, Beckett's clown, and above all Hašek's Schwejk: "Sprenger spielt das Feige und das Würdelose mit einem so konsequenten Aberwitz (und manchmal schon surrealen Zuckungen), daß nicht er der Dumme ist, sondern die Welt als Wahnsystem erscheint." There was considerable confusion as to the main thrust of Flimm's interpretation, Rolf Michaelis judging it as more heavily weighted towards the farcical, and Ulrich Schreiber extracting the message, "daß die Frauen die wahren Leidtragenden der Männerherrschaft sind"; however, the critical consensus remained appreciative of Flimm's effort: "Die Inszenierung demonstriert genau und unaufwendig die fortbestehende Aktualität Kleists, mit all der Irritation, die daraus folgt."[63]

The next two 1982 productions did not fare as well with the critics. Erwin Axer's version for Vienna's Akademietheater, despite Sylvia Lukan's "zauberhafte Alkmene, voll reiner Naivität,"[64] failed in the opinion of many to capture the inner spirit of the work and to establish any sense of rapport between the stage action and the spectator. As an example of this shortcoming, Karin Kathrein and the reviewer for the *Neue Zürcher Zeitung* (21 June 1982) both mentioned the unsuitable conclusion: "[Die] Erhebung der einen Amphitryon-Gestalt in den Götterrang wirkte unbefriedigend, Merkurs

Abflug nahm sich wie aus einem Raimund-Märchenspiel [Kathrein also refers to the action's being raised "ins Märchenhafte] aus, und Alkmenes 'Ach' haftete ein Hauch von Operettenhaftigkeit an." Oddly enough, Jens Wendland of the *Süddeutsche Zeitung* (17 September 1982) levelled the same criticism at Adolf Dresen's poorly reviewed staging for the Frankfurt Schauspiel: "Das Ende löste sich operettig auf." Given the scepticism of the average twentieth-century theatre-goer, many directors are at somewhat of a loss to know how to deal with the apotheosis, but even for Kleist, the *deus-ex-machina* expedient represented the ironic extrication of an exalted power figure from an embarrassing situation potentially damaging to his credibility: "Verflucht der Wahn, der mich hieher gelockt!" (1512) Dresen's production exhibited several other weaknesses, including actors unable to deliver Kleist's verse, the cutting of one of the best comic scenes (Charis's kneeling before the real Sosias as if he were the god[65]), the miscasting of a young actress, Almut Zilcher, who played Alkmene "ohne Liebreiz und Neugier"[66], and the absence of a clear, unifying interpretation. The one enduring recollection left with most reviewers seems to have been the opening flash of lightning and sonorous clap of thunder at which a massive, thick cloud descended upon the stage over Sosias and his double, Mercury. In synchronic movements they rolled themselves a cigarette, the one serving as a mirror to the other. The only other memorable contribution noted in almost all the commentaries was Manfred Zapatka's portrayal of Amphitryon: "Dem Darsteller des Amphitryons dagegen, dem silbengenau sprechenden Manfred Zapatka, wäre der Glanz des Göttlichen schon zuzutrauen."[67]

Nicolas Brieger's interpretation for Munich's Kammerspiele, the last major production of 1982, managed to escape many of the pitfalls into which Dresen fell (e.g., "Geist und Schönheit von Kleists Sprache [durften] immer wieder triumphieren"[68]), although more than one commentator remarked on the absence of a unifying principle.[69] However, the director, while recognizing the difficulty of the play – "Je mehr man an die Figuren heranrückt, desto mehr verästeln sie sich, sie werden immer schwieriger" – stressed in an interview that what he saw as the general theme was, "die Konfrontation einer Frau mit der Männergesellschaft, mit dem männlichen Ich, das sich autark setzt und sich selber genug ist"[70] – a feminist bias also evident in some earlier stagings. Hans Schwab-Felisch remarked, "Die Komödie kommt zu ihrem Recht," especially in the introductory sequence where a turtle crawling across the stage served as a repository for Sosias's lantern. But to complete the Schwab-Felisch quotation: "und doch hat [die Komödie] einen Zug zur Bitterkeit, der sich zunehmend verstärkt, auch wenn sich die beiden so unterschiedenen Amphitryone am Ende für einen herzlichen Moment in den Armen liegen." This tragic potential manifested itself in the central function of the identity crisis felt even by Jupiter and particularly in the conclusion with Alkmene's bitter "Ach!". In this respect Brieger appears to have provided an adequate realization of his own analysis: "Bei aller Tragik hat Amphitryon so viel Anteil am Komischen wie Sosias bei aller Komik auch am Tragischen. Wenn Leute in eine verzwickte Situation geraten, sind sie ja meistens beides, tragisch und komisch."

After Jürgen Kloth's respectable but generally ignored "werknahe Inszenierung"[71] for the Stadttheater in Konstanz (February 1983), an interpretation which stressed the play's tragicomic closeness to our own times, and "Winni Victors mißglückte *Amphitryon*-Inszenierung" in Gießen (January 1984), which "als Theaterspaß zu langweilig, als Psycho-Stück zu albern [war],"[72] the next version to attract critical notice comparable to that enjoyed by Flimm's was a guest performance of Bonn's Stadttheater production from the fall of 1985, directed by Jossi Wieler for the Mannheim Schiller Festival in May 1986. While remaining true to the text and its basic message, Wieler, in the estimation of several critics, did not convey "Einheitlichkeit im Gesamtkonzept,"[73] the by now conventional criticism of almost every interpretation; but all the reviews acknowledged that despite weak moments – the middle part was found to be long-winded and the conclusion unbelievable –, the evening furnished overall "spannendes und intensives Theater," including some imaginative dramatic innovations. In an attempt to create an intimate acting space, seats were placed upon the stage; however, this arrangement led to an initial delay of more than half an hour that did not put the spectators in the most receptive frame of mind. In the first scene, the audience had to contend with a set in total darkness – the director took Kleist's stage direction "*Es ist Nacht*" (p. 247) quite literally – except for the flashlights held by Sosias and Mercury. In one of the early highpoints of the evening, Mercury, in the light of his flashlight, began his metamorphosis into the servant and "schließlich dem Sosias in Kleidung, Gesichtzügen, Stimme so ähnlich wurde, daß die Irritation über dessen Identitätsverlust durch Identitätsverdoppelung insgeheim aufs Publikum übergriff."[74] When Jupiter and Alkmene subsequently appeared before the house, a crack of light from the open door illuminated the parting lovers, Alkmene (Tanja von Oertzen), dressed in transparent white, embraced by a Jupiter (Günter Lampe) in a red cloth. This cloth turned out to be his only piece of clothing during the scene, a bold stroke which, according to Christel

Heybroch, Wieler brought off with dignity and sensitivity. The set devised by Anna Viehbrock emphasized in a unique fashion the discrepancy between Amphitryon's sphere and that of his divine counterpart. The mortal half of the stage consisted of a gymnasium complete with parallel bars, pommel horse, mats etc., from which the staging derived some unforgettable effects: Amphitryon relived in painful imagination the love union of his wife and Jupiter, while seated on the pommel horse and, in his rage, forced Sosias to perform deepknee bends in a puddle below the horizontal bar. While the human characters had to make their less-than-graceful entries across an obstacle course of sports equipment, Alkmene and the Olympian intruders could descend majestically via an elegant staircase at the back of the stage. Because the costumes did not focus on any specific historical period and combined older with more modern dress, they tended to underscore the comedy's contemporary relevance. In view of Robert Hunger-Bühler's depiction of Amphitryon as a volatile, authoritarian, intellectually limited career officer in uniform with boots and binoculars, it is not surprising that Alkmene's final "Ach!", expanded by Wieler into a leitmotif throughout his production,[75] suggested "ihr erwachendes Bewußtsein von der entgöttlichten, all-täglichen Wirklichkeit" (Heybrock). Notwithstanding a protest exodus part way through the performance, "großer Beifall"[76] brought the evening to an end.

In April 1986 *Anfitrione* returned to the Italian stage (Torino) in a production of the Gruppo della Rocca under the direction of Guido De Monticelli. The general thrust of this interpretation, as described by Renato Palazzi (*Corriere della Sera*, 19 April 1986), became imme-diately evident in Paolo Bregni's set, a conglomeration of enormous wooden machines, mechanical gadgets, and pulleys evoking a textile factory, windmills, or the complicated interior of a music box. Against this background the characters, dressed in neoclassical costumes, walked about stiffly as if oblivious to the surrounding mammoth structures. The aim was to underscore the modernity of Kleist's comedy as a delineation of "la crisi dell' uomo dalla fede illuminista al dubbio romantico," (the crisis of man from enlightened faith to romantic doubt) the transition from the optimistic view of the eigh-teenth century to the traumatic experience of the industrial revolu-tion, the nightmare to which we have all fallen heir. The drama thus constitutes a prophecy of the loss of childlike trust in the "totalità dell' uomo," (the totality of man) who now places his faith in the machine. The themes of "perdita d'innocenza" (loss of innocence) and technology as fate Monticelli skilfully combined in the image of spinning (the Fates): the audience first viewed Alkmene (Dorotea Aslanidis) at the spinning wheel and some of the wooden props were reminiscent of mechanical looms. Palazzi greatly admired Monticelli's *Anfitrione* (translation by Roberta Paola De Monticelli), calling it "un bel coup de théâtre" that made extensive but rewarding demands upon the mind of the spectator. Although the actors failed to reproduce fully the subtlety of the director's vision, they nevertheless made their contribution to a "successo ... assai caldo" (lukewarm success).

In the final year I shall examine, 1987, three directors staged an *Amphitryon* that drew press coverage: Carsten Bodinus for the Badisches Staatstheater (Karlsruhe, January), Dieter Bitterli for Freiburg's Stadttheater (February), and Inge Flimm for Zürich's Schauspielhaus (May). In the first two instances, the directors mounted the comedy as a farewell offering before moving to a position at another theatre. As a further parallel, both German versions set the play partly in the dramatist's period as suggested by the costumes, which ranged from Prussian guard uniforms (Karlsruhe) to an Alkmene decked out "im weißen Kleid der Preußen-Königin Luise"[77] (Freiburg). While Marion Breckwoldt and Dina Sikirić successfully conveyed the naive, unaffected aspect of the heroine in the initial scenes, Rüdiger Krohn faulted the latter in the second half as "eine Alkmene ohne innere Not."[78] Similarly, Renate Braunschweig-Ullmann found Breckwoldt unequal in the second part to the task of projecting "die Verwirrung, die Zweifel an der Wahrheit des eigenen Gefühls." As an oblique indication of the histrionic inadequacies of the principals, critics singled out for special mention the actresses playing relatively minor roles. In a description of the Karlsruhe version, one reads: "Eine Glanzleistung lieferte Sibylle Brunner als Sosias-Gattin Charis, die durch ein grandioses Talent für komische Rollen überraschte und der Aufführung jene Höhepunkte bescherte, die die Protagonisten der zentralen Handlung ihr nun einmal nicht geben konnten" (Rüdiger Krohn); and Gerhard Jörder wrote in reference to the Freiburg production: "Lebendiger hingegen der Kontrapart Sosias-Charis: Rosmarie Brücher gibt der Rolle energische, resolute Farbigkeit." Both productions experienced serious difficulties in coming to terms with the finale and resorted to the usual operatic expediency – thunder-and-lightning effects – but with especially devastating consequences in Freiburg: the whole cast fell to their knees before a radiant Jupiter set against a copy of the giant, star-studded celestial dome designed by Karl Friedrich Schinkel for Mozart's *Die Zauberflöte*. "Da zielt die Regie hoch hinaus – und landet hart auf dem

Bauch. Kleists Seelendrama geht im Bühnengetöse und im fröhlichsten Gelächter des Premierenpublikums unter, Alkmenes 'Ach' ist nur noch ein bedeutungsloses Suffix."[79]

In the May 1987 production in Zürich's Schauspielhaus, performed in Napoleonic dress, the director Inge Flimm sought, according to Reinhardt Stumm, to accent a feminist thesis by presenting the comedy as a "Kommentar ... zu den Herrschaftsansprüchen von Männern über Frauen."[80] But, in pursuing this objective, she emphasized the physical and concrete – "reine Äußerlichkeiten"[81] – to the detriment of the Kleistian verse and the psychologically subtle interplay between the protagonists. When, for example, Alkmene (Charlotte Schwab) learned the true state of affairs, "verkrampft sich ihr Unterleib, von Schmerzen gepeinigt, keucht sie an die Rampe" (Stumm). In the excessive use of gestures, the delicate nature of her inner life apparently never came across. Peter Brogle's Jupiter lacked "die göttliche Souveränität" (Der Bund) associated with his role, and to make matters worse, "Königlich ist hier auch der göttliche Amphitryon nicht."[82] The "kühle Sachlichkeit" (Neue Zürcher Zeitung) of Alkmene's concluding "Ach!" only seemed to reinforce the generally pragmatic interpretation of this poorly received staging.

On the basis of Amphitryon's stage history to date, the director who decides to mount Kleist's "Lustspiel nach Molière" has several problems to overcome. These include the difficulty of finding actors trained to recite Kleist's challenging verse, the necessity of achieving some sense of balance between the comic and the tragic elements, the conflicting and, in the eyes of some (Goethe), incompatible demands of the ancient and the modern, the pagan and the Christian, the pitfalls of a conclusion which the current theatre patron may find embarrassingly ludicrous, and the inevitable comparison with other dramatic versions of the same theme from Plautus's Amphitrio to the present. And yet Kleist's adaptation, one that really amounts to a new emphasis away from the male protagonist to the female – he might more fittingly have called his drama Alkmene – looks back more to the first recorded treatment of the myth, a lost tragedy by Euripides, than to Molière's galant, socially satirical comedy. Kleist's substantial revisions and rewriting reflect his own view of life, the "unerklärlich[e] Einrichtung der Welt,"[83] according to which we are all helpless isolated victims of forces beyond our ken or control. Not despite, therefore, but because of the many discrepancies or tensions in the comedy, directors have quite justifiably chosen to focus on the modernity of a play in which identity crises or the search for some degree of certainty in an absurd world play a central role. Kleist's Amphitryon has had its detractors but also its champions, among the most distinguished of whom one must count Thomas Mann: "Das ist das witziganmutvollste, das tiefste und schönste Theaterspielwerk der Welt"[84] – very high praise indeed. The proof of the play, however, is in the performance, and to judge from *Amphitryon*'s nearly one-hundred-year record on stage, the shortest history of all his dramas, his "Lustspiel nach Molière" will continue to figure prominently in theatre repertoires on account of the wealth of interpretations to which it readily lends itself.

## CHAPTER FOUR

# *Penthesilea*

Of Kleist's seven completed plays, *Penthesilea* is undoubtedly the most exacting one to stage effectively, partly because of the peculiarity of its style and partly because of the technical difficulties it presents. The particular nature of the author's poetic vision led him to avoid any division into acts, for this would only serve to retard the momentum of the dramatic movement, and in so doing, he created a structure at variance with the theatrical tradition of the eighteenth and nineteenth centuries. Since the work calls for a large number of female actors, most theatres have been obliged to combine roles for lack of adequate personnel, but the main obstacle has frequently been the difficulty of finding an actress capable of fulfilling the exceptional demands placed upon the titular heroine. Even in more recent times critics and directors alike have expressed the view that *Penthesilea* is simply unperformable, and the origin of this view may be traced back in part to Goethe's disapproval of the *Penthesilea* fragment published in *Phöbus*: "Mit der Penthesilea kann ich mich noch nicht befreunden. Sie ist aus einem so wunderbaren Geschlecht und bewegt sich in einer so fremden Region daß ich mir Zeit nehmen muß mich in beide zu finden."[1] Kleist's play had very little, if anything, in common, with the Weimar stage style with its idealized language and gesture and a balanced, dignified approach; more significantly, its content could not be made to conform with the ethical and aesthetic standards of classicism. In a conversation with Johannes Daniel Falk, Goethe commented:

Beim Lesen seiner Penthesilea bin.ich neulich gar zu übel weggekommen. Die Tragödie grenzt an einigen Stellen völlig an das Hochkomische, z.B. wo die Amazone mit einer Brust auf dem Theater erscheint und das Publikum versichert, daß alle ihre Gefühle sich in die zweite noch übrig gebliebene

Hälfte geflüchtet hätten, ein Motiv, das auf einem neapolitanischen Volkstheater im Munde einer Kolombine, einem ausgelassenen Policinell gegenüber keine üble Wirkung auf das Publikum hervorbringen müßte, wofern
ein solcher Witz nicht dort, durch das ihm beigesellte widerwärtige Bild
Gefahr liefe, sich einem allgemeinen Mißfallen auszusetzen.[2]

Goethe's repudiation became widely known and has been held largely
responsible for the fact that the tragedy had to wait seventy years
for its first performance.

On 23 April 1811, the actress Henriette Hendel-Schütz gave a
pantomime display of certain passages from *Penthesilea* in the concert
hall of Berlin's Königliches Schauspielhaus. Her husband, Professor
Schütz, delivered a lecture in which he offered an explanation of the
work and then recited scene twenty-three as an accompaniment to
his wife's silent acting. Hendel-Schütz had achieved considerable
renown as a mime and for a short time had even succeeded in
rendering pantomime fashionable, but clearly she only desired to
exploit Kleist's tragedy as a means of self-advertisement at the
expense of the work's true greatness – the spoken word. Although
the critics generally acknowledged her virtuosity, the *Vossische Zeitung*
(25 April 1811) did not even mention Kleist's name and the *Stuttgarter
Morgenblatt* blamed the play itself for the failure of the evening: "Die
Ankündigung pantomimischer Darstellung von Mad. Schütz
bewirkte einen überfüllten Saal, da zumal die Künstlerin aus den
früheren Bildern alles gewählt hatte, was auf die Berliner Eindruck
machte. Doch die einzige neue Darstellung, die *Penthesilea* nach
einem Gedichte des Herrn von Kleist, eignete und gestaltete sich
nicht, weil die Aufgabe zu verwickelt war. Auch das von Herrn Prof.
Schütz zur Erklärung gelesene Bruchstück des Gedichtes langweilte
und war zuwider durch verrenkte Sprache und gemeine Malerei im
Ausdruck."[3]

Not only classical writers, but also the romantics could not come
to terms with this barbaric woman, because she clashed so violently
with prevalent social and literary conventions. Even Ludwig Tieck,
who admired Kleist and was responsible for the first publication of
his collected works, found himself caught between his moral abhor-
rence of "dieses seltsame Ungeheuer" and his aesthetic admiration
for so much "Schmuck echter Poesie."[4] What saved the work from
total oblivion was the more positive reception enjoyed by the other
Kleistian plays. Since *Penthesilea* obviously could not at that time be
performed as written, Salomon Hermann Mosenthal sought to make
it more stageworthy through accommodation to current theatrical
practices. To have offered the original in an uninterrupted production

would have taxed the most patient audience and hence Mosenthal divided the work into three acts. A second major issue was the question of scene changes. Did Kleist intend there to be only one permanent set? The noted director Eugen Kilian remarked at the beginning of the twentieth century: "Kleist hat für eine völlig unreale Bühne geschrieben, für ein Theater, 'das da kommen soll'."[5] The difficulty was eventually resolved with the advent of the revolving stage, but Mosenthal saw no way out of this dilemma other than advocating two main sets with four changes. Essentially, his adaptation strove to popularize the work by making it conform to the taste of the court theatre. Although he commendably added very little of his own invention, he still felt obliged to cut about one thousand lines, to reduce forty-five speaking roles to eighteen, to give the language a more classical flavour, to eliminate any offensive parts, and to bring the tragedy into line with the heroic style that people were accustomed to seeing and hearing in the playhouse.

The Berlin *première* was made possible partly through the intervention of the emperor but above all through the enthusiasm of the then celebrated actress Clara Ziegler who, not unlike Henriette Hendel-Schütz, sought to utilize the tragedy as a vehicle to promote her own career. "Im Jahre 1876 [25 April] führte ich [Clara Ziegler] die Tragödie [*Penthesilea*], eine Perle der deutschen Dichtkunst, auf der Hofbühne in Berlin ein. Kaiser Wilhelm I befürwortete die Aufführung, die dann dreimal wiederholt wurde und spendete ihr lebhaften Beifall. Aber man hatte damals in maßgebenden Kreisen nicht den Mut, das Original auf die Bühne zu bringen; ja man riet mir, von einer Aufführung ganz abzusehen."[6] All interest was concentrated on the central protagonist so that the rest of the cast, with the exception of Maximilian Ludwig's fiery Achilles, failed to make any impact whatsoever. Taking advantage of the tragic pathetic style of acting, Ziegler reportedly achieved notable effects in the quieter passages, where she made extensive use of gestures or monumental poses, but when called upon to express great emotions, she resorted to a "sing-song" tone so that her words became incomprehensible. Her costume, which she changed three times during the performance, also underscored the heroic. The production lacked a unified point of view, and this has been blamed largely on the acting. Three of the performers were guests and thus unaccustomed to working together, while the casting, especially that of Stolberg as Prothoe, revealed a total lack of foresight. To quote the *Vossische Zeitung*: "Allerdings hatte diese Prothoe das Längenmaß, um ein Pendant zu Penthesilea zu bilden, aber der sanfte Charakter der Rolle, der schönsten im ganzen Stück, der einzigen, für die man ein menschliches Mitgefühl haben kann, war verloren gegangen."[7] When the Amazon army appeared, each warrior wearing modern, black canvas boots with small high heels, the spectators broke into peals of laughter. Moreover, "[d]as gute Dutzend meist zarter Gestalten mit zimperlichen Stimmen" representing the female army did not speak well for the courage of the Greeks, their worthy opponents, and the resulting merriment in the audience did obvious damage to the attempt to suggest an overall ominous atmosphere. Although there were three more performances, the production could not be considered a breakthrough, and despite Mosenthal's efforts audiences remained antagonistic to the play. The critics described the production as an interesting venture but felt that the work, aside from its excesses, lacked the necessary tragic motivation to maintain dramatic interest, since the catastrophe hinged upon a mere misunderstanding: "So kann schließlich zusammenfassend gesagt werden, daß das erste Erscheinen der *Penthesilea* auf der Bühne nichts zu der besonderen Wertschätzung dieser Tragödie beigetragen hat."[8]

Although Clara Ziegler was claimed as the perfect Penthesilea in a Nuremberg production of 16 October 1877, detractors frequently pointed to the Berlin *première* as proof positive of the play's unstageworthiness. Blaming the failure on Mosenthal's inadequate adaptation, Ziegler continued to campaign for a *Penthesilea* performance in the original, but it was only with the advent of naturalism in the 1890s and its stress on the animal side of human nature that she dared put forward her own reworking of Kleist's text, based substantially upon that of her predecessor, Mosenthal. This new version, which preserved more of the original but still toned down the sensual passages, was first presented in the Königliches Hof- und National-Theater in Munich on 15 June 1892 with Clara Ziegler in the title role, and its qualified success was again attributed by the critics almost exclusively to the actress, not to the play, which one critic rejected as undramatic.[9] Refusing to be swayed by the mixed reviews of what was generally classified as a "Kuriosität", Ziegler took the Munich staging on tour to Cologne, Nuremberg, Mannheim, and Schwerin, the last performances (1893–94) of the nineteenth century. There was therefore only one Penthesilea in the last century, that of Clara Ziegler who gave ample evidence of adaptability in her move away from the heroic stage style of 1876 towards greater theatrical realism in 1892: "Gerade die Fähigkeit, den wuchtigen Klang der Heroinensprache völlig abzulegen und in der Verwirrung des entzückten Herzens durch mädchenhafte Naturtöne zu ersetzen, war hier zu bewundern. Oft war es nur ein kurzes Moment, ein liebestrunkener Blick, eine schmachtende Gebärde, eine Geste voll

Verlangens, in welcher die Leidenschaft sich kundgab, aber in diesen plastischen Posen lag soviel des Ausdrucks, daß man es übersehen durfte, wenn in der Deklamation nicht überall das Kleistische Pathos bewahrt blieb."[10]

The first twentieth-century staging, on 17 October 1908 in Weimar, did not augur well for the future of the tragedy. To begin with, it availed itself of a new adaptation, or better stated, distortion, fabricated by Hermann Schlag whose sole principle was to please the public. He wrote an exposition to inform the audience immediately of the background to the conflict and changed the plot so that Penthesilea did not join her dogs in ripping apart Achilles (she only showed them the spot to attack), and finally stabbed herself with one of her arrows. The production, directed by Karl Weiser, to commemorate the hundredth anniversary of the work, proved to be a complete disaster because of the ill-informed adaptation, the inappropriate casting (Achilles [Adalbert Herzberg] came across as a salon lover), and the generally poor acting. Schneider's Penthesilea was found totally inadequate in her "übertriebene Gewaltsamkeit,"[11] while the Amazon army, wearing cute little dresses, could scarcely conceal the fact that it had been recruited from the *corps de ballet*. The critic of the *Weimarische Zeitung* was even left with the impression that what he had witnessed had been Offenbach, not Kleist!

Despite this setback, other signs remained favourable for a more positive acceptance of the drama. Germanists had created a greater awareness of and appreciation for Kleist's genius and a new literary movement began to make its influence felt upon the stage. Not only Kleist's work but also his life came to be viewed as one of the first manifestations of expressionism in German letters. *Penthesilea* profited extensively from this new trend, becoming the most popular Kleistian play of the period. The hundredth anniversary of Kleist's death in 1911 witnessed no less than six new adaptations and ten stage productions. In his widely played version Paul Lindau avoided for the first time any change in scenery, on the grounds that Kleist had provided through his stage directions a great variety of lighting effects, from sunrise to sunset, which would preclude any boring uniformity. Although he cut about one third of the original, including the sixth scene with the "Rosenjungfraun" and the captured Greeks, still considered alien to contemporary taste, he nevertheless remained closer to Kleist than any previous adaptor. The Königliches Schauspielhaus in Berlin elected to produce this adaptation on 16 September 1911. However, only a week later, the Deutsches Theater, also in Berlin and then under the general management of Max Reinhardt, opened its staging of *Penthesilea* directed by Ernst Stern in a version by Theodor Commichau that came even closer to Kleist's text (the sixth scene was reinstated). The most noteworthy technical innovation was the efficient application of the revolving stage. "Es ist durch die Drehbühne möglich," Stern commented, "offene Verwandlung vorzunehmen, während man weiterspielt."[12] It was feasible not only to keep the same basic scenery, but also to preserve the logic of the plot. While Lindau made extensive use of illumination, basically for realistic purposes, Stern went one step further and exploited colours as a stylizing, symbolic device in what amounted to an impressionistic approach, where the décor and colour reflected the mood of the protagonists. The choice of costumes underscored this same distinction: Lindau's actors wore clothing emphasizing "das echt realistische Moment,"[13] but Stern's costumes remained as rough and barbaric as the sets. The Amazons exposed wide expanses of flesh, suggesting their close affinity with their animals.

As expected, the critics were divided in their assessments of the two productions, a diversity especially apparent in their reviews of the very different interpretations of the title role. In the staging for the Königliches Schauspielhaus, Rosa Poppe conveyed, in the words of Kurt Lowien, a "modern realistisch-heroische Darstellung"[14] in line with Lindau's approach. In contrast to Clara Ziegler, she apparently made great efforts to avoid rhetorical and gestural extremes, in order to suggest the internalized, mental tragedy of the heroine, but in so doing she neglected to put across the primitive, strongly irrational element in her psychological makeup. "Gertrud Eysoldt [Deutsches Theater] dagegen will die Penthesilea in das überreizte, feinnervige, dekadente Ichsgefühl ihrer Tradition und künstlerischen Umwelt bannen." She was the first actress to give a pathological-psychological interpretation of the part by overstating the sadistic, sexual aspect of Penthesilea's personality, but neither she nor Poppe succeeded in giving or even hinting at the conflicting loyalties that make up the heroine's complex character. Waldemar Staegemann, playing Achilles for the Königliches Schauspielhaus as "einen witzigen burschikosen Leutnant," lost in a primitive, natural society, failed completely, while Alexandro Moissi's humourless Achilles constituted only a partial success. One reaches the inevitable conclusion that Lindau's aim to stage Penthesilea's death as a victory in the heroic vein of a Schillerian tragedy did as much injustice to Kleist's drama as Stern's view of Penthesilea as a woman possessed by an obsession which ultimately consumes her.

When Franz Herterich became the new director of the Burgtheater, he proclaimed his support for expressionism, the prevailing modern trend, by first producing one of Franz Werfel's expressionistic dramas and then by offering the Viennese *première* of *Penthesilea*. As Liselotte Schmidinger remarked: "Auch [Penthesilea] wächst in einer Umwelt auf, die in ihrer absurden und unverstandenen Natur die naive Gefühlsstärke Penthesileas vergewaltigt, da schlägt es hart auf und zerstört sich selbst. Dies ist aber nichts anderes, als die weltanschauliche Lage des Expressionismus."[15] Complementing this literary bias, Remigius Geyling designed, in a decidedly abstract style, cubistic sets which unfortunately clashed with the costumes. "Hier [i.e., in the costume department] strahlte üppig-phantasievolle Farben- und Formenpracht, ein fast operettenhaftes Gepränge." Another problem lay in the inability of the cast to capture the musical rhythms of the play, one of the aspects of *Penthesilea* which first attracted the expressionists. Although Auguste Pünkösty managed to suggest the naturalness of the title role, she tended to tone down the queen's immoderate behaviour and hence failed to present an expressionistic Penthesilea. The *Wiener Zeitung* (9 October 1923) observed: "Frau Pünkösty spielte als Penthesilea ein wonnevolles Käthchen von Heilbronn. Die Worte, 'den / Ida will ich auf den Osa wälzen' flüsterte sie verzückt vor sich hin." Ranol Aslan's Achilles evidently left much to be desired in the utterance of his gallant lines, almost as if he refused to take the whole matter seriously. But this defect only served to reinforce the generally ironic impression which this staging, with its propensity to gloss over Kleist's realm of emotional extremes, left behind.

In the National Socialist era, *Penthesilea* was produced at several local festivals along with the other more popular Kleistian plays. For example, it appeared together with *Die Hermannsschlacht* during the Kurmärkische Festspiele in 1937 and was also one of the works performed on the occasion of the Bochum Kleist-Woche sponsored by the Nazi party. However, these productions, designed with a specific propaganda purpose in mind, did little to encourage a greater appreciation of this difficult tragedy.

The first production after the war had to wait until 1954 when the avant-gardist Heinrich Koch offered an interpretation in Hamburg's Deutsches Schauspielhaus. For the first time, in keeping with the dramatist's intention, the tragedy ran a full two hours without interruption. Despite the fact that Koch provided a well organized performance with considerable attention to the peculiar nature of Kleist's verse, his greatest success, in the opinion of Johannes Jacobi, was his staging of the initial expository scenes. Maria Wimmer displayed the intelligence and discipline necessary to convey a Penthesilea caught in the dilemma of conflicting demands. But when she appeared with the body of Achilles, "war [sie] eine Schäferin des Schäferspiels mit der Attitude Ophelias, wo doch Brünhilde an der Bahre Siegfrieds hätte stehen sollen."[16] Heinz Baumann's approach to the figure of Achilles most clearly exposed the conflict between Koch's modern approach and Kleist's tragedy: "Vom tragischen Liebhaber Kleist zeigte Baumann jedoch kaum eine Spur. Er war ein Spielmann der Liebe von 1954: verhalten, unterkühlt im Ausdruck und ironisch den Bekenntnissen eines Weibes lauschend, um plötzlich fordernd gegen den girrenden Sex appeal die Macht des Besitzers mit aller zeitgemäßen Brutalität anzumelden." The critics commended the acting of Dagmar Altrichter (Prothoe) and Peter Schüttle (Odysseus) and found the remaining roles to be satisfactorily performed. Ita Maximowna's set, which consisted of a simple sloped expanse on a revolving stage, reinforced Koch's effort to update the play. By turning the stage, various perspectives could be achieved: the highpoint of the slope was used symbolically and for impressive effects, while intimate scenes were played with extreme simplicity before the cliff-like reverse side. When the curtain fell, there was considerable applause but, in Johannes Jacobi's opinion, of a decidedly polite, noncommittal nature: "Aus einer zeitlosen Liebestragödie wurde das Intermezzo einer Mänade, wurde das Zwischenspiel eines Griechenhelden, der vor Troja bei seinem Urlaubsabenteuer umkam."

After Jean Vilar had achieved fame with his celebrated *Le Prince de Hombourg*, Jean-Louis Barrault appealed to the poet, novelist, and critic Julien Gracq, noted for his surrealistic sympathies, to write a stage version of *Penthesilea*. Both of them were fully aware of the dramatic and casting problems faced by a director producing this work, with its reputation of being "armchair theater."[17] Convinced that Kleist's tragedy represented "a self-sufficient world of silent tensions,"[18] Gracq emphasized its symbolic content, suggesting three possible points of view: "the Germanic message," with its glorification of war (an anticipation of Nietzsche's blond beast), the subjective-Romantic element (Kleist as Goethe's antipode), and the psychological element (the symbolic portrayal of the battle of the sexes). Gracq's prose translation was supposed to be staged during the fall of 1955 in the Théâtre Marigny but Barrault withdrew the project without explanation. However, on 20 July of the same year, in the Théâtre Hébertot, director Claude Régy presented *Penthesilea* to the Festival de Paris in a translation by Charles Floquet and Maurice Clavel. This French *première* met with a mixed critical reaction. H. Magnan of *Le Monde* (23 July 1955) gave his enthusiastic endorsement, although he still felt obliged to defend the play against charges of sexual and sadistic excesses. Jean Nepveu-Degas of the *France observateur*, while praising the lyrical quality of the play, the excellent directing of Régy, the sensitive interpretation of the titular heroine by Sylvia Manfort, and the black and white sets which complemented the acting, still found fault with the work's dragging tempo and frequent repetitions.

In 1923, the noted critic Alfred Kerr remarked: "Kleist [sic] *Penthesilea* steht und fällt mit der Penthesilea."[19] However, as noted by Rolf Michaelis, a novel symbolic staging directed by Friedrich Siems in 1960 for Mannheim's Nationaltheater seemed to belie this observation. Siem's utilization of symbolism extended to the costumes, to details of the sets devised by Paul Walter, and above all to the pervasive presence of colour. A violet shade permeated the whole production and tended to merge into the two basic tones of the play, red and blue. The former, in all its variations – the red clothes and turbans of the Amazons, the pink of the flower girls, the rust-brown of the priestess, the glowing torches – reflected the blood-red of Penthesilea, the colour of the love she sought and the death she provided. Blue, on the other hand, became associated with the Greeks and especially with a shining aquamarine Achilles. According to the demands of the plot, the set was bathed in black, violet, or bright red, while a weak sun shone in a constantly changing sky: "Das Ungefüge von Kleists hartem Versrhythmus ist ins Optische übersetzt. Bei so rationalisierender Symbolregie droht allerdings stets die Gefahr, daß die Tiefendimension des Trauerspiels verlorengeht."[20]

On 18 November 1961 a review of the Tower Theatre production of *Penthesilea* in a new translation by Neil Curry appeared in *The Times*. The anonymous commentator spent more time finding fault with Kleist's play, its inherent weaknesses, than in describing the performance. Achilles, we are told, is merely "a spoiled child, a booby and doesn't suspect it." But above all Kleist was criticized for "not [coming] out into the open. He neither exposes the pretensions of his Greeks and Amazons, nor tries to convince us that they themselves believe in those pretensions, even if we cannot." Drawing attention to the fact that this play "has hardly ever been acted in its country of origin," the critic implied that a "new version" was required if the work was to receive a favourable reception and that Curry's translation, by revising the dialogue, had bestowed a compactness upon the action which Donald Kirkman's directing managed to sustain. Reading between the lines, one may assume that uninspiring individual efforts contributed to the negative reaction to the English *première*: "Mr. Val Homes' setting and Mr. Hugh George's lighting make some of the acting look undistinguished by comparison."

The immense importance to this difficult work of the quality of acting was vividly illustrated by a much heralded production in Zürich by the Schauspieltruppe under the direction of Robert Freitag and played without the use of a curtain and without an intermission. Although the commentator of the *Neue Zürcher Zeitung* (12 October 1962) objected to Freitag's use of a mixed adaptation (the "Buchausgabe" of 1808, the manuscript of a copyist corrected by Kleist, and the *Phöbus* fragment) and felt that the Amazon army came across as "zarte Nereiden," not as fierce warriors, he had only praise for Maria Becker's interpretation of Penthesilea: "Diese große Schauspielerin erfüllt noch heute wie ehedem die unerhörten Ansprüche der Rolle, auch wenn sich die Gestaltung natürlicherweise von den starken Impulsen jugendlicher Kraft zum bewußteren Differenzieren aus überlegenem Kunstverstand hin gewandelt hat. Sie trägt Herbheit zur Schau, strafft immer wieder ihren Körper, das Haupt in den Nacken gebogen. Ihre innere Spannung ist auch in der Verhaltenheit stets fühlbar, in einer reizbaren Empfindlichkeit und im Umschlag zu sprunghaften Ausbrüchen." Above all, she made the audience willing prisoners of her consummate skills as an actress during the mad scenes, which ranged in intensity from the battle howls of a wild dog to the gentle soft voice of an unsuspecting maiden: "Von diesem Augenblick an bis zum großartig gestalteten Sterben waren die Zuschauer atemlos still, ja selbst die Mitspieler auf der Bühne schienen aus innerer Erschütterung heraus am Spiel Maria Beckers zu wachsen." Complementing Becker's excellent performance was that of Gerhard Riedmann as Achilles, who managed to convey the physically endowed, self-satisfied but psychologically naive Greek hero: "Gerhard Riedmanns Leistung durfte neben Maria Becker bestehen. Die beiden Gestalten beherrschen die Bühne, sie beschäftigen unsere Phantasie noch, wenn Botenberichte und Schlachtschilderungen von ihnen künden." The fact that these two lead roles were given excellent support by the remainder of the cast (with only two exceptions: Dietlinde Lougear as Meroe and Margarete Fries as the Oberpriesterin) guaranteed an enthusiastic reception of what has been recognized as one of the highpoints in *Penthesilea's* stage history: "Im gesamten erstaunte es, wie sicher Robert Freitag seine zu einem großen Teil doch noch sehr jungen, kaum erfahrenen Darsteller durch alle Fährnisse des heiklen Stücks geleitete, so daß bei allen Rangunterschieden zwischen den einzelnen Kräften eine schöne Ensembleleistung möglich wurde."

Karl Heinz Stroux's staging for Düsseldorf's Schauspielhaus in September 1969 exposed the danger of not having a clear concept of *Penthesilea* and its dramatic difficulties; but the even greater danger of imposing on the work an arbitrary interpretation which ignores its real strength, the poetic idiom, came to the fore in the controversial, sensation-seeking production of Klaus Michael Grüber, a student of Giorgio Strehler, for Stuttgart's Staatstheater in November 1970. Odysseus wore nothing but a G-string and a pair of black sunglasses; the Amazons appeared in earth-brown bikinis with exotically made-up faces; and during the love scene Achilles (Giovanni Früh) seemed "zum Showman für ein Body-Building-Institut degradiert."[21] Scenes and speeches which followed one another in the text were presented synchronically, so that the language, a challenge in its own right, now became totally incomprehensible and the audience had considerable difficulty in following the threads of the plot: "Grüber benützt die Verse nur als akustisches Material seiner Collage aus Wort, Musik und Bewegung."[22] Not only the press and the audience expressed their disapproval, but the actors themselves protested, and with some justification. At one point, Rosl Zech (Penthesilea) had to remain rigid, lying on her back with her legs in the air for ten minutes, and the director further required her to give a pantomimic rendering of the concluding mad scene which "mit Hilfe des Rotstiftes, von einem der genialsten, lebendigsten Dialoge deutscher Dramatik zu einer Art von Opern-Schluß ... umfunktioniert worden war."[23] What most of the reviewers of this production objected to, in addition to the obvious lack of faith in Kleist's drama and its language, was the total absence of a unifying principle: "Nicht einmal die hervorstechendste Eigenschaft, die der manieristischen Bizarrerie, war folgerichtig durchgeführt." Günter Schloz suggested that Grüber endeavoured with his irreverent approach to destroy that pathologically destructive, totally egocentric consciousness so characteristic of the protagonist, but if this were indeed his intention, then he evidently fell prey to the very subjective illusion he found so reprehensible in Kleist: "Der Regisseur hat nur *seine* [Schloz's emphasis] Interpretation inszeniert und nicht das Stück."[24]

As previously noted, Claude Régy's production came to partial grief because of *Penthesilea*'s notoriously static quality, the fact that most of the action is only reported by messengers or the chorus. Jean Gillibert, experienced with the Greek theatre, succeeded in overcoming this obstacle in his highly regarded staging of Julien Gracq's adaptation for the Théâtre de Châteauvallon in 1973. "En disposant ses personnages sur les divers niveaux de la scène qui surplombe la mer, en leur faisant commenter par le mouvement les péripéties des combats que nous ne voyons pas, il élargit à l'infini le cadre du jeu pour le ramener parfois à un simple cercle de lumière lorsqu'il faut cerner en un gros plan l'un ou l'autre des protagonistes."[25] This excellent stage management helped to create an ever increasing tension as the characters gradually lost their weapons and their heroic proportions to become mere human beings, the slaves of their passions. But the real success of the performance depended to a large degree upon the inspired portrayal of the titular heroine by Maria Casarès, around whom Gillibert constructed his interpretation. "Lorsque Maria Casarès, sous le casque d'or de Penthésilée, a descendu les marches de l'amphithéâtre antique pour gagner le proscénium où l'attendaient les Amazones, il semble que toute la nature environnante ait approfondi son silence. C'était une menace d'orage qui se profilait sur les étoiles du ciel. Elle apportait avec elle le vent et la tempête des âmes qui constituent le thème fondamental de la *Penthésilée* de Kleist."

The year 1973 witnessed another "storm wind," the successful revival of the Swiss composer Othmar Schoeck's one-act opera *Penthesilea* in the framework of the International Music Festival of Lucerne (Luzerner Festwochen). This work, a late romantic contribution to musical expressionism, originating about the time of Berg's *Wozzeck* but *premièred* in Dresden in 1927, had been kept alive with several performances in Zürich (in 1968, for example). Music historians have classified it as a sequel to Richard Strauss's realistic one-act operas *Salome* and *Elektra* and indeed several parallels do exist, especially with the latter. (Ironically, Strauß wrote to Zweig in May 1935: "Kleist ist unkomponierbar."[26]) Musically, however, Schoeck's score makes less concession to traditional tastes and is considered more avant-garde than those of Strauß: "Vor allem geht die Harmonik über die Spätromantik weit hinaus: Sie ist vorwiegend polytonal, mit tonalen Episoden – hauptsächlich in lyrischen Momenten – und aufregenden Dissonanzen."[27] Schoeck obviously took great liberties in his libretto, reducing Kleist's text to a one-act drama with a mere eighty minutes of playing time (he actually cut about three quarters of the verses). To achieve this extreme abridgement, he concentrated on the love interest ("Niederlage und Gefangennahme der Fürstin gehen der Begegnung voraus, ihr folgen die Ermordung des Peliden, der Tod Penthesileas"[28]) to such an extent that the "Ringsumstehenden ... nur Staffage, Erzähler, schauderndes Volk [sind]."[29] Although such a practice must inevitably do some damage to Kleist's poetic tragedy of the word, no less an apologist than Emil Staiger came to the enthusiastic defence of the opera: "Amazonen, die Schoecks Orchester gleichsam auf die Szene schleudert, bedürfen keiner Beglaubigung mehr; und eine Penthesilea, die singt, so singt, wie Schoeck sie singen heißt, durchbricht von vornherein die Grenzen des irdisch möglichen Daseins so, wie Kleist sie durchbrochen haben wollte. Das Knirschen des Dichters über die Unzulänglichkeit seiner künstlerischen Mittel verwandelt sich in der Oper in einen Triumph des angemessenen Ausdrucks. Denn eine Musik, die selbst dem grandiosesten Sprecher versagt bleibt, sie teilt sogar den höchsten Grad der Ergriffenheit, das Verstummen, noch mit."[30] Schoeck's score managed to convey the underlying tragic tone by a predominant "bronzene[n] Klang" (Adam). He limited the orchestra to woodwinds, brass, pianos, violas, cellos, bass viols, and only four violins. As part of this lower register, a mezzo-soprano and baritone have the main roles in a new musical dramatic form: "In den Stimmen wechselt Schoeck von freier Rede über rhythmisch pointierten Sprechgesang zum Gesang, zur emotionellen Kantilene wie zum Aufschrei" (Adam). The composer insisted that "das Stück vorüberrauschen [muß] wie ein Sturmwind, daß der Hörer überhaupt nicht zum Aufatmen kommt und erst zum Schluß aus der Spannung entlassen wird."[31] The only respite offered to the listener is a beautiful duet between Penthesilea and Achilles composed after the *première* for a Zürich production in 1928. The 1973 revival, the result of the cooperation between the West-German Radio Network of Cologne and the management of the Lucerne Festival, proved to be the highpoint of the Swiss season, "eine bedeutsame kulturhistorische Leistung."[32] Carol Smith in the title role sufficiently projected a "dunkeldramatische Ausstrahlung" but did not always meet the enormous demands of the deep register: "Der Heldenbariton Roland Hermann war als Achilles ein überzeugender Gegenspieler." As a decisive indication of the importance of this musical event, the cast was reconvened in 1975 for a recording session with the Cologne Radio-Symphony Orchestra under the baton of Zdenek Macal and the results were subsequently made available on cassette and LP.

France's love affair with *Penthesilea* continued with productions by Michel Hermon and Lucien Melki for the Théâtre de la Tempête, December 1976 and by Gabriel Blondé and Luce Berthomme at the Théâtre du Lucernaire, 1977, the latter version transforming "l'un des plus grands poèmes de l'histoire du théâtre" into "un mélodrame de brigands, style Second Empire du côté des barrières."[33] This latter staging received a generally bad press, but Hermon's experiment enjoyed enthusiastic reviews both in France and Germany. Before Hermon and Melki offered *Penthesilea*, they spent months carefully working on the text based on Julien Gracq's adaptation. On the purely technical side they had to contend with the "cartoucherie" as a theatre, an unheated powder shed from the old days in a distant eastern suburb of Paris. (During the performance three horses stabled in the adjacent stalls added their snorts to the text.) The collaborators directed most of their attention to a theoretical problem: "[Dans] le même lieu, la scène, et dans un temps défini – le temps de la représentation – les personnages parlent, agissent, se souviennent, rêvent et meurent sans que jamais ces différents états soient nettement distingués. Le temps que vivent les spectateurs est tantôt le temps réel, d'une action qui se déroule sous leurs yeux, tantôt le temps raccourci du récit du rêve, du souvenir, de l'épopée."[34] The dream was carried over, however, into the action, and this provided the drama with a dynamic, surprising dimension. Because of this concern with time, Hermon and Melki avoided presenting *Penthesilea* as an ancient Greek tragedy and placed it instead securely into Kleist's own nineteenth-century environment: "Die Griechen stecken in Stiefeln und abgenutzten Fräcken 'jener' Zeit, in der das Gedicht entstand. Die kriegerischen Frauen verkörpern, weil, wie gesagt zeitlos, eine bühnenmäßig denkbare Lösung. Nicht einmal graue, eher farblose lange Röcke, natürliches Haar ohne historische Anspielung: Frauen, die gezeichnet sind wie Asketen und Wahnsinnige, welche keinem Stand mehr angehören. Denn so gehören auch diese Geschöpfe, die der Weiblichkeit rationell entsagt haben, ihrem Stand, ihrem Geschlecht nicht mehr an."[35] There was only one interpolation. When called upon, two Amazons were instantly converted into a pianist and a Lieder-singer who together performed works by Brahms. Despite this questionable interlude and the attempt to relativize what is in fact a universal myth, the critics unanimously lauded the thought and the care that went into "eine durchweg künstlerische Umsetzung eines (und welchen!) theatralischen Themas." This French performance made such a strong impact on the Paris correspondent of the *Frankfurter Rundschau* that she recommended it be staged in Germany, "zur Information, zum Vergleich, vielleicht zum Gewinn."

While the French production strove to suggest a timeless aspect by imposing myth upon the Napoleonic era, the Battersea Salt Theatre in London decided to present the tragedy as an "ultimate sex-war play"[36] in a modern setting. The usual difficulties of dealing with the poetic language and the long reports of battles were simply ignored: "No problem: the lights go down, a catlike figure glides across the floor, and with the line 'Hello, soldier' the first guard bites the dust." Then the audience observed Achilles and Odysseus playing a game with old tin cans while discussing the siege "in round south London tones." A scene followed in which Penthesilea (Sandy Maberly), wearing a tracksuit, warmed up with her fellow-Amazons for the impending match. The reported battles of the Kleist original were now acted out in tracksuits, with bamboo swords and fencing masks as illustrations of "the contemporary situation of sexual roles vis-à-vis the women's movement." The abstract, stylized décor, reminiscent of a gymnasium with scaffolds and movable partitions, destroyed any vestige of historical accuracy. Indeed, Irving Wardle of *The Times* was left with the impression that he had viewed a rather innocuous athletic contest between two rival private schools, which reached a climax "when the head girl's two prefects [turned] against her for letting down the side." "But the aimless chases over the scaffolding, duels with anonymous Trojans and the obliteration of dialogue under playful rough and tumble and kite-flying, leave one longing for one of Kleist's messengers to arrive and describe the events instead." Any resemblance to *Penthesilea* was purely accidental.

Another partially successful attempt to modernize *Penthesilea* took place in May 1978 in Frankfurt's Schauspielhaus. Director Frank-Patrick Steckel intentionally did away with a set or any form of decoration and placed the 450 spectators directly on three sides of the stage in unnumbered seats. According to Steckel, "Ein Stück, in dem die Frauen herrschen – da hat man das Bedürfnis, auch eine paradoxe Zuschauersituation zu schaffen."[37] At first the observers were forced to listen to a deafening drumming noise and then to witness a battle enacted through pantomime. "Der Text des Stücks hat die Neigung, sich auszusprechen," Steckel noted. "Nur: wo ist da noch ein Platz zum Spielen? Man kann allenfalls eine Annäherung zum Text bringen: einen Kommentar." This new adaptation shortened the original text by about one half, a reduction made in the name of stageworthiness which harks back to nineteenth-century criticism of the play. For instance, through cuts and revisions the production almost immediately set before the audience a Penthesilea (Marlen Dieckhoff) who, when she first appeared, seemed tired, exhausted and desperate, as if she were already at death's door. In order to reduce the almost superhuman qualities of the heroine and render her more human, Steckel frequently removed Penthesilea from the centre of the action and concentrated upon the other women. To this end the narration of the Amazons' history was relegated to the high priestess. Achilles was also brought down to a very human level: "Geschunden plagt sich Christian Redl über die Lehnen der leeren Sitzreihen des Parketts nach vorn in seine erste Szene. Ein etwas dümmlicher Sportsmann, Unverständnis im Blick. Er ist nackt bis auf einen Lederschurz, läßt sich wie ein Fighter den Leib massieren."[38] The other Greeks, dressed in motorcycle helmets and football uniforms, treated him with care. The empty auditorium accentuated the isolation of the individual which this production sought to underline. When Penthesilea set out to kill Achilles, she dragged herself away from the acting area towards a spotlight in the orchestra pit which, of course, dazzled her, thus conveying her blind love-hate relationship with her rival: "Das ist ein schön erfundenes Bild und vielleicht der stärkste einzelne Eindruck, den die Aufführung schafft." The representation of Penthesilea's self-willed suicide brought another novel effect: her companions proceeded to wrap her head in a bright cloth and, almost unnoticed, she apparently suffocated. The critic Georg Hensel (*Frankfurter Allgemeine Zeitung*, 14 March 1978) maintained that since she was led off stage by two Amazons, her attempt at self-destruction also ended in failure: "Suizid durch Sprache, dies hält die Regie offenbar nicht einmal bei Kleist für möglich." For this scene the attendant women seemed strangely transformed into figures reminiscent of tragic heroines from Hebbel to Brecht. For example, Elisabeth Schwarz's Prothoe, now wearing a long dress, played "mit den Pistolen Hedda Gablers"[39] – or did Steckel intend this as a veiled allusion to Kleist's death? The scope of critical reaction to this attempt, "*Penthesilea* ... nicht als dramatisches Gedicht, sondern als Drama so realistisch wie irgend möglich zu spielen" (Hensel), ranged from enthusiastic endorsement – "Selten sieht man heute leider nur eine so treue und dennoch ganz moderne Interpretation eines klassischen Stückes"[40] – to polite rejection – "Abzubuchen als interessant mißlungener Versuch, sich der *Penthesilea* zu nähern."[41]

Years ago I read a German play called *Penthesilea* by Heinrich von Kleist. I liked it so much I commissioned a translation, which turned out to be an excellent one, by Humphrey Trevelyan; and I published it in my anthology *The Classic Theatre*. Much as I admired Kleist, I could not see things his way at all, and when one of my U.B. [University of Buffalo] students, Linda Lavorgna, told me I was preoccupied with men and should write about women for a change, I resolved to re-write Kleist's story my way. The result is before you.[42]

With the statement quoted above Eric Bentley sought to justify in the program notes his very free adaptation of Kleist's tragedy, entitled *The Fall of the Amazons*, which had its first performance on 26 April 1979 in the Center for Theater Research in Buffalo, NY. On the basis of *Penthesilea's* nineteenth-century reception and more recent productions there would seem to be some justification for the liberties taken with the original source. Bentley did follow the basic outline of Kleist's plot and preserve many of its memorable images (the arch, the oak tree), but he added a prologue and an epilogue, consisting of dialogues between Ulysses and Agamemnon, and he transformed the work into a discussion of women's issues. His intent became particularly evident when Penthesilea no longer slaughters Achilles in the mistaken belief that he has rejected her as a woman – the more liberated queen knows beforehand that Achilles plans to surrender to her – but because she is led to believe that he intends to treat her as a woman according to the norms of a male-oriented society. The villain of the tale, Ulysses, presents this argument: "'When I [i.e., Achilles] pretend to lose, what will it mean? I've never lost. And I have shown that I can beat this female. ... At any time in the future I could win again. She will know that. If she ever forgets I will remind her. She cannot fail to know who's up, who's down, who's master and who's slave!'"[43] To expose the illusion of masculine superiority, the epilogue reveals that there is an attempt to conceal the fact that "it was a woman who killed Achilles" by promoting the myth that Achilles slew Penthesilea, "the right kind of woman – sexless, dumb and rather good at sewing" (p. 49). One senses the influence of Brecht both in the decision to adapt the play (Brecht concerned himself primarily with adaptations of classics during the last years of his life) and in the collaborative approach to mounting it: those involved contributed their thoughts to Bentley, who "re-wrote his script again and again,"[44] both before and during rehearsals. To suggest the larger-than-life dimensions of the warrior women, the director Saul Elkin "hit upon the notion of the Amazons as a 'tribal unit' decked out in fur and feathers, trained in the use of the sword and lance, and in the martial arts."[45] Bob Groves, in his review of the staging for the *Buffalo Courier-Express* (27 April 1979), commended the witty dialogue, the choreography of the battle scenes, the functional costuming ("except when the men's armor looks like Dr. Denton-Captain Video space suits and when the women appear to be hippies in flesh colored thermal underwear"), and the two leads: "David Lamb [Achilles] is both valiant and vulnerable. Lorna C. Hill is both touching and a terror as the feminist queen." Although Groves viewed the play in the more generally accepted, English-speaking context of the Shavian tradition, the adaptation does not appear to have made any lasting impression.

In December 1980, Frankfurt again hosted a *Penthesilea* production which, inviting comparison with Steckel's version, met an even more negative reaction from audience and critics alike. "Frank-Patrick Steckels Inszenierung damals war kein großer Wurf, aber sie war dramaturgisch und schauspielerisch dem neuen Versuch doch weit überlegen."[46] This new attempt represented Wilfried Minks's first offering as the new co-director of the Frankfurter Schauspiel, a responsibility shared with Johannes Schaaf. Minks, who gained considerable acclaim as a designer (he planned the sets for Grüber's 1970 Stuttgart *Penthesilea*), at least achieved novelty. Jürgen Holwein

(*Stuttgarter Nachrichten*, 8 December 1980) described the stage as "ein tief gelegener, rechteckiger Raum, von drei Seiten von Zuschauerplätzen begrenzt, eine von rostigen, gleichwohl farbigen Ölfässern gerahmte Arena." The oil drums, some 150 of them, dominated the production and helped to sustain a depressing atmosphere. Actors were forced to make their entries and exits by climbing over this industrial-waste mountain, while individual oil drums functioned as a makeshift altar (complete with smoke for the high priestess), as a "monströses Sexualsymbol"[47] when mounted by Penthesilea, or as a rain barrel for a Greek soldier who plunged into one to escape the heat and flies. "Mein Nachbar," reported Rudolf Krämer-Badoni, "zählt bewundernd die Sekunden, die er [Greek soldier] mit dem Kopf unter Wasser bleibt."[48] Kleist's great play was reduced to the trivial, indeed to the comically trivial, as the staging focussed attention on the many war-games fought with the omnipresent stage props at the expense of Kleist's verse. "Aber wie soll," asked Wilhelm Ringelband, "in diesem Tonnen-Getürm Kleists Sprache Gestalt gewinnen?"[49] This adaptation showed an almost total disregard for the poetic language, resulting in the "Verlust des Kunstwerks," according to Peter Iden, and to make matters worse, the actors had no feeling whatsoever for what little of Kleist's text remained. Almost without exception the critics deplored this condensed version of Kleist's play. The history of the Amazon state related to Achilles by Penthesilea more than half-way through the drama (scene 15), was narrated instead by the high priestess as a prologue. The production, running uninterrupted for almost two and a half hours, deleted "alle tiefenpsychologischen Zeichen, aus denen die Tragik einer großen Seele spricht" (Krämer-Badoni), for example, Prothoe's perceptive defence of her mistress: "Und jeder Busen ist, der fühlt, ein Rätsel" (1286) – "Nichts also vom Wahnsinn, nichts vom Widerspruch, vom unbedingten Gefühl, von der Lebensgefahr der Liebe, von der Vernichtung der Individuen, nichts von Kleists kritischer Wucht."[50] Manuela Alphons depicted a neurotic housewife rather than an heroic Penthesilea, and the critical consensus deplored Michael Altmann's interpretation of Achilles as "brummig, träge, desinteressiert."[51] The "scheußlich kostümierte[n]" (Ringelband) women seemed much too small and fragile to be Amazons and thus, when they carried on stage the captured, seminaked Greeks upon their shoulders, smeared their arms in blood or raped their captives, the scene struck the reviewer as either comical or highly improbable. The one innovation that garnered some approval came at the conclusion, when Penthesilea dragged behind her by a rope the body of Achilles wrapped up in a brown bag. When she regained consciousness and wanted to see the corpse, she did not expose the face but rather the butchered middle section: "Dies ist so etwas wie ein objektives Korrelat zu einer dieser Kleistschen Visionen, die noch unsere Gegenwart erhellen" (Hensel). Except for one or two lukewarm assessments (e.g., "Minks gelingt eine herausfordernde, entmythologisierte Wiedergabe der Kleistschen Fabel"[52]), the critical reception proved to be decidedly negative: "Man wird an den großen Bühnen lange nach einer ähnlich mißglückten Arbeit suchen müssen."[53] The traditional view is repeated yet again in Hensel's conclusion: "Eine vollendete 'Penthe-silea-Aufführung' wird es nie geben. Das Stück ist unspielbar: Kleist weckt Erwartungen, die kein Schauspieler erfüllen kann."

As if in response to Hensel's implied challenge, Joachim Kramarz, in a review of a June 1981 production, remarked: "Das Stück gilt als unspielbar, und es wurde auch nach dem Krieg in Berlin nicht ein einziges Mal inszeniert. Daß das Stück aber doch immer wieder gespielt werden muß, beweist Hans Neuenfels im Schiller-Theater."[54] Presenting *Penthesilea* in the context of the "Preußen-Jahr" and as a contrast to his earlier production of Goethe's *Iphigenie*, also with Elisabeth Trissenaar in the title role, Neuenfels announced that his staging amounted to a world *première* (Welturaufführung), thereby implying that he, for the first time, would present the tragedy in a manner faithful to the author's intent. When the numerous[55] critical verdicts came in, there was general agreement, "daß er die Schau-spieler in einer Weise führt, die Kleist in seinem vollen Ernst wie auch in seinen gelegentlichen komischen Momenten gerecht wird."[56] As noted earlier, one of the seemingly insurmountable problems facing any theatrical realization of *Penthesilea* lies in the predominance of long speeches describing actions off stage. In fact, the highpoints of the plot: the combat scenes between the two main protagonists, the history of the matriarchy (so crucial to an understanding of the heroine's mentality), and the death of Achilles, are narrated at con-siderable length; and what dialogues do arise, evolve largely out of reactions to reported events. Endeavouring to preserve as much of Kleist's poetry as possible and rejecting the temptation to adapt the text, Neuenfels recreated on stage many of the powerful images contained in the verses. Prothoe's concluding speech: "Die abgestor-bene Eiche steht im Sturm, / Doch die gesunde stürzt er schmetternd nieder, / Weil er in ihre Krone greifen kann" (3041–3) helps to explain the presence of "ein[e] brandenburgisch[e] Ur-Eiche,"[57] the focal point of the novel stage setting. Any departure from a strict reading strove above all to stress the fateful love-hate relationship between Penthe-silea and Achilles or "die Unmöglichkeit der Liebe selber"[58] with the aid of modern psychoanalysis – and in the estimation of several reviewers, with noteworthy success: "[Die] Glorie [dieser Berliner Inszenierung] ist die psychologische Treffsicherheit im Liebes-, Lust- und Trauerspiel."[59] To support this approach and to demonstrate as well the tragedy's eternal relevance, Neuenfels depicted several eras simultaneously. Some of the Greeks wore Prussian army uniforms and powdered wigs from the Napoleonic era (the high priestess, dressed in a classical costume, strongly resembled portraits of Queen Luise of Prussia), but other Greeks, sporting only a G-string, suggested a savage prehistoric past. The Amazons in their dainty white dresses evoked in the minds of several observers members of the Nazi Bund deutscher Mädchen. "Achilles und Penthesilea wirken wie Fremde in dieser Umgebung: Sie sind die einzigen 'modernen' Figuren, er im weißen Anzug, sie im schlichten Sommerkleid."[60] To reinforce even further this temporal coalescence, Neuenfels included four black-and-white film sequences, in which the Greek and the Amazon hordes appeared in the parks and pavilions of Charlottenburg and Glienicke, a collage effect rejected by some as an annoying intrusion which weakened the effect of Kleist's language. The two chief actors, however, gained the unanimous approval of both reviewers and audience: "Elisabeth Trissenaar ist Penthesilea, schön, wild, berauscht in den leisen Tönen des Liebeseingeständnisses wie im Wahnsinn der schreienden Tötungslust"[61]; "Hermann Treusch als Achill ist kein strahlender Muskelheld, sondern eher ein Melancholiker, der eine gewisse Mühe hat, die ihm von seinen griechischen Kameraden abverlangte Rolle zu spielen."[62] In view of this endorsement, it comes as a surprise that a supporting role won the highest praise, Katharina Thalbach's portrayal of a street-wise Prothoe: "Die Thalbach kann alles; aus Kleist reproduziert sie die Herztöne und zeigt sie vor mit dem Hauch von Komik, der in ihrer Rolle zu entdecken ist. Für sie gab es den stärksten Beifall" (Weber).

Much of the controversy surrounded, not unexpectedly, the bestial slaughter of Achilles, the sequence most responsible for *Penthesilea's* notoriety as "das meist gefürchtete Drama deutscher Sprache" (Wirsing). When the queen learns of Achilles' renewed challenge and interprets it as his repudiation of her as a woman, she incites her dogs and Elizabeth Trissenaar, in a conscious effort to transform a verbal image into a visual one, "auf allen vieren kriechend, bellt die Verse heraus, wird hechelnd eins mit der unsichtbaren Meute" (Grack). The atrocity itself is narrated by an older Amazon to the audience from a position at the very front of the stage, with only her face sharply outlined by a spotlight. Penthesilea entered pushing a wheelchair with three blood-smeared suitcases containing the cut-up remains of the hated loved one. She removed the cases and placed them about her person as if escaping behind a fortress of insanity: "Die Aufführung schlägt hier eine Brücke zwischen dem 'klassischen' Fall, wie ihn der preußische, todessüchtige 'Romantiker' ausgedacht hat, und den Wahnbildern, die uns in Sexualverbrechen überliefert sind."[63] To conclude a four-and-a-half-hour production, taxing the attention-span of the most well-meaning patron, the audience witnessed a film depicting the heavily guarded, walled border with East Germany to the accompaniment of dogs howling, the only sound in the otherwise silent film. This prompted Günter Grack to speculate: "[L]assen es [das aggressive Gebell] nun die Wachthunde der Vopos [East-German border guards] hören oder die Jagdhunde der Penthesilea?" One gathers an overall positive impression from the many articles dealing with Neuenfels's interpretation: "Ein großartiger Abend, mit diskussionswürdigen Einzelheiten, aber ein mit Abstand wahrhaft theatralisches Ereignis" (Weber).

Whereas Michel Hermon used a powder shed next to a horse stable for his 1976 Paris production of *Penthesilea*, André Engel, characterized by Guy Dumur as "le plus *radical* [Dumur's emphasis] de nos metteurs en scène"[64] and noted for presenting his readings in nontheatrical settings such as hangars and hotels, finally opted in June 1981 to stage the tragedy in the Théâtre national de Strasbourg. (He had given thought to using the Roman baths.) Ticket-holders had to wait until the last moment before gaining entrance to the auditorium, because, as they were informed, "on est en train de faire la neige. Elle ne tient que deux heures" (Dumur). The orchestra section was quite literally filled with artificial snow: "Eine weiße Schnee- und Gletscherfläche, mit Eistürmen und Verwehungen bis zu den vorderen Sesseln";[65] "[Nicky] Reiti, parfait illusioniste ... a reconstitué un paysage glaciaire inspiré de Caspar David Friedrich" (Dumur). Patrons had to feel their way to their seats since blankets of fog substantially reduced visibility and thereby aided the director "to destroy, or at the very least, to confuse the link between auditorium and stage."[66] In this dimness the spectator gradually became aware of male silhouettes, Greeks in long, thick coats discussing in whispers their conflict with the Amazons and gazing with fearful apprehension into the distant fog bank. Suddenly, out of the mist, the enemy materialized, "[s]chicke, junge Damen in Lammfellhüllen, mit mondänen roten Schneggerlfrisuren, Rauhlederhosen und hohen Stiefeln, schnüffelnde Schlittenhunde an der Leine" (Hohlweg). This adaptation by Bernard Pautrat, based on three separate French translations, concentrated on the love-hate relationship between Penthesilea (Anne Alvaro) and Achilles (Gilles Arbona), the only two figures to stand out, however briefly, from the all-encompassing cold and gloom. What Georges Schlocker called "[e]ine Überromantisierung ..., die überaus kennzeichnend ist fürs heutige französische Theater"[67] was also present in the sets (the predilection for a moonlit landscape reminiscent of a C.D. Friedrich painting) and in the conscious attempt at mythologizing, especially in the characterization of Achilles. He embodied the ancient Greek warrior in the traditional form, "un fantôme antique [qui] vient parler aux fantômes de notre temps" (Dumur). Further support for Schlocker's assessment was provided by Dumur's review in which he saw this play and Kleist himself in the context of the Greek goddess Hecate: "Cette lune, ce brouillard, cette neige, ces chiens, ne serait-ce pas l'accompagnement obligatoire de la virginité d'Hécate, déesse de la mort? ... Kleist le solitaire, le dramaturge maudit, trouvant dans l'antiquité un surcroît de romantisme pour écrire cette épopée sado-masochiste."

The main objection raised by all commentators was the disservice done to Kleist as poet by the manner in which what little remained of the original text was whispered by the actors, so that the audience heard even less. When criticized for this shortcoming, Engel defended himself by saying that he wanted the spectator to make a special effort to hear, "afin de participer, par cette tension, à ce drame du solstice d'hiver, à cette fête païenne aux bruits et aux cris assourdis par la neige et le brouillard" (Dumur). This "großartige Son-et-Lumière-Show" (Hohlweg), by virtue of its impressive images, garnered glowing reviews: "[J]'ai rarement vu quelque chose d'aussi beau au théâtre. Engel est décidément un grand artiste" (Dumur); and in April of the following year it was taken for a two-month run to the Théâtre de Chaillot, where the Parisians welcomed it just as warmly: "Pourquoi le nier? On est saisi par ce mystère, cette magie, cette beauté."[68] But to quote the same critic, "Même Kleist, même nous, [remain] modestes spectateurs."

In a literary essay analysing Neuenfels's staging of *Penthesilea* and Robert Musil's *Schwärmer*, Christoph Müller contended: "Es sind dies, wie einig oder uneinig man mit dem Inszenierungsergebnis im einzelnen auch sein mag, die symptomatischen Aufführungen des deutschen Theaters zu Beginn der achtziger Jahre."[69] Whatever *Penthesilea* may be symptomatic of – Müller saw the central character as a "Sprachschwärmerin" – Kleist's unplayable play saw an additional realization in 1981, this time in the capital of the Federal Republic of Germany, Bonn. Peter Eschberg chose the tragedy to inaugurate both a new season and the beginning of his tenure as director. His wife, Carmen-Renate Köper, assumed the title role. The reviewers found fault with almost every feature of the production: the inability to articulate Kleist's verses, the elimination of all the descriptive passages, an inappropriate set ("Im krassen Gegensatz zur Aufführung von Minks stürzen sich bei Eschberg die Frauen zwecks psychischer 'refreshments' ins Wasser, ... und schnuppern sich dort, nach kleinen Tauchrekorden, am Ufer einer Insel in Gestalt eines Pferdeschädels"),[70] but above all a failure to understand the dramatist: "Kleist wirkt in dieser Bearbeitung und Inszenierung merkwürdig albern und belanglos."[71] Despite a reduction in playing time to two hours, Lothar Schmidt-Mühlisch wrote of a boring evening, while Günter Engelhard went as far as to interpret Eschberg's misreading as indicative of a national characteristic: "Das Stück strebt nicht Entlarvung an, sondern Aussöhnung: Die Katastrophe der Deutschen besteht darin, es nicht genau lesen zu können. Kleist hat unter anderem wegen solcher Verständigungsschwierigkeiten Selbstmord begangen."

In response to the implication that the director could be held responsible for having exacerbated these "Verständigungsschwierigkeiten," a visitor from Cologne who had attended a performance demanded the return of his DM 36 on the grounds that he was the victim of a misrepresentation: "[Ü]berhaupt sei diese Bonner *Penthesilea* lediglich *nach* [reviewer's emphasis] Kleist inszeniert worden und nicht, wie angekündigt, eine Aufführung *von* [reviewer's emphasis] Kleist gewesen."[72] Since the theatre refused to make a refund, the patron took his case to court, arguing that consumer-protection laws should also apply in this instance. Judge Blüm's decision warrants being quoted at length, for it addresses a crucial issue: the justification for the "Umfunktionierung" (Brecht) of a classical text by a contemporary director:

Unstreitig ist in der vorliegenden Inszenierung der *Penthesilea* der Originaltext von Heinrich von Kleist rezitiert worden [according to the plaintiff, only 38%!]. Die vom Regisseur vorgenommenen Kürzungen und Regieanweisungen müssen daher als zulässig angesehen werden. Nach dem heutigen Kunstverständnis ist nämlich die Regiearbeit als künstlerische Arbeit anzusehen. Hierbei muß dem Regisseur eine gewisse Gestaltungsfreiheit eingeräumt werden, die seiner künstlerischen Eigenart entspricht und es ihm erlaubt, in seinem Werk seine individuelle Schöpferkraft und sein Schöpferwollen zum Ausdruck zu bringen.[73]

The plaintiff should have taken fair warning from the press reviews and thus, to cite Ute Naumann's tongue-in-cheek conclusion, "Justitia hat Kohlhäschen abgeschmettert."

Despite four-and-a-half months of concentrated preparation, the students of the Otto-Falckenberg-Schule could not live up to the demands made by *Penthesilea* in their five-hour version for Munich in May 1982. According to C. Bernd Sucher,[74] the troupe's excessive dependence upon the Schaubühne model established by Peter Stein and others accounted largely for the failure of this staging (directed by Gerd Kaminski), which simply ran out of steam after the intermission. In August of the same year, the Salzburg Festival presented in the Felsenreitschule the Austrian *première* of Schoeck's *Penthesilea* opera. This first performance, with the ORF Orchestra of Vienna under the baton of Gerd Albrecht, was a concert rather than a stage performance, a decision that left the audience to recreate the plot from their imagination and prior knowledge of the play.[75]. However, both Helga Dernesch (Penthesilea) and Theo Adam (Achilles), two of the greatest singers of their generation, gave strong vocal interpretations that more than compensated for the lack of visual representation: "Als Träger seiner Gesangspartie möchte man [Theo Adam], trotz der Konzertsituation, eher Darsteller als Sänger nennen – so sehr stand bei ihm die gestaltete Persönlichkeit im Vordergrund."[76] The laudatory reviews of what one critic called the "bedeutendst[e] Konzert dieses Sommers" (Klaus Adam) and the "frenetisch[e] Jubel" (Endler) of the full house augured well for Albrecht's dedicated effort to gain recognition for Schoeck's largely ignored work.

Although there were no major productions of *Penthesilea* in German-speaking countries in 1983, the year provided ample evidence of a growing international awareness of this problematic play. As part of a "stagione tedesca" (German season) Italy saw no less than three attempts to acquaint the public with Kleist's tragedy, one of them being the national *première* in Genoa of a filmed version of Hans Neuenfels's interpretation during a seminar on the staging of classical works. More significantly, after several Italian directors, including Luca Ronconi, had met with disaster in their endeavours to produce the drama, two avant-gardists, Mario Ricci and Carlo Quartucci, took up the challenge. The more traditional of the two, Ricci, based his concept on an expressive recitation in a meagre setting consisting of only pyramids and cubes covered in black cloth. All aspects of this Rome production were designed to focus attention on Penthesilea's inner turmoil at the expense of the male roles, including even that of Achilles: "ein rosenwangiger Jüngling, bestenfalls schöner Gigolo [Walter Mramor]."[77] Since Delia Boccardo had constant recourse to exaggerated "stereotype Gestik and Mimik," she never came close to putting across the heroine's complex, contradictory emotional life.

A totally different approach, Quartucci's interpretation in Bologna, a "'Soloversion für Schauspieler und Tonband'," deleted the first twelve scenes and played the remaining eleven as a requiem mass with accompanying electronic music in a ritual style composed by Giovanna Marini. In the middle of the stage stood the isolated figure of Carla Tatô before a music stand, motionless, except when she struggled with the pages of her score which repeatedly fell to the floor, or when she emphasized her words with gestures: "Sie ist nicht Penthesilea, sondern Kleist, der einem imaginären Wieland den visionären Text vorführt, spricht, schmettert, brüllt, schreiend flüstert." This individual performance with musical accompaniment, although it recalled the tragedy's first public performance in 1811 by the mime actress Henriette Hendel-Schütz and her husband, was based upon the "Camion" group's avowed goal of seeking to transcend dialogic convention in order to create a new "Totalität des Theaters." Because Quartucci had previously failed in his attempt to produce *Penthesilea*, he regarded this more modest 1983 experiment as the first stage of a greater project, the second being a film version to be shot in Berlin, and the third the staging of the whole drama.

The other foreign production in 1983 marked the return of *Penthesilea* to England. "In mounting [Kleist's] grandiose Romantic drama on a diminutive stage [The Gate at the Latchmere, Battersea], Michael Batz, the director, has gone for a small-scale realism with television virtues: physical immediacy, harshness, abrasiveness."[78] Notwithstanding what could be only termed a moderately successful evening, at least this time the English reviewers showed a greater knowledge[79] and appreciation of Kleist's importance. Writing for the *New Statesman* (9 December 1983), Christopher Edwards, in his description of the relationship between the two main protagonists, observed: "The motive for their reciprocal violence is ... love, and the play proceeds to analyse the relation of eros to thanatos with the boldness and 'modernity' that characterises Kleist's work and endears him to contemporary audiences." John Barber, however, reviewing "Heinrich von Kleist's grandiloquent drama" for *The Times* (28 November 1983), faulted "the great passionate speeches [which] lack intellectual substance and spill over into bombast." The latter criticism may in part be attributed to Robert Nye's translation, since it "alternates sensitive and faithful passages with deliberately flat slang" (Hofmann). Batz chose to highlight the war theme with a distinct emphasis on the brutal, nonheroic aspects. The dark scenery, made up of pyramids, a catwalk, scaffolding, and camouflage netting, strongly suggested to one critic (Hofmann) a foxhole. Whereas Susannah York's Penthesilea received contradictory assessments – "Susannah York, baring her teeth and using a thrilling deep voice, makes a formidable impression as Penthesilea" (Barber); "[S]he completely lacks severity or the least vestige of a martial presence" (Edwards) – Paul Moriarty's Achilles, "a dour, crop-haired, greying man," lacked passion and thus failed to project the larger-than-life dimensions demanded by the text. Batz's illusionless portrayal of war, the "Schmutz" rather than the "Glanz" of Kleist's soul, may have dictated this cold interpretation.

In the twentieth century, where some writers have insisted that the traditional forms have been exhausted, originality has become next to impossible, and parody remains the only viable alternative, *Penthesilea* has often lent itself to the most outrageous readings that depend upon theatrical gimmicks and have little or nothing to do with Kleist. A special case in point would seem to have been Hans Hollmann's staging for the Schauspielhaus in Zürich in December 1984: "Kleist bleibt, wenn auch mit seinem schwierigsten Text, in Zürich unerforscht."[80] There was much to censure. The costumes presented the Amazons "dick geschminkt in scheußlichen Cocktail-kleidern" with champagne glasses, and the Greeks "in lächerlichen Kolonialarmee-Uniformen,"[81] while the love scene featured an Achilles in tights stretched out on a psychiatric couch that bridged a shiny metal trench separating the male and female territories (sets by Wolfgang Mai). Behind the couch stood Penthesilea (Reinhild Solf), and farther back a bandaged oak tree seemed to rise from a shelf. Except during the conclusion, the actors screamed and yelled their lines.[82] Odysseus presented the confused battle exposition as a comic-strip projection on a white screen, and when Penthesilea threw down her champagne glass in anger, an Amazon quickly appeared with dustpan and brush to remove the fragments. As for the casting, "[e]ine Katastrophe, die das Stück bisweilen zum Lustspiel degradierte, war Fritz Schediwy als Achilles."[83] If a message did emerge from Hollmann's "Trivialisierung des Stoffes aus der Perspektive unserer Tage,"[84] his "sado-masochistischen Ritual" (Schaub), it was the nightmare of the male suddenly confronted by a stronger, uncontrollable female, a vision apparently excluding the text's more gentle accents of love. The reviewers deplored with almost one voice the director's disservice to the dramatist, his transformation, however unintentional, of a difficult but great tragedy into a near comedy: "[Hollmann] hat die *Penthesilea* der Lächerlichkeit preisgegeben,"[85] and thus they concurred with the public condemnation: "Die heftigen Buhs und Pfiffe in der Pause und für Schediwy und Hollmann am Schluß waren berechtigt" (Benesch).

In 1985 there were two noteworthy productions of *Penthesilea*, one directed by Pierre Politz in the pathos transport Theater in Munich (February) and another concert performance of Schoeck's opera in

Zürich (November), again with Gerd Albrecht on the podium. The stage version, set in a contemporary Greek tavern, employed only seven actors: "Männer (im Macho-Look), die sich bei Wein und Tanz (Sirtaki) den Tag vertreiben; zwei blonde Mädchen (Touristinnen mit Koffern), die eingebrochen sind in diese fremde Männerwelt."[86] Politz moved the fourteenth scene which begins, "Penthesilea! O du Träumerin!" (1538) to the opening of the play so that, perhaps in imitation of Peter Stein's celebrated interpretation of *Prinz Friedrich von Homburg*, one of the blondes (Sara Thiemann), after fainting, regains consciousness but is now in Penthesilea's dream-like state of mind. Male privileges clash with emancipated female attitudes and result in violence and destruction. The only review I could find of this generally ignored experiment in modernization contained largely praise: "Diese 'Kleist Penthesilea' heute funktioniert erstaunlich gut, weil Pierre Politz mit streng komponierten, kühlen Bildern und einer spannungsvollen Musikdramaturgie der Gefahr der Trivialisierung entkommt."

In the context of the Othmar Schoeck-Gedenkkonzerte, Albrecht essentially repeated his Salzburg production, with Helga Dernesch again in the title role, for the Zürich Tonhalle and gained even more outstanding notices than in 1982: "Wer hätte noch vor zehn Jahren zu wagen gehofft, daß diese hochexpressive Kleist-Vertonung ein heutiges Zürcher Publikum zu solchem Enthusiasmus [ten minutes of nonstop applause at the conclusion] hinzureißen vermöchte?"[87] Radio DRS (Deutsche und Rhätoromanische Schweiz) carried the performance live. The fact that the obvious success of the concert format contrasts vividly with the failure of an operatic realization in Bern in the spring of the same year, would seem to give further justification to the claim that *Penthesilea* as a drama is simply "unspielbar." As noted by Peter Hagmann in his review of the Zürich concert (*Basler Zeitung*, 9 November 1985): "Hier kam das Werk zu höchst eindringlicher Wirkung, weil der Ausdruck ganz vom Musikalischen ausging, wo das pathetische Expressivo in Bindungen formaler Natur aufgehoben ist, während alles andere der Phantasie des Zuhörers überlassen blieb." In the same way, the positive reception of the operatic version in Düsseldorf in 1986, conducted by Peter Erckens, had little to do with Werner Düggelin's monotonous staging, but everything to do with the music: "Am Ende, wenn Penthesilea [Gail Gilmore] in ihre Innerlichkeit wie in einen Schacht steigt, um dort ein tödliches Gefühl hervorzuheben, erleben wir wie in kaum einer anderen Oper dieses Jahrhunderts den Untergang einer Figur als Implosion: Revolte und Verinnerlichung in eins."[88]

According to Rolf Michaelis (*Die Zeit*, 13 December 1985), the East German director Jürgen Gosch fully recognized the strong appeal to the imagination contained in *Penthesilea*, and just as Schoeck's music manages to exploit this dimension (Staiger), Gosch sought to achieve the same objective through an extreme stylization: "Diesem ganz im Kopf, im Traum, im (Liebes-) Wahn – und aus dem Wort – lebenden Trauerspiel sucht Gosch ein sprachliches und szenisches Äquivalent." In his pursuit of this equivalent, he was apparently inspired by an amateur theatrical performance in the auditorium of his son's school: "[S]o 'einfach' wie jene Schüler müsse man auch die Tragödie Kleists angehen, mit einer gewissen 'Ärmlichkeit' der Mittel."[89] Reduction therefore became the overriding principle of his controversial staging for Hamburg's Thalia Theater in December 1985, beginning with the one permanent set: "Bis auf ein trapezförmiges weißes Segel (ein schwarzes parallel verdeckt dahinter) und einen Streifen Sand hat Axel Manthey [set designer] Zelte und Schlachtenhügel vor Troja verkürzt. Ein roter Vorhang begrenzt das Halbrund der Szene."[90] The white sail frequently functioned as a canvas upon which spotlights projected the shadows of the protagonists caught up in their dance of love and death. All the Greeks wore gold-tinsel togas, rendering movement at times awkward, and the Amazons white ones drawn over the right shoulder to expose the left breast. The uniformity extended as well to the action or the lack of it: "ein in strenger, oft quälend langsam gezogener Choreographie sich entladendes Ritual, das Entsetzen, Bewußtlosigkeit, Lähmung und Ohnmacht gleichsam in einem Dauer-Ritartando vorführt."[91] The male members of the cast performed a slow-motion ballet with spears to open the evening, a routine later complemented by a similar display by the females with bows and arrows. The strictly regulated movements put many reviewers in mind of the puppets from Kleist's famous essay or the trance-like mentality of Käthchen or Homburg, but the choreography also resulted in a contradiction: "Während sie [the actors] von unbändiger Raserei reden, bewegen sie sich wie eine Zeitlupe" (Berndt). This slow-motion technique was not limited to the action: "Es schleppt sich auch der Vers."[92] Although he undoubtedly wanted to circumvent the criticism levelled at Hollmann or Neuenfels by paying close attention to the language – "Die Sprache tritt in den Mittelpunkt"[93] – his interpretation called for a monotonous, tiresome, dirge-like recitation, whispered, for the most part, in order to force the spectators to concentrate more upon the verse. Not surprisingly, this taxed the audience's patience to such an extent that a considerable exodus took place during the intermission.

As the first winner of the "Theaterpreis des Europarats" (1985) for his much heralded production of Sophocles' *Oedipus*, Gosch had a considerable reputation to live up to, and this may partly explain the extensive coverage his Hamburg staging received. While a few commentators partially defended him – "Gosch macht mit dieser *Penthesilea* unbedingtes Theater, mit dem Mut zu jungen Schauspielern [an allusion to Lena Stolze in the title role, in the opinion of most a "Fehlbesetzung"]"[94] – a majority, together with the audience ("Am Ende buhte das Publikum den offenbar verschreckten Regisseur aus und räumte fluchtartig das Haus" (Berndt)), rejected his effort as simply boring: "Über drei Stunden hinweg ergibt das eine Veranstaltung von bohrender Langeweile, eine Übung in Geduld, bei der man vielen schönen Standbildern ... zuschaut."[95]

When the Staatsschauspiel in Dresden (GDR) produced *Penthesilea* in the spring of 1986, the reviewer for *Neues Deutschland* (15 May 1986), Gerhard Ebert, found fault only with Jochen Finke's set – a much too cramped battlefield before Troy. Otherwise he admired every aspect, including the casting of the various roles, the "prosaic" costumes indicative of "normale Menschen," and the directing: "[Wolfgang Engel] erreicht hier ... eine künstlerische Reife, die ihn in die erste Reihe der Schauspielregisseure unseres Landes rückt." Although much of Ebert's review amounts to a plot summary, it nevertheless reveals that the director adopted a conservative, traditional approach, avoided the gimmicks frequently resorted to in the West, and interpreted the tragedy as the conflict between civilized Greek values and the unnatural demands of a matriarchal society: "[Christoph] Hermanns Achilles verkörpert eine neue, humane Welt und Auffassung gegenüber dem in die Krise geratenen Barbarentum der Amazonen." With this emphasis upon the human side of the tragedy, the love relationship became the highpoint of the evening: "Diese Liebesszene zwischen Penthesilea [Cornelia Schmaus], die als gesundes Weib zu empfinden und zu regieren vermag, und dem selbstbewußt-bescheidenen Achilles wird zum Glanzpunkt der Aufführung." But one wonders how such an interpretation could ignore those extreme aspects, which are equally if not more typically part of Achilles' personality:

ACHILLES    *steht auf und reißt sich die Kränze* [of the love scene] *ab.*
Die Waffen mir herbei! Die Pferde vor!
Mit meinem Wagen rädern will ich sie [die Amazonen]!
PENTHESILEA *mit zitternder Lippe.*
Nun, sieh den Schrecklichen! Ist das derselbe – ? (2265–7)

The cultural climate of the "other" Germany and its continuing fascination with the tragedy was again made evident in March 1987, when after six months of rehearsal Alexander Lang, "der berühmteste, aber in seinem Land gewiß nicht geliebteste Regisseur der DDR,"[96] employed an almost identical cast to interpret both Racine's *Phèdre* and Kleist's *Penthesilea* for the Kammerspiele in Munich. This director had already acquired a reputation in East Berlin for such experimental double *premières* as part of his strategy called "'Theater der Zusammenhänge', mit dem er das Publikum dazu bringen will, sich unter verschiedenen Gesichtswinkeln mit jeweils ähnlichen Problemen auseinanderzusetzen."[97] Program notes pointed out the analogies: "Die Parallelen zwischen beiden Inszenierungen sind klar herausgearbeitet: Zweimal zerstört der unterdrückte Trieb die rationale Ordnung, zweimal ist das Ziel der Leidenschaft der Besitz des anderen, zweimal erscheint die Liebe als Schwester des Todes – und zweimal sehen wir die Angst des Mannes vor der übermächtigen Frau."[98] The specific "problem" that drew Lang to the two notoriously difficult plays, separated by some 130 years, was the common theme of violent female passion in conflict with the accepted social norms. Despite the recognition of a tried and tested theme, in the words of Ursula Hübner: "Tradition existiert für Lang anscheinend nur, um sie hemmungslos zu desavouieren" (*Neue Zürcher Zeitung*, 7 April 1987). Goethe had remarked that *Penthesilea* frequently hovers on the brink of "das Hochkomische" because of its extreme situations and language, a peril in any production for a director trying to present the tragedy seriously, but as Barbara Schmitz-Burckhardt so aptly put it: "Der Regisseur Alexander Lang, und das ist eine raffinierte Form der Feigheit, macht nicht sich, sondern das Stück, die Stücke lächerlich" (*Frankfurter Rundschau*, 3 April 1987). In other words, this reading evidently attempted to avoid the risk of involuntary humour by transforming the tragedy into a comedy with a tragic conclusion. The battle sequences reminded several critics of cabaret scenes, the cowardly, comical Greeks of bedouins from the pages of Karl May, Achilles (Manfred Zapatka) of Lawrence of Arabia, and the Amazons dressed in black evening dresses of Wagner's valkyries or "Salondamen." Gags abounded. For example, as soon as the noise of battle drew near, Odysseus, played as a comic figure by Lambert Hamel, jumped out of his extravagant armour, and as a civilian in his nightshirt sought refuge in one of the "putzigen güldenen Pappmaché-Felsen, mit denen Volker Pfüller [stage designer] die Bühne bestückt hat" (Schmitz-Burckhardt). At the mere mention of the Amazons, Antilochus, out of fright, tripped over his own golf club, and during Penthesilea's account of her state's history a bored Achilles lit up a cigarette. Lang extended the comic mode even to the treatment of the verse – "Viel Gelächter entsteht, weil die Schauspieler Kleists Text herunterziehen, verharmlosen"[99] – and did not hesitate to reduce or adjust the content substantially in order to attain further humorous effects. When, for example, in scene 21 Achilles informed his fellow-Greeks of his intent to allow himself to be defeated, he suddenly observed: "Sie schwitzen" (537) – a comment which occurs in the fourth scene and refers to the horses. In Munich the four Greek officers stepped back in obvious embarrassment.

This comic emphasis in the first half proved detrimental to the emotional, darker side of the drama and created considerable difficulties in accommodating the serious theme of the second half: "[Die] Verse widersetzen sich wunderbar dem, was Lang den Geschichten in ihrer szenischen Zurichtung, zuweilen bei Racine, fast durchgängig bei Kleist, antut."[100] At least two critics, Renate Schostack (*Frankfurter Allgemeine Zeitung* (1 April 1987) and Ursula Hübner, found the generally positively received performance of Gisela Stein as both Phèdre and Penthesilea simply out of place or too manneristic (several reviewers alluded to the puppet-like choreography) to project the explosive irrationality of the thwarted queen: "Das Elementare bleibt sie schuldig. In einer Inszenierung, die den Schrecken durch Komik dämpfen will, muß diese Penthesilea im luftleeren Raum agieren" (Schostack). Several commentators, however, praised the love interlude: "ein spannende[r] Moment von zögernder Annäherung. ... Da wird, einmal, wirklich etwas spürbar vom Schrecken und vom Zauber der Liebe" (Schmitz-Burckhardt), and the final scenes as Penthesilea awakes "aus der Trance des Liebesmordes ..., da ist Gisela Stein ganz bei Kleist und schlägt damit Langs aus ideologischer Bedenklichkeit ins Komische abgedrängte Schreckensversion einer universalen Unordnung die ironische Distanz weg" (Wiegenstein). When Penthesilea collapses upon the body of her desecrated lover, "fällt ein Blütenregen vom Himmel herab. Wind kommt auf, das Licht verlischt" (Höbel). On the opening night the audience booed the director and only applauded the actors, while the critics remained divided in their verdict: "Langs Doppelprojekt [*Phèdre* was better received than *Penthesilea*], das jeweils an zwei aufeinanderfolgenden Abenden gespielt wird, ist gewiß eine Reise wert. Doch letztendlich läßt diese Gewaltregie, die Passionen zu Beweisstücken degradiert und deren Erfolg am Ende nur Binsenwahrheiten sind, kalt" (Schostack).

The last two productions to be described both originated in France but came to Germany as guest performances. The first of these materialized as part of a highly successful double staging of *Penthesilea* and *Das Käthchen von Heilbronn*, performed by student actors from Patrice Chéreau's school of the Théâtre des Amandiers in the Paris suburb of Nanterre. According to Hellmut Kotschenreuther, who reviewed the two plays for *Der Tagesspiegel* (10 November 1987), director Pierre Roman was intent upon demonstrating the close relationship between both titular heroines: "[Auf] mich wirkten das Käthchen Aurelle Doazans und die Penthesilea Marianne Cuaus in der Tat so, als seien sie bei aller Unterschiedlichkeit der äusseren Erscheinung nur extreme Ausformungen dessen, was Kleist als 'ein und dasselbe Wesen, nur unter entgegengesetzten Bedingungen' bezeichnet hat." A common set was radically reduced to "eine dunkelgraue, kahle Spielfläche ..., auf der nur ein paar alte Tische, Stühle und Bänke herumstehen," in order to oblige the spectator to use his/ her imagination; and this set served to underscore the analogies even further. In the love scene, the "positive" Amazon queen conveyed the same potential for total surrender to the loved one (Achilles, Thierry Ravel) that one normally associates with the negative of the Kleistian equation, Käthchen. Both productions eventually made their way to the Avignon Theatre Festival in August and *Penthesilea* to Berlin in November of the same year. The latter tragedy, as mounted in Avignon, turned out to be particularly memorable because of a novel solution to the staging of the conclusion. After the action was interrupted briefly to allow the actors and the audience time to quit the austere setting of the monastery auditorium, the drama continued to its tragic end in the nearby Carthusian cemetery: "Das kleine Rosen-Geviert, umrahmt von den Bögen des Kreuzgangs, steigt sanft an zu einer kleinen Erhebung. Dort ragt eine Zypresse in den Nachthimmel. Auf diesem Totenacker, unter dem Licht von Mond und Sternen, im Brausen des Mistrals, der die Zypresse beugt, rast Penthesilea ... sich und den geliebten Mann in den Tod."[101]

It is particularly appropriate that the last production of Kleist's "schwierigstes und großartigstes Trauerspiel"[102] I shall consider, was stimulated by a negative reaction to Quartucci's experiment in Rome but, at the same time, recalls the dramatist's own reading of the text before an appreciative audience of friends and its first public exposure through the Henriette Hendel-Schütz pantomime rendition of 1811. Why *Penthesilea* has proven so difficult to stage has been consistently and correctly attributed by reviewers to the crucial role of language – in dialogue, monologue, narrative, and reports. Although the tragedy deals at a surface level with battles, the pervasive Kleistian *agon*, the real conflict concerns, as Cornelia Köster put it, "den Krieg der Seelen" (*Der Tagesspiegel*, 24 April 1988), expressed in a "Sprache, die an die Grenze der Grammatik rührt, weil der Kopf, der sie schuf, an die des Bewußtseins rühren mußte." As early as 1907, Robert Walser exclaimed: "Eine Million für den Schauspieler, der die götterhaft-korrekte Sprache eines Heinrich von Kleist sprechen kann!"[103] and eighty years later an actor would seem to have earned Walser's million in Jürgen Syberberg's unique Parisian production in the Théâtre des Bouffes du Nord: "[Im] Zentrum der Aufmerksamkeit steht in der Tat nur Kleists Sprache" (Grathoff). Syberberg abridged the text, basing it upon the *Phöbus* fragment and, as in Quartucci's staging, one person spoke all nine roles, but with absolute fidelity to Kleist's verses: "Demut vor dem Text forderte Edith Clever – und praktizierte sie nun in Paris: Die Skepsis, die in Rom noch artikuliert wurde, schwand in Paris" (Grathoff). The critics were united in extolling the "Wogen des Cleverschen Sprechgesangs" (Klöster), clearly a great dramatic tour de force:

Edith Clever geht bis an die Grenzen der schauspielerischen Leistungsfähigkeiten in den dreieinhalb Stunden in Paris. Sie schreitet das gesamte Repertoire sprachlicher Artikulationsmöglichkeiten aus, von verhalten-sanft geflüsterten Tönen bis zu ekstatisch wilden Schreien, von leicht ironisierender Komik bis zu würdig-machtvoller Empörung und dem Entsetzen über das Unfaßbare. Wer meint, nach zwei Stunden müßten ihre Kräfte doch schwinden, wird erstaunt, ja fasziniert das Gegenteil bemerken: sie steigert sich, je länger das Spiel nur währt. Dieser Penthesilea glaubt man endlich den Wahn, wenn sie am Schluß in das Geheul ihrer Hunde einstimmt, um in einem kannibalischen Rückfall den Körper des geliebten Achill zu zerreißen (Grathoff).

Syberberg's staging itself did not fare as well in the critical appraisals. To accentuate the superiority of the spoken language over the printed text, Clever, after having read from Helmut Sembdner's critical edition, would tear a page from the book, while still reciting her lines, and either burn it in one of the many candles illuminating the house or drown it in a water pitcher. Both on the stage and throughout the auditorium, Syberberg placed plaster-of-paris busts, statues, and relief tablets featuring classical figures or personages from Prussian history, such as Frederick the Great. This Prussian message gained further prominence with the inclusion of Kleist's patriotic poem, "Das letzte Lied," as an exposition in spite of its anti-French sentiment: "Insgesamt [griff] die direkte Bezugnahme auf

Preußen ein wenig kurz" (Grathoff). A number of the busts depicted
Goethe, and as the tragedy approached its Dionysiac climax, Clever
began to cover up the German Olympian, presumably so that he
would be spared the gruesome depiction of Achilles' slaughter. In
the guest appearance in Berlin (the production also went to Frankfurt), Goethe completely disappeared from sight to signal Kleist's
ultimate victory over his rival in the twentieth century. Although the
Clever-Syberberg collaboration was acclaimed as "grandios unzeit-
gemäß" (Grathoff) or as "die 'authentischste' Aufführung der *Penthesilea* ..., seit sie geschrieben wurde" (Klöster), Clever's skill in
making the tragedy come alive in the spectator's imagination almost
exclusively through the medium of the spoken verse accounted for
the success of the production.[104]

*Penthesilea* has fully earned its notoriety as "das meist gefürchtete
Drama deutscher Sprache"[105] since its official *première* in 1876. Even
in that Mosenthal adaptation, a radical rewriting dictated by the
prevailing practices, the problems that would plague subsequent
efforts are evident: the failure to master Kleist's language, the sheer
length of the work (Mosenthal cut 1000 lines), the very real risk of
provoking a humorous reaction where none is intended (the first
audience laughed at the attempt to modernize the Amazon army),
and the considerable demands made upon actors assigned the minor
parts. It also says something about this tragedy that to date many of
the most successful realizations have been solo performances of an
actor or concert performances of Schoeck's operatic version, both of
which depend heavily upon an appeal to the spectator's own fantasy
and upon music, "Sprechgesang," to expand the limits of what can
be portrayed on stage. However, in order to refute H. Lehmann's
assertion, "*Penthesilea* ist kein häufiger Gast auf den Bühnen der Welt"
(*Badische Neueste Nachrichten*, 3 April 1987), one has only to examine
the ten years from 1978 to 1987, during which "[das] vielleicht hei-
kelst[e] aller Bühnen-Ungeheuer"[106] experienced more than twenty
different stagings in West and East Germany, Austria, Switzerland,
France, Italy, the United States, and England. This fact alone would
seem to indicate that *Penthesilea* will continue to provide, in the words
of Dirk Grathoff, "[eine] Herausforderung für das heutige Theater."[107]

## CHAPTER FIVE

# Das Käthchen
# von Heilbronn

Since Kleist found the theatrical situation of northern Germany to be, in his words to Goethe, "gar zu niederschlagend,"[1] and because he found himself to be in serious financial straits, he chose to write one decidedly popular play with a Viennese audience in mind. Appealing to his friend and enthusiastic promoter, the Austrian dramatist Heinrich Joseph von Collin, he remarked: "Das Käthchen von Heilbronn, das, wie ich selbst einsehe, notwendig verkürzt werden muß, konnte unter keine Hände fallen, denen ich das Geschäft lieber anvertraute, als den Ihrigen. Verfahren Sie ganz damit, wie es der Zweck Ihrer Bühne erheischt."[2] Collin did not hesitate to take advantage of Kleist's offer, and a version of *Käthchen* presumably made by the director, Franz Grüner, sought to satisfy the tastes and demands of the Theater an der Wien. This, the last work to be performed in the author's lifetime, had its *première* there on 17 March 1810.[3] This particular adaptation, one of a long series which continued well into the twentieth century, has been lost, but from contemporary reports there were few departures from the original (i.e., the "Buchausgabe" of 1810): several minor characters disappeared, the emperor became a mere duke of Swabia to avoid censorship problems, and Kunigunde was condemned at the end to the dungeon. With its wealth of historical colour, including bridges, castles, mountains, and horses, the Theater an der Wien offered *Käthchen* in the tradition of the knightly spectacular play, the colourful genre so popular with a large segment of the Viennese theatre-going public. The performance was generally praised by the press, which singled out the "meisterhaft[e] Darstellung des Wetter von [sic] Strahl [[Grüner] und d[ie] täuschend[e] Natürlichkeit des Käthchen [Christiane Dorothea Pedrillo]."[4] The *Österreichische Annalen der Literatur und Kunst des In- und Auslandes* assessed the play as "eine ängstlich treue Nachbildung der Jungfrau von Orleans [Schiller]," but one which had achieved "unter allen in diesem Jahre erschienenen neuen Darstellungen ... den ersten Rang";[5] however, both *Der Österreichische Beobachter* (18 March 1810) and *Der Sammler* (22 March 1810) classified it respectively as a work "ohne Kraft und Einheit" and "ein ziemlich unzusammenhängendes Gerippe einer Rittergeschichte" held together by the generally first-rate quality of the acting. Already at the *première* a tendency manifested itself which was to become characteristic of all the early productions, a propensity to reduce the play to a spectacle. This approach can be readily verified in the *Dresdner Abendzeitung* review (15 December 1819) of the staging in Dresden: "Das Szenische des Stückes, die Gefechte, die Prozession am Ende, die neuen Kostüme, alles erhob diese Vorstellung zu einer der erfreulichsten, die wir seit einiger Zeit gesehen haben. Alles ging rund und pünktlich. Die Dekoration des Schloßbrandes machte solche Wirkung, daß ihr besonderer Beifall ertönte."

After essentially the same production was presented with limited success in Graz, the next city to host *Käthchen*, Bamberg, witnessed both a high and a low point in the history of the drama: the manager and director of the Sodensches Theater, Franz Holbein, took it upon himself to improve the play, and thus he paved the way towards greater acceptance of Kleist, but at the same time, as Reinhold Stolze noted: "Es ist die erschütternde Tragik in dem Bühnenleben des hochpoetischen *Käthchen*, daß es nur als Aschenbrödel in dem grauen Alltagsgewande, das ihm Holbein umhing, ein halbes Jahrhundert hindurch, auf vielen Theatern sogar bis in die jüngste Gegenwart dem deutschen Volk erscheinen durfte."[6] In all, Holbein devised three versions: the Bamberg (1811), the Karlsruhe (1814) (which Ludwig Börne classified as "ein ganz eigenes Kapitel des Jammers"[7]), and the book form (1822). Totally without any appreciation of the work's structure or poetic beauty, Holbein proceeded to convert it into a popular melodrama, a guaranteed box-office success. He changed Kunigunde's physical ugliness into moral depravity, shortened the elder-bush scene drastically, created a new tavern episode, simplified scenes or altered their order, almost rewrote the fifth act, and transformed the count into a lachrymose, weak-willed mother's boy. And yet by 1822 the Karlsruhe adaptation was being used in no less than thirty theatres and enjoyed in total more than 1200 performances.

Little information has come down to us about the Bamberg staging. Holbein himself commented: "[E.T.A.] Hoffmann und der talentvolle Schauspieler Holdermann malten die Dekorationen, ich machte die Modelles [sic] der Maschinen; und so wurde auch in dem Ausstattungsfache, ungeachtet großer Sparsamkeit, Genügendes und

Originelles geleistet. Von Handwerkerei war keine Spur vorhanden. Die ganze Arbeit glich vielmehr einem Liebhabertheater, für dessen künstlerische Erhebung jeder mit Aufopferung, Lust und Liebe wirkte."[8] On the whole, the production was well received, especially Hoffmann's sets and the acting of Marie Johanna Renner (later Frau Holbein). Hoffmann, who particularly admired *Käthchen* – commentators have interpreted the importance of the "Holunderbaum" in *Der goldene Topf* as a secret homage to Kleist – objected to Holbein's treatment of the original, while Renner, noted for her naturalness, genuine naiveté and ability to identify completely with the role, was the first to gain a national reputation as an interpreter of Käthchen. The Karlsruhe performance, also enthusiastically acclaimed, with Holbein as the count and Madame Renner in the title role, led to guest performances by its two stars in Mannheim, Magdeburg, Bremen, Cologne, and Aachen in 1815, and in Braunschweig and Hannover in 1816, while the stage version came to be used in almost all the major cities, including Munich (Isartortheater, 6 March 1816 and National-Theater, 16 April 1827), Hamburg (13 December 1816), and Frankfurt am Main (15 September 1816). In Frankfurt, Karoline Lindner's Käthchen scored a noteworthy triumph. Scarcely able to contain his enthusiasm, Ludwig Börne remarked: "Gewiß und wahrhaftig, das demütige, gottgefällige, wundersüße, heimgefallene Kind hätte wahrer, lieblicher und rührender nicht dargestellt werden können. Es war nur ihre Schuld, wenn man es vergaß, wie schwer die Schlafrednerin zu spielen sei."[9] The most famous nineteenth-century Käthchen appeared on 21 April 1824 in a Berlin Hoftheater staging, which was directed by Count Moritz von Brühl and enjoyed six full houses in succession. This success was attributed almost exclusively to the innocence and pure heart of the titular heroine as portrayed by Luise von Holtei. The *Abend Zeitung* went so far as to say that she had been born for the role, but the *Vossische Zeitung* recognized certain limitations: "Sind nur auch Motive darin, die größere Mittel fordern, als der liebenswürdigen Schauspielerin zu Gebote standen, so dürfen wir dennoch der Zufriedenheit beistimmen, die das Publikum äußerte."[10] Contemporary criticism soon saw in Holtei's performance Käthchen's ideal image, and by its lavish praise contributed to the establishment of a theatrical convention to which any new budding actress had to conform, if she wished to gain public recognition.

On 23 June 1817, the theatrical manager of the Nationaltheater zu Breslau, Professor Gottlieb Johann Rhode, staged *Käthchen* as closely to Kleist's text as the demands of his playhouse would permit. Although his example gained little influence, being soon supplanted by the Holbein adaptation, Rhode's production did have the merit of bringing together the most famous pair to play the lead parts, Heinrich Anschütz (Strahl) and Emilie Butenop (Käthchen). Describing the performance in his memoirs, Anschütz claimed: *"Das Käthchen von Heilbronn, das ganz nach dem Original, selbst mit der gewagten Badeszene zur Darstellung kam, hatte einen Erfolg, der außerordentlich zu nennen war, nämlich für die Darstellerin (Jungfer Butenop), meine jetzige Frau. Ich kann diese Leistung mit keiner andern Darstellerin vergleichen. Diese Rolle wurzelte so tief in dem ganzen Wesen meiner Frau, daß sie beinahe ein Abdruck ihres eigenen Naturells zu nennen war. ... Diese Rolle steht weit über allen anderen Leistungen meiner Frau und bildet gleichsam ihr künstlerisches Kleinod."*[11] The objectivity of Anschütz's praise of his own wife is, however, called into question by a review published in the *Dresdner Abendzeitung*, characterizing her as "im gewöhnlichen Konversationston sprechend und handelnd, ... ganz hoch-pathetisch, süß-sentimental und naiv geziert."[12]

Indicative of *Käthchen*'s growing popularity, is the fact that this was the first Kleistian drama to be performed outside the German-speaking countries. On 14 April 1819, *Das Berliner Morgenblatt* (Nr. 89) reported: "Bei der Veranlassung der Geburtstagsfeier der Königin und der Kronprinzessin [28 October 1818] ward auf dem Königlichen Theater [Copenhagen, Denmark] gegeben: Das Mädchen von Heilbronn, Drama, bearbeitet nach Kleist von Rosenhilde." The staging seems to have had little success; it even caused a minor scandal, apparently attributable to the Danish adaptation, which was, in fact, a translation of Holbein's version.

Joseph Schreyvogel who became director of the Burgtheater in Vienna in 1814 tried to free himself from the prevailing dependence upon the Holbein adaptation and to return to Kleist. However, although he made few changes in the first two acts and used the conclusion as first written, Holbein's influence can still be detected. But Schreyvogel managed at least to convey more of the poetic qualities of the work by cutting several of the adapter's so-called improvements on Kleist's language. Because the *première* of *Prinz Friedrich von Homburg* had met with public rejection on 3 October 1821, Schreyvogel postponed the staging of *Käthchen* until 22 November 1821, a significant date, for it marked the drama's acceptance into the repertoire of one of the most outstanding and influential German-speaking theatres. The Anschütz's once again assumed the lead roles, Heinrich receiving special accolades for his interpretation of the count: "Hr. Anschütz zeigte als Wetter von [sic] Strahl, daß er die Macht besitze, eine Darstellung aus dem Innersten der Brust geschöpft, mit hellen Farben an das Licht zu stellen; daß er für jeden Effekt Ton und Gebärde richtig zu handhaben wisse, kurz, daß er Meister der Kunst sei. ... [Den] Kulminationspunkt erreichte er im fünften Akt in der Szene mit Käthchen, in welcher das überströmende Gefühl der reinsten Liebe in schmelzend-melodischen Akkorden Worte findet."[13] Karl Ludwig Costenoble, praised for his Theobald, was highly critical of the sets and the costumes, maintaining that Anschütz was made to look like "ein herumfahrender Seiltänzer."[14] This production, despite the lack of a coherent approach, met with considerable success and had thirty-four performances by the year 1835; it was even deemed worthy of a parody in Leopoldstadt, a suburb of Vienna.

Since Kleist wrote his "großes historisches Ritterschauspiel" for the Viennese stage, it continued, not surprisingly, to enjoy its greatest popularity in the Austrian capital. Heinrich Laube, who had been inspired to renounce theology and devote himself to the theatre by a staging of *Käthchen* in Breslau in 1828, decided to create his own version, endeavouring to remain as true to the author as possible, but at the same time following "Tiecks Rate," a reference to the following comment made by Ludwig Tieck, Kleist's first publisher: "In dem vorliegenden dramatischen Werke des Verfassers ist der größte Übelstand und für die Empfindung am meisten verletzend, daß die Hauptperson sich am Ende als die Tochter des Kaisers ausweiset. ... Vielleicht ließe es sich von einer geschickteren Hand dahin abändern, daß Käthchen die Enkelin des alten Waffenschmieds ist; seine einzige, schöne Tochter ist an der Geburt des Kindes gestorben."[15] This so-called "father problem," born out of the prudery and aristocratic prejudice of the times, necessitated many adjustments to the original, especially in the fifth act where Theobald became a mere foster father. Although Laube did succumb to the demands of narrow-minded propriety, his adaptation went further than Schreyvogel's in restoring the authentic text and did contribute to undermining the authority of the Holbein version.[16] The production, first performed 11 December 1852, was a great success, ascribable largely to Laube's excellent casting and staging. Singled out for high acclaim were Schönhoff's Käthchen, Heinrich Anschütz's Theobald, and Christine Hebbel's Kunigunde. Käthchen's rival has consistently posed a major problem for all directors as a consequence of her seemingly dual personality. At first Kleist supposedly conceived of her as a Melusine (water-nymph), but when he came to write down the play he transformed her into a deceptive cosmetic artist – a change which the dramatist allegedly made because of a misunderstanding between himself and Tieck.[17] It is indicative of the problematic nature of Kunigunde that it required an actress of Christine Enghaus-Hebbel's stature to create some respect for this role. As a sign of the production's fame and official recognition, a special performance took place on 13 March 1853 at the request of the emperor following his convalescence from an illness after an attempt on his life; and it continued to draw large audiences, primarily because Laube managed to engage outstanding young actresses, such as Maria Seebach, Marie Bossler, Friederike Gossmann, and Auguste Baudius.

There were several other adaptations, for example, that of Eduard Devrient for a staging directed by him in Karlsruhe, 8 October 1854, but Dingelstedt's version written for a production in the Burgtheater on 10 October 1876 proved to be one of the most polished and poetic and closer to the original than Laube's adaptation. Theobald became once again Käthchen's (Antonie Janisch) legal father, and Kunigunde (Zerline Gabillon) retained her physical deformities. Whereas Laube sought to emphasize acting skills and care with the spoken word, Dingelstedt chose to accentuate the visual, decorative aspect of the drama, offering a virtual feast for the eye. In the *Neue Freie Presse* (10 October 1876) review which lauded the fidelity to the original, the skilful set changes, and the scenic effects (especially the collapse of the castle), one can still detect traces of the criticism levelled at past spectacular stagings: "Das Publikum war ganz verdonnert. Wie man sieht, laufen wir unwillkürlich dem Dichter davon und dem Maschinisten nach; aber so erzieht uns das Burgtheater. ... Was die Aufführung nach ihrem künstlerischen Teil betrifft, so erhob sie sich manchmal über das Mittelmäßige. Frau Janisch als Käthchen und selbst Herr Krastel als Friedrich Wetter hoben sich von den übrigen Mitwirkenden nicht unvorteilhaft ab."

While both Laube's and Dingelstedt's approach tended towards extremes of understatement and overstatement respectively, the Meininger selected the middle path. The high esteem enjoyed by the Meiningen court stage was due in large measure to its director, Duke Georg II von Sachsen-Meiningen, a man who was blessed with genuine artistic appreciation and understanding and who made it his goal to coordinate all aspects of a performance according to one overall conception. To ensure this unified approach, the director availed himself of near dictatorial power over every detail of a production, from the most trivial to the most significant. For the first time, a staging of *Käthchen* kept as closely as possible to Kleist's text, so that there were no arbitrary additions or alterations except for the omission of the grotto scene. Indeed, the Meininger made it their task to gain public acceptance of the original throughout Germany by close adherence to what they considered to be its unique and unifying style. The first step in this commendable endeavour was their guest performance in the Friedrich-Wilhelmstädtisches Theater in Berlin on 1 May 1876. Despite the growing tendency amongst writers to insist upon the unembellished presentation of real life, a tendency about to culminate in naturalism, the Meininger version underlined the fantastical, dream-world aspect. (Theodor Fontane himself insisted that the work should be viewed as "ein dramatisiertes Märchen" and that great pains should be taken not to break the magic spell of this realm.[18]) One of the few criticisms directed against this, their most famous, production concerned the too frequent set changes which cut the play into approximately fifteen sections and did serious damage to the poetic mood. However, most of the reviewers were prodigal in their praise, and Paul Lindau's commentary, which lists the basic strengths of the Meininger, warrants being quoted at length:

Durch die Richtigkeit der Kostüme, die glückliche Zusammenstellung der Farben, die Treue der Gerätschaften und die künstlerische Ausführung der Dekorationen erhielt das ganze Stück den Charakter des Echten und Wahren. Es war ein wirkliches Ritterstück, das wir sahen. Die Gruppierung der einzelnen Szenen, namentlich der in der Schenke, in der jede Figur eine charakteristische Stellung einnahm, und des Gruppenbildes auf dem Schloßplatz zu Worms mit dem Kaiser in der Gerichtslaube, umgeben von seinen Rittern und dem Volk, das sich zu dem prächtigen Schauspiel herandrängt, waren von wunderbarer malerischer Wirkung. Es waren lebende Bilder von einer Schönheit, einem Geschmack und einem Kunstverständnis, wie man sie sonst nur auf Festlichkeiten der Künstler zu sehen bekommt.[19]

The actors all excelled themselves, but Adele Pauli was found especially noteworthy for her lovable and natural portrayal of Käthchen, particularly in the elder-bush scene. From 1 May 1876 till 11 May 1886 (Mainz), the Meininger gave a total of eighty-three performances in such cities as Berlin, Vienna, Budapest, Prague, Düsseldorf, and London.

Although the Meininger's triumph can be explained in part by their reverence for the original text, adaptations, albeit much closer to Kleist than Holbein's distortion, continued to flourish. One was made, for example, by August Förster, and it was dramatized by Adolf L'Arronge for the Deutsches Theater in Berlin on 23 December 1885. However, the Meininger's influence can still be detected in the overall tone of this staging, characterized by Otto Brahm as reflecting "den Geist des deutschen Märchens und des deutschen Volksliedes."[20] In the very midst of the literary controversy surrounding naturalism and its advocacy of "une tranche de vie," this romantic work still managed to command a considerable public following: "Als eine Weihnachtsgabe von schönster Art wurde uns das *Käthchen* dargebracht; und es war eine Freude, zu sehen, wie die Hörer von dem einheitlichen Zuge, der durch diese Aufführung ging, immer lebhafter erfaßt wurden."[21]

When Max Reinhardt, after acquiring a reputation for outstanding innovative work in several small Berlin theatres, was appointed general manager of the Deutsches Theater, he elected to inaugurate his directorship with a new production of *Käthchen*. Ignoring the example of the Meininger, Reinhardt tampered extensively with the text, especially with the second half. On the one hand he was accused of having completely ignored the organic unity and division into acts of the original, so that the conclusion was rendered totally incomprehensible (Stolze, 106–7); but on the other hand the normally uncomplimentary critic Maximilian Harden remarked: "Of the text of the poem, you [Reinhardt] retained as much as one evening permitted."[22] The reviews were not overly enthusiastic, for it was generally felt that "der Meister der Farbentöpfe"[23] had emphasized scenic spectacle at the expense of the poetic and dramatic content. The audience broke out in applause each time the curtain was raised. The sets made use of plastic trees, authentic bird calls, real grass, and live spruce set up on stage, with the result that the house smelt "wie auf dem Weihnachtsmarkt."[24] Siegfried Jacobsohn was highly critical of this attempt to recreate the environs of Heilbronn, pointing out: "[Kleist] kommt nicht zu seinem Recht – nicht sein Geist und nicht einmal sein Wort"[25]; but Harden defended Reinhardt against the charge of having had recourse to excessively detailed sets: "Your [Reinhardt's] production was more meagre than any I have ever seen in a performance of this play – almost too meagre. Think of all the money the Duke of Meiningen spent on this drama! And no one has ever had a word of censure for him."[26] Another criticism levelled at this production was its duration. Although Reinhardt was able to turn to account a revolving stage, it still moved slowly, necessitating the use of a drop-curtain, and thus only served to destroy the fairy-tale atmosphere which the director was anxious to suggest. But again Harden came to Reinhardt's rescue, claiming: "Your *Käthchen* kept us under her charming spell for almost five hours. We went home exhilarated."[27] As for the acting, only the two lead roles met with some qualified enthusiasm. "Your Friedrich Wetter (Friedrich Kayssler) lacks radiance; as a boy, he did not learn to laugh, and as a man, he never yielded to fun and mischief";[28] but it is precisely this aspect of Kayssler's portrayal which the critic of the *Berliner Tageblatt* (20 October 1905) found admirable: "Oft scheint die Eigenart des jungen Darstellers ein wenig trocken monoton. Doch gerade für diese Rolle dürften auch solche Töne nicht fehlen." Lucie Höflich's Käthchen, according to Harden, was "young, clean, lovable, sheerly charming under the elderberry-bush";[29] however, she "hat [Siegfried Jacobsohn] merkwürdig kalt gelassen."[30] And finally: "old Theobald, whom [Reinhardt] played [himself], [Harden] did not like at all."[31] Notwithstanding the mixed reviews, Reinhardt's staging enjoyed considerable success and could boast of a further twenty-nine performances in seven months: "On the whole, the performance was certainly the best that our drama had seen for decades; much more refined than the Meiningen company's had been, much more in the poet's own spirit than that of the L'Arronge theater, even considering Sorma's [she played Käthchen] participation."[32]

Because almost all productions, including those of the Meininger and Reinhardt, maintained the consistent tone and atmosphere of the fairy-tale, Jürgen Fehling's production in the Staatliches Schauspielhaus in Berlin, on 1 February 1923 constituted a real innovation, a departure from the traditionally held view: "Mit dieser Inszenierung fügte Fehling so viel leichte Ironie und Travestie in ein Stück, das bisher als Ritterstück gespielt und in den Veränderungen der damaligen Darstellungstechnik kaum noch für spielbar gehalten wurde, daß es ein Vergnügen wurde."[33] As Siegfried Jacobsohn pointed out, "Mit der Sicherheit künstlerischen Geschmacks sieht und hört [Fehling] jede Komödienwirkung heraus,"[34] even in the choice of the sets designed by Caspar Neher who transformed the stage into "einen primitiv bemalten Karton." Above the prompter's box hung a tavern sign with the drama's title, and red and blue putti surrounded the famous elder bush, all of which encouraged the audience not to take the performance too seriously. A touch of irony apparently pervaded the court scenes: the most varied groups from robber barons and pragmatic burghers to respectable aristocrats were set off against one another, and yet at the same time they merged into one another. The delineation of several minor figures gained a new comic dimension. Arthur Kraussneck rendered the servant Gottschalk as a lovable rascal, while Ernst Gronau's interpretation of a timid innkeeper, Jacob Pech, aroused laughter. The tavern scene with the Rhine count and his followers was converted into "ein Idyll der Betrunkenheit"[35] and what once constituted the main obstacle for a nineteenth-century audience, the so-called "father problem," the director now exploited as travesty: "Bei Fehling wird aus dem erhabenen Herrscher so etwas wie ein romantischer Kaiser aus der Welt Raimunds."[36] Carl Ebert, "nicht gerade der strahlendste, nicht gerade der hinreißendste Friedrich Wetter" gave a generally satisfactory performance, while Lucie Mannheim, "ein angenehmes Durchschnittstalent,"[37] presented a portrayal of Käthchen which was totally lacking in vitality. This experiment proved to be "ein [ ... ] ansehnlich[er], mit sehr viel Beifallsfreude anerkannt[er] Erfolg."[38] In summary, Jacobsohn observed: "Fehlings Ausgangspunkt, Motto, Leitmotiv, Endzweck: daß der Scherz nie sein spezifisches Gewicht, nie seine klare Süße verliert. Fehlings einziger Fehler, daß er die Szenenfolge beseitigt hat, wo Strahl Kunigundens Toilettenkünste entdeckt. Wie hätt' er da schmunzelnd austuschen können! Nachdem man vier volle Stunden im Stadttheater gesessen hatte, war man nicht etwa übersättigt, sondern noch auf diesen einen unterschlagenen Gang hungrig."[39]

As a result of Kleist's elevation to the status of *the* classical writer, indeed the prophet of National Socialism, *Käthchen* continued to be offered after the Nazis' accession to power in 1933. Its privileged position is evident from the fact that it was selected to inaugurate the open-air festival in the courtyard of the castle in Heidelberg in August 1935 (Heidelberger Reichsfestspiele). Despite the inevitable domination of the theatre by Nazi ideology, certain directors such as Fehling managed to adhere to the high artistic standards of the past, as evidenced by his new production for Berlin's Staatstheater on 23 December 1937. Once again this highly creative director brought a fresh approach to the play, as noted by K.H. Ruppel: "Jürgen Fehlings neue *Käthchen* Inszenierung unterscheidet sich von allen gewohnten Aufführungen dieses dichterisch blühendsten und dramatisch konfusesten Werks Heinrich von Kleists dadurch, daß sie nicht den Versuch macht, die Unvereinbarkeit der Elemente, aus denen es besteht, zu verwischen, sondern daß sie sie betont und unterstreicht."[40] According to Ruppel, Fehling correctly recognized the two diametrically opposed elements of the play, the poetic and the theatrical, and decided to emphasize first one aspect and then the other. For example, the elder-bush scene, the highpoint of the evening, was transferred into the poetically magic realm of the fairy-tale, because Käthchen – for Fehling a passive figure – embodied the lyrical, not the dramatic; but at the same time he revealed his flair for visual effects with a sensational representation of the castle conflagration, harking back to the days of the Meininger. Käthe Gold and Paul Hartmann, supported by a first-rate cast, excelled in the lead roles: "Ein kühnes, neuartiges und unkonventionelles Kleist-Bild hat sich in dieser Aufführung durchgesetzt."

The make-believe atmosphere called into question by Fehling returned with Gustav Rudolf Sellner's production for Darmstadt in 1953 where the performance concluded with a laugh, invented by the director, aimed at the unmasked Kunigunde: "Mit diesem Gelächter wird die Endstation Märchen deutlich markiert."[41] The focal point of this interpretation, an idealization of Käthchen and her unshakable faith in her feelings (what the critic Georg Hensel called the "Entwirklichung der Realität und Verwirklichung des Traums"), was supported by the sets (designed by Frantz Mertz), which underscored the symbolic nature of the action. Four years later, Sellner again directed *Käthchen*, but this time for the Schillertheater in Berlin. On this occasion, to emphasize even more his symbolic intent, Sellner added a surrealistic flavour, supported by the décor of Jörg Zimmermann, which sought to create "eine träumerische, surrealistische Distanz."[42] This collaboration between set designer and director was nowhere more apparent than during the most crucial moment of the play, the elder-bush scene played on an almost empty stage. The only item visible was a hovering sphere on which, with imagination, one could perceive a surrealistic elder bush: "Doch eben in der linearen Klarsichtigkeit, mit der Sellner die Szene anlegt, erhält sie jenen zauberischen, transparenten Glanz, jenen mächtigen Sog von Zartheit und Größe, der sie von aller stofflichen und Zeitgebundenheit befreit und ihre romantische Substanz herausdestilliert. Hier wird, als Höhepunkt einer ungemein kunstvoll präparierenden Inszenierung, der Nerv des Stückes bloßgelegt, und doch beherrscht lauterste Poesie die Szene."[43]

In the first half of the nineteenth century, Heinrich Heine, living in exile in France, brought a translation of *Käthchen* to Alexandre Dumas in the hope of persuading him to have it produced in Paris. Dumas apparently admired the character of Käthchen, but felt that the work was "not at all suitable for the French stage."[44] Although an adaptation of the play by Paul Morand was broadcast by the Radio Diffusion Française in the 1950s, *Käthchen* had to wait until June 1960 for its French stage *première* in the Théâtre de l'alliance française under the direction of Bernard Jenny, as part of the "Concours des Jeunes Compagnies." Since he had been raised in the tradition of Jean Cocteau, Jenny resorted to several film practices and techniques. In his review of the competition, Guy Dumur felt that the undertaking proved decidedly too ambitious for a young theatrical group with little experience and talent.[45] Filled with praise for Kleist's romantic drama, Dumur recognized that the staging and acting requirements would tax the skill and resources of a well established troupe and that this accounted in part for most of the inadequacies of Jenny's experiment. The critic also deplored the use of an unsatisfactory translation and the inappropriateness of Wagner's music (*Parsifal* and *Die Götterdämmerung*), whatever the composer's admiration for Kleist's plays.

To commemorate the 150th anniversary of Kleist's death, the Landestheater Württemberg-Hohenzollern in Tübingen offered a new version, adapted and staged by Hannes Loges who, according to one reviewer (USE.), for the first time treated the play as a conflict between Käthchen and Kunigunde. For this purpose, Loges went to great lengths to humanize the problematic Kunigunde and make her into a real rival: "Gleichgewichtig standen weibliche Machtgier gegen mädchenhafte Hingabe, Märchensinn gegen hintergründige Parodie, kalte Künstlichkeit gegen traumsichere Natur."[46] Needless to say, Käthchen (Elisabeth Kergl) and Kunigunde (played by Frauke Grund, "die halb an Shakespeare, halb an Wedekind denken ließ") came to dominate the production, and even the role of the count (J. Kraus) could be seen as evolving from his reaction to and interaction with the two female leads.

With the twentieth century's propensity for taking great liberties with a classic in order to provide a radical approach more in keeping with contemporary taste, *Käthchen*, as already noted, became the subject of several imaginative interpretations, ranging from parody to symbolism and surrealism. The risk involved in diverging too far from the original clearly manifested itself in the failure of Jean Anouilh's adaptation and staging in collaboration with Roland Pietri for the Parisian Théâtre Montparnasse in 1966. The only positive aspect singled out by the critics was the portrayal of the title role by Caroline Cellier: "Alle anderen Darsteller [haben] entsprechend den Anweisungen des Bearbeiter-Spielleiters wie seelenlose Marionetten gespielt und mit Emphase gesprochen."[47] Very rarely could the audience sense the romantic, mysterious element, while a flat, banal tone, occasionally inciting laughter, tended to impose itself upon the production. Anouilh felt himself irresistibly attracted to the figure of Käthchen as the incarnation of the absolutely loving woman and proposed that an incident from Kleist's life may have served as her inspiration. In 1803, Christoph Martin Wieland's thirteen-year old daughter had fallen in love with Kleist and from all reports the sentiment was returned. Although Wieland gave his consent to a marriage, Kleist fled from the scene, maintaining: "Ich habe das Haus mit Tränen verlassen, wo ich mehr Liebe gefunden habe, als die ganze Welt zusammen aufbringen kann."[48] In response to this episode Anouilh asked: "Ist dieser Furcht vor der absoluten Liebe eines Kindes nicht die Existenz des *Käthchens* zu verdanken?" Since the French author was himself drawn to heroines driven by an inner compulsion, it comes as no surprise that Anouilh chose to see Käthchen almost exclusively from this angle, with the result that the emperor gave the appearance of being an "Einfaltspinsel," the aristocrats acted like "lächerlich[e] Figuren," and Kunigunde was reduced to a mere witch. In summarizing his assessment, Edgar Schall noted: "Dem Schreiber dieser Zeilen scheint es aber, daß Jean Anouilh nur sich selbst treu geblieben ist, indem er sich auf seine Weise für das junge Theatergenie Kleist einsetzte."

In the last twenty-five years, Kleist's romantic drama has partly justified its classification as "ein Sorgenkind unserer Bühne."[49] The dilemma, simply stated, is this: how can one combine the fairy-tale, romantic element, the grand medieval knightly spectacle, with the more pragmatic, more realistic, if not cynical, approach of many trends in the German theatre from Brecht to the present? For example, Karl Heinz Stroux's staging of March 1967 for Düsseldorf only rarely achieved great poetic moments. In the elder-bush scene Käthchen (Nicole Heesters) came across as an embodiment of female cunning ("Verführung durch Unschuld"), the knightly scenes as parody, and the miracle of Käthchen's rescue from the fire as an everyday event. Hellmut Matiasek's production for the open-air theatre of the Luisenburg Festival (summer 1968) consciously sought to downplay the poetic idiom and offer an abundance of action: "Er [Matiasek] jagte Kleists Dichtung als ausladendes Ritterstück über Stock und Stein der Luisenburg. ... Kleists Sprache rollt fast harsch und unmutig daher."[50] Both Kai Braak (October 1968, Kassel)[51] and Kurt Hübner (July 1972, Schwäbisch Hall)[52] sought in their respective productions to bring Kleist's work up to date and to lessen or eliminate the "naive" aspect by presenting it as an obvious parody. Not unlike Sellner in his Berlin version, Braak, making do with a mere slope and a minimum of props, avoided the ostentatious romantic pageantry, with the result that during the trial by fire a ladder remained the only object in the audience's field of vision. No sharper contrast with the visual extravaganza proffered by the Meininger is conceivable.

A guest appearance by the Teatro Libero di Roma (8 August–2 September 1972) clearly demonstrated the dangers of the search for novelty. The noted director, Luca Ronconi, drawing his inspiration from the water spectacles of the seventeenth-century Italian princes, devised the idea of exploiting water's continual movement in a production designed for performance on the lake of Zürich near the city of the same name. The plan included an abundance of smaller and larger floating stages on pontoons, by means of which the actors would sail from one artificial island to the next while the audience would follow the action on its own free-moving float. However, the lake of Zürich can be quite unpredictable and is capable of becoming treacherous in a matter of a few minutes, a point driven home during a rehearsal when one of the actors, a nonswimmer, jumped onto his make-believe horse, but was suddenly thrown from his saddle into the lake by an unexpected wave and almost drowned. As a consequence, the Zürich water police intervened and prohibited the use of the moving floats. Instead, Ronconi had to content himself with one stage on pontoons surrounded by three audience floats, all four of which were securely tied to the shore. This initial setback marked only the beginning of a long series of misfortunes. During one performance, at a highpoint of the action, Käthchen (Gabriella Zamparini) slipped and fell into the water, from which her rival Kunigunde, – who in the context of the play would like nothing better than to see her dead, – rescued "die pudelnasse Poesiegestalt."[53] Giorgio Zampa's new Italian translation made the mistake of retaining the German word "Fräulein" which for those familiar with Italy during the Second World War had a very uncomplimentary connotation. Even the most effective of the sets, the secret court, came across "wie eine Verschwörerszene aus *Ernani*, voll großem italienischem Opernpathos," and to compound the difficulty, designer Arnoldo Pomodoro, upset at the distortion of his original concept, insisted that the program include an announcement of his refusal to accept responsibility for the necessarily abbreviated stage décor. In all fairness to Ronconi it must be stated that his view of theatre relies heavily upon the skilful use of action and space. The close proximity of the audience brought about by the makeshift arrangement of the four floats reduced the scope of the production almost to the level of an intimate open-air theatre. Since Ronconi required his actors to speak in a conventional, uninspiring fashion, "vom Schauspieler her [war] diese Aufführung nicht zu retten. Ihm kommt in der Konzeption des Theaters, welches Raum erschließen und im Raum erst seinen Kunstwert manifestieren kann, nur eine zweitrangige Bedeutung zu."[54] The reviews were devastating in their rejection of this interpretation: "Da ja Wasser genug zur Verfügung stand, hätte man aus dem schweizerischen Nationalcircus Knie zwei Bälle jonglierende Seelöwen hinzuziehen sollen. Dann wäre wenigstens etwas Nettes zu sehen gewesen, und mit Kleists *Käthchen von Heilbronn* hätten sie ebensoviel oder -wenig zu tun gehabt wie Luca Ronconis Wasserregie."[55]

In direct contrast with this arbitrary treatment of the text, Walter Felsenstein's much acclaimed staging for the Burgtheater of January 1974 revealed such enormous faith in Kleist, "daß er sich striktest jeglicher sogenannten Aktualisierung verschließt, jeglicher Verfremdung auch, jeglicher Zutat an Regieeinfall und Gag ...: Kleist [wird] in dieser Inszenierung mit unerbittlichem Ernst beim Wort genommen ... und nur beim Wort."[56] Felsenstein, who began his three-year contract at the Burgtheater with this version, insisted upon having double the normal number of rehearsal hours before the *première* and utilized this extra time to perfect the very aspect Ronconi chose largely to ignore, the spoken word. "Felsenstein hat Vorzügliches in der Sprachschulung der Darsteller geleistet."[57] The fairy-tale aspect tended to be understated: "Felsenstein ließ sich von Rudolf Heinrich Bühnenbilder entwerfen, die keineswegs ein deutsches Märchenland nachbilden, sondern in ihrer schönen, atmosphärischen Weiträumigkeit der Phantasie viel freien Raum geben. In diesen Räumen agieren zwei junge Menschen, die in holder Naivität und Grazie das Wunderbare als Realität erleben und vor allem Bösen, das sie bedrängt, bewahrt bleiben."[58]

After a careful examination of the original texts, Felsenstein resolved to drop the last scene as too pompous and conclude with the dialogue between Käthchen, believably portrayed by Maresa Hörbiger, the outstanding performer of the evening, and the count, played by a too old Joachim Bißmeier. Arm in arm, they disappeared into a background landscape highly reminiscent of a Caspar David Friedrich painting.

When Winfried Roesner of the *Stuttgarter Nachrichten* (13 November 1975) interviewed director Claus Peymann, the latter remarked in connection with his new version of *Käthchen*, "Der Traum verträgt die Kollision mit der Wirklichkeit, sprich: Übergang zur Ehe, nicht mehr. Da ist Kleist schon ungeheuer weit. Und das wollen wir in einem sehr schönen Schluß zeigen: Die Hochzeit geschieht mit einem ohnmächtigen Käthchen." The beginning of the production proved to be even more unusual. Designer Achim Freyer had set up on the stage a tent of transparent plastic and a high-tension wire, and as the curtain rose, "[lärmen] die Schauspieler als seiltanzende, sich überkugelnde, auf die Pauke hauende Zirkus-Truppe auf die offene Bühne."[59] This initial impression was consciously sustained throughout: slapstick in the tradition of Charlie Chaplin dominated the knightly scenes, the cavaliers rode bicycles instead of horses, and the costumes and props ran contrary to any sense of historic accuracy, the count (Martin Lüttge) appearing, for example, in armour and blue jeans, while an old typewriter could be heard pounding away during the secret court's interrogation. The servant Gottschalk (Branko Samarowski) was portrayed as a clown, Kunigunde (Kirsten Dene) as "ein[e] mondän amerikanisch[e] Femme fatale mit Barmusik, Hüftgewackel und Girrlauten,"[60] dressed half in leopard skin, half in leather, and the emperor (Gerhard Just) as "ein Zirkusdirektor im Flitterfrack mit Nero-Lorbeer."[61] The director chose to view the play as a fairy-tale, but a fairy-tale in a Freudian or Jungian sense as a naive vehicle with which to express and come to terms with one's deep-seated psychological fears. As Donald Crosby put it: "Peymann, in effect, merely substituted a modern parody of life – the distortion of a circus – for an antiquated one."[62] At one point in the performance Kunigunde actually ensnared the count with a ball of string, an alienating image of the predatory seductress. Later, when she climbed out of a lion-footed bathtub to appear to the astonishd count as a decrepit conglomeration of false limbs, Peymann attempted to suggest the unconscious male fear of being betrayed and overwhelmed by the deceptive female siren: "Als ... der Ritter erkennt, daß seine Braut nur aus Prothesen und Versatzstücken besteht, wird sie in der Stuttgarter Aufführung auf einmal echt erbärmlich und elend ängstlich. Sie weiß, daß sie nur zählt, wenn sie für den Mann schön ist."[63] "Part *Machtweib*, part *Märchenhexe*," noted Crosby, "this incredible amalgam of cosmetics and prosthetics somehow metamorphoses, in Frau Dene's protean performance, into an almost believable woman!"[64] This psycho-analytical interpretation can also be detected in the following assessment of the love between Strahl and Käthchen: "Martin Lüttge und Lore Brunner [Käthchen] spielten deftiges, gescheites Volkstheater, spielten den Kinderglauben, der, wie die Seiltänzer am Anfang der Aufführung über die sexuellen Abgründe des Stücks hinwegtanzt – ins Happy-End." Although this controversial experiment met with a somewhat mixed critical reaction, on the whole it turned out to be such a box-office success that the production went on tour to Vienna (Theater an der Wien, June 1976), to Zürich (11 June 1977), and finally, as the first West German theatrical offering to the Edinburgh Festival, where its one performance encountered an unfavourable press. *The Times's* correspondent J.W. Lambert referred to it as "a jollied-up version" of "this dotty schoolroom classic,"[65] a not unexpected but still not very encouraging reaction to the first twentieth-century production of *Käthchen* to appear in the United Kingdom.

Kurt Hübner again proved in Berlin's Freie Volksbühne (September 1976) that an honest attempt to adhere to Kleist's poetic word, when supported by capable young actors, can still captivate and enthrall a receptive audience. Moreover, since *Käthchen* contains a veritable plethora of heterogeneous dramatic material – partly as a result of Kleist's acknowledged effort to please a not-too-discriminating public taste – directors have yet to exhaust its potential for diverse, often diametrically opposed interpretations, as illustrated by Hans-Joachim Heyse's staging in Bonn to commemorate the dramatist's 200th birthday (1977). Heyse took as his point of departure a quotation from Kleist's essay "Über das Marionettentheater," which, appearing on the curtain, emphasized in Brechtian fashion the puppet angle.[66] And Weimar, where Goethe once condemned the play as "[ein] wunderbares Gemisch von Sinn und Unsinn",[67] hosted an East German *première* directed by Professor Fritz Bennewitz for the Deutsches Nationaltheater in February 1978.[68]

To judge by the numerous references and comparisons to Peymann's highly successful production, it exercised a significant influence on other directors, which may in part explain the extensive revival enjoyed by *Käthchen* in 1979, a year that witnessed no less than five major productions. The first of these, a staging in Bochum by Werner Schroeter in January, aroused the least critical interest and was generally rejected for its "wütend[en] Angriff auf die Kleistische Märchen- und Ritterwelt"[69] or the "entzaubernd[e] Demontage der Sprachpartitur":[70] "Schroeter inszeniert in Bochum seine Ansicht von Kleist und brachte ihr das *Käthchen* zum Opfer. Nicht die Zertrümmerung dieses 'großen historischen Ritterschauspiels', das szenisch ohnehin nur noch glaubhaft gemacht werden kann durch Demontage, ist ihm zum Vorwurf zu machen, sondern die verbissene Bewußtlosigkeit, wie er mit dem Material des Stückes und mit den Schauspielern umgeht."[71]

Whereas Schroeter's version demonstrated a consciously cultivated disrespect for the original, the next production to appear, taking the play quite seriously, attempted to preserve the atmosphere and the structure "im durchaus konventionellen Umgang mit den Mitteln des Theaters."[72] However, this interpretation by Johannes Schaaf for the Schauspielhaus in Düsseldorf went, in the opinion of nearly all the reviewers, to an extreme reminiscent of the nineteenth-century Meininger spectacles. His set designer Erich Wonder provided a visual extravaganza, a "Bühnenbildinszenierung" (Schulze-Reimpell), which sought to translate poetic metaphors into stage images, while Schaaf's fidelity to the text resulted in a four-hour performance that strained the audience's patience. The reviewers expressed admiration for the decorations: "[Erich Wonder] versieht Schaafs Inszenierung mit magischen Lichträumen und gespenstischem Wald, mit Nebellandschaften und aus Dampf gefertigtem Wasserfall";[73] but a majority deplored the domination of the optical display, the over-emphasis upon the theatrical to the detriment of the language and the acting: "Johannes Schaaf flüchtet sich vor den Problemen, die Kleist aufgibt, in eine Theatralisierung, in der sich letztlich alles in Wohlgefallen und schönen Bildern auflösen läßt."[74] The audience was immediately confronted and apparently captivated by one of those beautiful images.[75] A high box bathed in a dull blue light housed the opening "Vehmgericht" scene. In the foreground rose a plexiglas pillar in which water dripped. Käthchen (Susanne Granzer), released from a straight-jacket, appeared as a contrasting point of light against the black, anonymous circle of judges surrounding her. Unfortunately, Strahl's trial became somewhat of a trial for the spectator as well, lasting almost a full hour. During the battle to secure the release of the captured Kunigunde, the staging conjured up a ritualistically performed samurai duel with wooden swords and brightly coloured masks from traditional Japanese theatre, with the intention of achieving a *V-Effekt* through ridicule and exoticism. For a final pageant the heroine ascended a high wooden structure and assumed a position upon a podium from which her wedding dress descended like a curtain to the ground below: "Hier zielt alles auf die Geste, das Ritual – auf Theater: Käthchen findet sich am Ende nicht an der Seite ihres Geliebten, sondern wird auf ein Podest gestellt, zum 'Bild' erhöht."[76] Although the Schaaf/Wonder production did much to highlight the "Schau-"aspect of *Käthchen*, it still did serious, in the view of many, irreparable damage to the equally important "-spiel" dimension.[77]

Jürgen Flimm, who allegedly admired Peymann's achievement,[78] nevertheless followed Schaaf's example by taking *Käthchen* seriously, but managed to achieve a more balanced production with which to inaugurate his directorship of Cologne's Schauspielhaus. As it turned out, Flimm's staging won high praise from the audience – some reviewers saw his reading as an attempt to ingratiate himself with the public – but received mixed, at times contradictory notices from the critics in their attempts to interpret the interpretation. Georg Hensel, for instance, writing for the *Frankfurter Allgemeine Zeitung* (9 October 1979), maintained: "Er [Flimm] paßt das *Käthchen* der Gegenwart nicht an. Er zeigt, daß sie in unserer Gegenwart ein Fremdkörper ist, nicht von dieser Welt." On the other hand, Peter Iden of the *Frankfurter Rundschau* (12 October 1979) contended: "Von allen Aufführungen des Stücks während der letzten Jahre … ist diese am meisten bemüht, den Traum Käthchens auf Gegenwart zu beziehen, ihn 'wirklich' zu machen." Iden's assessment proved to be more in keeping with the intent of the production as outlined in the preview announcement: "Der Traum ist gefährlich, weil er vom Alltag handelt, nicht von ferner Zeit,"[79] and most commentators went to considerable lengths to stress the links Flimm established between Kleist's dream world and our contemporary reality in order to create, in the words of Heinz Klunker, "ein Stück realistischer Utopie."

The relative sparseness of the décor – described as an "Antithese zu Erich Wonders tödlicher Opulenz der Düsseldorfer Schaaf-Inszenierung"[80] – sparked some controversy. Set designer Rolf Glittenberg had two boats constructed, one, from which trees grew and which was located in the auditorium, and another directly opposite at the back of an almost empty stage filled with misty vapors. A ramp joining the boat in the midst of the audience to the stage made possible a novel entrance for several players, especially the blindfolded Käthchen when she approached the court. The area in between the two boats was largely bare, thus stressing the fact that Flimm wanted to concentrate on the acting and above all on the language.[81] Peter Iden offered the most ingenious analysis of the props and their possible relationship to the message: "Das ist ja ein altes Motiv der Kunst: das Narrenschiff, Metapher für die Lebensfahrt, die Lebensirrfahrt ist, immer gefährdet, bedroht von Illusion und Täuschung – und dennoch fortgesetzt, meistens mit Überzeugungen, Ideen im Sinn, Plänen für Morgen." This interpretation also provides a useful frame of reference for the unique manner in which Flimm concluded the show. When Käthchen lost consciousness upon hearing of her imminent marriage to Strahl, her body remained in isolation upon the floor, abandoned by the other characters who withdrew to the rear. This arrangement suggested anything but a happy ending. Suddenly, a large window was disclosed in the back wall of the theatre, offering a view of Cologne's Krebsgasse. The actors then reappeared on the outside of the building looking in upon the empty stage and waiting for a traffic light. When the latter finally turned green, they were last seen heading for the parking garage.

Nina Ritter's costumes also toyed with the dream/reality tension. According to Georg Hensel, those persons who held the dramatist's own beliefs and convictions, especially "wo das unerschütterliche Gefühl den gemeinen Verstand ins Unrecht setzt," wore clothing consistent with Kleist's own period; the characters drawn from the romantic world of the knightly novel sported the armour associated in popular imagination with that bygone age; and finally the figures belonging to Kunigunde's realm of artificial deception and greed were dressed in modern outfits.

Hensel's evaluation, "Kein großer Abend, aber ein sympathischer," summarizes fairly accurately the overall critical response to Flimm's production. Its great popularity with audiences has been attributed to Katharina Thalbach's "bemerkenswertes Käthchen, [sie] hat tief anrührende Töne, und daß sie die Weltentrücktheit von Käthchens Hingabe an ihren hochgestellten Herrn mit einem Hauch von Komik überzieht, macht die vorzuspielende bedingungslose Liebe nur glaubwürdiger,"[82] and to Elisabeth Trissenaar's portrayal of Kunigunde as "eine gegenwärtige Frau von jener Sorte, die man in Amerika Goldgräberinnen nennt" (Hensel). As a further sign of its public appeal, the zDF (Zweites Deutsches Fernsehen) network presented a filmed version of the staging in November 1980, May 1984, and again in December 1986: "Auch am Bildschirm gehört die Aufführung zu den großen Abenden, die man nicht entbehren möchte."[83]

After his highly acclaimed film *La Marquise d'O* (1975), Eric Rohmer again turned to Kleist, this time for his first stage enterprise, *La petite Catherine de Heilbronn* performed in la Maison de la culture de Nanterre in Paris. This constituted the fourth major production of 1979, inviting and receiving the inevitable critical comparisons with its German predecessors: "Die deutschen Inszenierungen der letzten Jahre, von Peymann, Schaaf und Flimm, waren alle kräftiger, reicher, auch entschiedener in den Bilderwelten, die sie entworfen haben."[84] Rohmer translated and adapted the text himself, rewriting the iambic pentameters into blank verse and preserving the contrast between prose and poetry. Because he chose to focus on the love interest – "Die Aufführung konzentriert sich ganz auf diese beiden Figuren [Käthchen und Strahl]" (Peter Iden) – the exposure of Kunigunde's treachery occurred before the elder-bush scene and the disclosure of Käthchen's true parentage, so that the heroine's dream confession ensured the happy ending on which the evening came to a close. While Rohmer sought to respect the text, he did make some additions: a few drops of the poison meant for Käthchen accidentally fell upon some flowers which instantly expired and filmed re-enactments of the "Sylvesternachtträume" were projected upon transparent stage curtains.

A fairy tale about a man caught between two women, the good princess and the bad princess, is how Rohmer read the play: "Die heutigen deutschen Aufführungen versuchen, das Stück zu entmystifizieren. Im Gegensatz dazu möchte ich [Rohmer], daß der Zuschauer sich willig gefangennehmen läßt von diesem Märchen."[85] In an attempt to recreate the naivety of this genre, he used simple but beautiful, suggestive stage decorations by Yannis Kokkos and engaged young, relatively inexperienced actors whom he trained rigorously for two months until he achieved an amazing and, for some, undesirable uniformity of action: "Eine höchst raffinierte Bewegungsregie bestimmt den Handlungsablauf, der auch sprachlich keinem Fortissimo Raum gewährt" (Ruth Henry, *Süddeutsche Zeitung*, 22 November 1979); "[T]out se dévide dans la monotonie, sans rythme, une suite de tableaux séparés par des noirs pendant lesquels on entend une musique, toujours la même (Colette Godard, *Le Monde*, 13 November 1979).

Rohmer's first venture onto the stage elicited a wide range of critical reactions, ranging from "das Preziöse eines Kunstmärchens" (Hensel) to "die prosaischste, preußischste aller Kleist-Inszenierungen" (B.H.

*Die Zeit*, 16 November 1979). While Colette Godard of *Le Monde* denied Rohmer any knowledge whatsoever of the theatre and joined with the sarcastic reviewer (P.M.) of *Le Figaro* to repudiate the staging as "[le] comble de l'amateurisme,"[86] Ruth Henry came to Rohmer's defence, maintaining that the director's approach "erhält die märchenhafte Anschaulichkeit des Stücks" and pointing to his vindication through the audience's reception: "Und die Reaktion des Publikums – für welches, im Prinzip, ja Theater gemacht wird, – unterscheidet sich, wie so oft, vom Urteil der Profis." This verdict was called into question by Guy Dumur's article for *Le Nouvel Observateur* (26 November 1979) which reported "des ricanements saugrenus." "Ce n'était pas seulement de Rohmer dont on se moquait, mais, j'en témoigne, de la pièce elle-même, trop étrangère aux goûts du jour." However, nearly all commentators, including the most censorious, recognized the childlike but nonetheless dignified portrayal, the almost aristocratic refinement and sensibility which the unknown Pascale Ogier, with the large, haunting eyes, brought to the title role: "Pourtant, ce spectacle est sauvé par la présence de Pascale Ogier" (Dumur); "Doch wird das Märchen nun in der Pariser Katharina wahr" (Iden). The production generated sufficient interest to warrant greater public exposure through French television on 6 August 1980.

The last major staging in 1979, that of the principal dramaturge and director of Munich's Kammerspiele, Ernst Wendt, achieved the questionable notoriety of being the longest: "In viereinhalb Stunden wurde keine Silbe des *Käthchen von Heilbronn* ausgelassen."[87] "[E]her konzeptionslos" and feeling his way "neugierig von Szene zu Szene," Wendt spent two months attempting to come to terms with the play's ambivalent world. When asked to explain the current "boom" in *Käthchen* productions, he replied: "So wie es eine Klassiker-Welle gab, pendelt es sich jetzt auf einen empfindsameren Autor namens Kleist ein. Das ist fast schon eine Widerstandswaffe gegen die immer robusteren Erscheinungen um uns herum."[88] Although Wolfgang Johannes Müller (*Bayern Kurier*, 12 January 1980) deplored the omission "einer tragenden Konzeption," Wendt believed he had found one in his respect for the miraculous content: "Man muß wirklich an Wunder glauben," he remarked, "sonst braucht man das Stück nicht zu machen oder zu sehen."[89] In the opinion of some he did manage to convey in a convincing fashion this faith in the fairy-tale dimension: "Von allen Aufführungen dieses Stücks in den vergangenen Monaten ist diese die am lebhaftesten eine wunderbar-märchenhafte Geschichte erzählende, selbst voller Erstaunen über die sonderbaren Wendungen der Handlung, sich manchmal verwirrend in den Wechselfällen, die von der gebrechlichen Einrichtung der Welt herrühren ..., dem Zauber verfallen, mit Zweifeln auch, aber das Wunder ist stärker."[90] Consequently, special care was expended on those scenes featuring the "höchst sensibl[e], fast legendenhaft unschuldig agierend[e] Lisi Mangold" (Colberg) as Käthchen. Johannes Schütz's black set, which never changed throughout the evening, depicted in the opening "Vehmgericht" sequence an underground cavern in which three judges sat with their backs to the audience and from which a ladder ascended to the world above. As Theobald presented his case before the tribunal, Strahl leaned against the ladder and later Käthchen made a theatrically stunning entrance, climbing "in einem weißen Kleid wie Silber gleißend, die Leiter herunter: sie scheint nicht von der Erde oben, nein von weiter oben, aus dem Überirdischen, in dieses finstre Erdloch Licht zu bringen" (Hensel). This ladder, exploited as a visual leitmotif, reappeared in the first scene of the second act for Strahl's monologue (the upper end of the ladder, not visible in the cave, now emerged from the ground, a neat optical link between the two acts), during the conflagration, and at the beginning of the fourth act for the pursuit (where it became a bridge). The other image singled out by most critics occurred in the scene praised by Peter Iden as the "schönst[e] Szene der Aufführung," the elder-bush episode. Here the stage remained in darkness except for a cone of light that fell upon Strahl and Käthchen asleep within a loosely constructed, transparent gauze box, over the edge of which hung her stockings. There was a striking effect when Strahl, suddenly gaining insight into the miraculously shared dream experience, stood up so that his head rose above the veil-like curtain.

Reviewers of the Munich production recognized the conflicting tension between the unconscious dream world, which Wendt took pains to recreate and emphasize, and the knightly realm, characterized by slapstick comedy and cheap theatrical gags (hobby horses, gigantic swords in slow motion, the silent-movie ladder routine) and intended as a satire on the "groß[e] historisch[e] Ritterschauspiel." Gerhard Pörtl spoke of "Traumbild und Zerrbild," "Kleist und Kleist-karikatur" (*Schwäbisches Tagblatt*, 19 December 1979), and Klaus Colberg of a "Theaterabend ... zwischen Wunderwelt und ganz und gar profaner Allzumenschlichkeit." Other dubious innovations included a younger Gottschalk (Markus Boyson) in love with Käthchen, a lesbian Kunigunde (Barbara Freier), and Charles Brauer's operatic travesty of the emperor. The *Käthchen* text does entail conscious parody (the first section of Strahl's long prose monologue) and satire (the main butt being Theobald), but for Horst Ziermann, Wendt overstepped the boundary of the theatrically permissible and thus failed to do justice to Kleist: "Wendt benutzt Kleist nur noch, benutzt ihn zur Hervorbringung von Spektakel und glattem Amüsement. So etwas deprimiert" (*Die Welt*, 18 December 1979). Nevertheless, despite conflicting judgments – "Ein Fasching-Scherz im Advent" (*Die Zeit*, 21 December 1979); "Man kann angesichts dieses Münchner Käthchen leicht ins Schwärmen kommen" (Iden), – Wendt's production, "ein schöner, lustiger Traum,"[91] won the support of those who persisted until the final curtain: "Am Ende ein jubelndes Publikum, Ovationen" (Iden).

In April 1981 Milan's Teatro dell' Arte presented *Caterina di Heilbronn*, the first attempt to mount *Käthchen* in Italian since Luca Ronconi's disastrous spectacle on the waters of Lake Zürich. Director Massimo Castri, in his psychological reading of the play, met with only marginally more success than his predecessor. In direct contrast to the Munich version, the space and time limitations imposed by the Italian theatrical scene obliged Castri to reduce the performance to a three-act work with a two-and-a-half hour duration. The staging used Giorgio Zampa's faithful translation in which the focal point remains "la rivelazione dell'amore in un cuore intatto" (the revelation of love in a sound heart);[92] however, Castri elected to transform *Käthchen* into "una sorta di prevaricazione fantastica maschile" (a sort of fantastic male prevarication) inhabited by "Lolite in gonnellini trasparenti," (Lolitas in transparent mini-skirts). As a result, the titular heroine almost disappeared as a real life character and became a male fantasy, a mere projection of the masculine mind, while Kunigunde, a Circe, embodied yet another manifestation of Käthchen: deceptive appearance. Such an interpretation necessarily limited the love triangle and its underlying or overt sense of rivalry. To reinforce the general theme: "l'uomo intento a percorrere un rabbrividito e balenante viaggio nella foresta del proprio inconscio" (man intent on making a terrifying and lightning-fast voyage through the forest of his own unconsciousness), Maurizio Balò built on stage a veritable forest of tree trunks, through which the hero had to pass on his solitary voyage of self-discovery; and he designed costumes that reflected the eighteenth century rather than the Middle Ages. Because Strahl's role, played by Virgilio Gazzolo, came to prevail, the two female leads, Zappa Mulas as Caterina and Carla Chiarelli as Cunegonda, were reduced to "due bambinacce" (two nasty little girls) with a tendency to view their participation as "una serie di corsettine, risatine e piccole riverenze" (a series of small runs, giggles and little curtsies). Although those who remained to the end of the confused, enigmatic evening applauded enthusiastically, this endorsement failed to dispel the overall negative reaction of reviewer Roberto De Monticelli.

Carsten Bodinus's staging for Karlsruhe's Großes Haus des Badischen Staatstheaters in October 1981 followed much more traditional lines but fared little better than Castri's. After a promising pantomime prologue, which evoked Kleist's suicide pact juxtaposed with the ideal embodied in Käthchen – "[Heinrich von Kleist] tötet gefühlsverwirrt eine Gliederpuppe, die tote Frau, während die in ihrer Gefühlssicherheit geborgene, lebendige, ruhig und fern ihr Lied singt"[93] – the performance began to flounder since it evidently lacked a uniform theme and depended heavily upon the audience appeal of "[e]inige wirkungsvolle Einfälle: die Gefechte der Ritter mit schweren Säbeln als Ballett zu Wagners 'Walküre'-Musik … oder Kunigundes Gemach als Folienzelt" (Waldecker). The realism of the burning castle – clouds of smoke spread to the auditorium – clashed with the more suggestive, symbolic style of the other sets, and there was no apparent justification for the night watchman's swinging on his bellrope above the heads of the spectators. Rüdiger Krohn (*Stuttgarter Zeitung*, 23 October 1981) deplored the extent to which the large stage seriously jeopardized any attempt to recreate the drama's intimate moments, and the audience was left with the visual impression of several helpless individuals arbitrarily dispersed over a wide expanse. Berthold Toetzke managed to project Strahl's underlying insecurity but did not succeed in conveying his suppressed emotional commitment to the *Bürgerstochter* in spite of his family heritage. Similarly, Angelika Bartsch (Käthchen) failed to put across "den selbstverständlichen Widerstand eines unversehrbaren Herzens" (Waldecker). The strength of the production in the analyses of both reviewers lay in the great care for and faith in Kleist's language, something which was apparent from the very first scene: "Bodinus läßt die mächtigen forensischen Redeblöcke des Femegerichts mit geradezu opernhafter Breite spielen; genüßlich zelebriert er den Text" (Krohn). Even this positive celebration of the spoken word, however, only served eventually to underscore the negative aspect, the general lack of dramatic action.

"Die Überraschung eines Weihnachtsprogramms von angestrengtem Glitzern war ein *Käthchen von Heilbronn*, das auf alle zu befürchtenden Mätzchen, Aktualisierungen und aufgesetzte Effekte verzichtete." In these words, Clara Menck, reporting for the *Frankfurter Allgemeine Zeitung* (28 December 1981), characterized Peter Beauvais's televised staging aired on Christmas Day 1981 (ARD). Although there had been other *Käthchen*s on the television screen before, notably Peymann's Stuttgart and Flimm's Cologne versions,

Beauvais, a television director by profession, made for the first time an original film on the basis of Kleist's text, rather than filming a stage production. For instance, he deleted the long monologues and rewrote Brigitte's narrative as a humorous dialogue between three old women. Parts of the film were shot in the studio, for example the private *Traumgespräch*, while the knightly episodes, complete with real horses, were filmed at the Löwenburg near Kassel. An inordinate amount of time and effort went into the planning of the costumes, devised by Gaby Jänicke in close collaboration with the director in order to steer a "Kostümkurs zwischen Mittelalter und Biedermeier,"[94] and into their making, the responsibility of the firm of Cerratelli in Florence. (This firm also furnished the costumes for Zeffirelli's film *Romeo and Juliet*.) "[Um] Kleists märchenhafte Geschichte der Vermählung von Licht und Liebe gegen das Dunkel (Kunigunde) [she wore dark, heavy velvet materials] sichtbar zu machen, findet [Jänicke] für Käthchen neben dem naheliegenden Weiß eine Menge leichter, lichter, durchscheinender Stoffe und heller, unmerklich abgestufter Pastellfarben" (Götze).

According to one review (BNB, *Frankfurter Rundschau*, 28 December 1981), the success of the two-hour production was due largely to outstanding individual performances: Manfred Zapatka's "sehr männlich[en] Walter vom Strahl," the unknown Marita Marschall's "ergreifend schlichtes Käthchen," Cornelia Froboess's "hexenhafte" and "dämonische" Kunigunde (*Mannheimer Morgen*, 28 December 1981), but above all to Dietrich Fischer-Dieskau's lightly ironic portrayal of the emperor, the baritone's début in an exclusively speaking role. Beauvais endeavoured to present the drama's most exalted personage in a less compromising light by downplaying the imperial indiscretion and its exposure. The middle part of his confessional monologue Fischer-Dieskau uttered at the conclusion in order to ensure a happy rather than the ambivalent ending with which Kleist's version leaves the audience. Instead of the ominous exchange – "KUNIGUNDE. Pest, Tod und Rache! Diesen Schimpf sollt ihr mir büßen! / DER GRAF VOM STRAHL. Giftmischerin!" (2681–3) – "schreitet Fischer-Dieskau auf die kaiserliche Empore, raunt sanfte Worte der Erinnerung, die er viel früher hätte sprechen müssen, und zieht einen roten Vorhang zu."[95] The overall evaluation of this interpretation was decidedly positive: "Heinrich von Kleists wundersam-wunderliches 'großes historisches Ritterschauspiel' war in der Fernsehinszenierung von Peter Beauvais ein Glanzstück im reichhaltigen Feiertagsprogramm" (Helmut A. Lange, *Schwäbische Zeitung*, 28 December 1981), a discordant note being sounded by only two critics, Rolf Michaelis and Thomas Thieringer (*Süddeutsche Zeitung*, 28

December 1981). The former took exception to the "schläfrig lieb" tone of the performance and to the emphasis upon the external violence of storm and fire to the exclusion of the inner violence done to human emotions, while the latter saw Kleist's play degraded to a "Ritter-Liebesspektakel" at the expense of the dramatist's language.[96] The film was, however, sufficiently well received to be repeated (March 1982) as the first offering in a series of five films, the others being Rudolph's *Amphitryon* (1975), Lietzau's *Der zerbrochene Krug* (1980), Rohmer's *La Marquise d'O* (1975), and finally the celebrated Stein staging of *Prinz Friedrich von Homburg* (1972).

"Klassiker Kleist wurde in Tübingen gewaltsam aktualisiert," announced Dieter Schnabel (*Badische Neueste Nachrichten*, 2 March 1982) in his review of Wolfgang Lichtenstein's controversial interpretation. The critics censured the caricatural acting, the lack of respect, if not scorn, for Kleist's verse, the one permanent set designed by Athanasios Soundoulidis (a grey wall in the rear, a tin-foil wall to the right, a partially torn-up parquet floor, with evergreens and several doors creating the impression of "ein Kabinett der tausend Türen, so daß ein nervendes Auf- und Abtrettheater geboten wird"[97]), and finally what Ulrich Wanner (*Stuttgarter Nachrichten*, 13 February 1982) called "die Aufdringlichkeit eines angemaßten Deutungspotpourris." The latter observation does in fact reflect the experimental intent expressed by the dramaturge Rainer Mennickern in a conversation reported in the *Schwäbisches Tagblatt* (10 February 1982): "Der Gedanke des realistischen, kritischen und spielerischen Überprüfens von Zuständen, Haltungen, Projektionen der Figuren wurde zum Ausgangspunkt unseres Inszenierungskonzepts." One reviewer (gam) pointed to the portrayal of sexual fantasies and fears as a possible unifying theme: "[M]an lernt, daß Kopulation eine Strafe sein kann." The evening began with Käthchen (Wieslawa Wesolowska) reading from Kleist's letters sentences punctuated by childish giggles indicative of her incomprehension. Then a puppet in armour, sitting on an elegant sofa, suddenly came to life, exposing the count (Christian Habicht). (Later in the production Strahl "exposed" himself even further when he appeared in the nude.) The judges of the fehmic court, wearing modern dress and using a tape recorder to register the proceedings, reminded one commentator (gam) of "einen gelangweilt blickenden englischen Altherren-Club." Rejected as a "manieriertes Schmierentheater" (Schnabel) or "eine Klassiker-Verkackeierung" (gam) by the press, the staging failed to elicit any support from the audience as well.

Pierre-Jean Valentin's production in Freiburg only a few months later met with substantially more approval than Lichtenstein's, but the reviews of the French director's staging were contradictory. Whereas Renée Buschkiel claimed in the *Badische Neueste Nachrichten* (28 April 1982), "Eine klassisch-werktreue Wiedergabe des 'großen historischen Ritterschauspiels'," Swiss critic Peter Burri (*Basler Zeitung*, 27 April 1982) maintained in reference to the same production: "Noch selten wurde ein klassisches Stück so konsequent verarscht." Nevertheless a consensus emerged that Valentin had sought to focus on the fairy-tale realm and its appeal to human fantasy while at the same time suggesting the underlying psychological theme – "[die] Unzulänglichkeit der Liebe, die im Augenblick der Erfüllung stirbt" (Buschkiel). For "einen Regisseur, der ganz in *Bildern* [critic's emphasis] denkt,"[98] Hans Georg Schäfer designed a series of predominantly dark sets with which to explore the inner dream world as suggested by shiny black curtains, clouds of fog, or mirrors. In the expositional court scene, Käthchen (Elvira Plüss), her eyes bound, made a sensational entrance from beneath the stage through a brightly glowing glass cylinder. Throughout this sequence she moved and reacted without the aid of her eyes but never faltered once, because she merely responded to the promptings of her infallible heart and, in keeping with a theme dear to Kleist (*Die Familie Schroffenstein*), she saw more dependably with closed eyes: "Sie vollzieht nur sehr einfach und überaus fremdartig schlicht die *Methode* [critic's emphasis] nach, in und aus der Kleists Käthchen lebt; die der sehenden Blindheit, des blinden Fühlens und Begreifens."[99] To follow the opening interrogation, Schäfer created the image of a gigantic black forest perforated by streams of light, through which Strahl (Rainer Kühn) made his way in another visually effective and memorable scene. After a long series of similarly impressive theatrical pictures, which in the estimation of Gerhard Jörder obscured the basic message of the text and omitted to establish the nature of the relationships between the drama's protagonists, the production culminated in a marriage spectacle (Buschkiel saw it as a stylized funeral, the death of true love), featuring a red-capped fool who announced the wedding, a puppet-like Kunigunde on stilts, and a Käthchen carried off into the night by her count. The production also made extensive use of music, ranging from Vivaldi, Mahler, and Orff to contemporary pop artists such as Jean-Michel Jarre – yet another sign for Reinhard Hübsch (*Stuttgarter Nachrichten*, 6 May 1982) of Valentin's overall "Konzeptionslosigkeit." The staging still earned good reviews, and even the most negative, that of Peter Burri, preserved a balanced judgment: "Die feine Mär, die Kleist in dieses Drama geflossen ist, wird hier zum Spektakel. Entertainment auf hohem Niveau. Was dabei ansatzweise verloren geht, ist die Poesie, die Doppeldeutigkeit des Geschehens."

This staging for Das Große Haus in Freiburg turned out to be the last major production up to 1987 to inspire extensive press coverage, even though there were at least five more attempts to mount *Käthchen*. In Bremen's Theater am Goetheplatz (March 1986), Torsten Fischer offered the play in the tradition of the "Volksschauspiel,"[100] but, in the judgment of the *Weser-Kurier* critic, by doing so, he did not do justice to the threat represented by the conscious, real world as it impinges upon the unconscious dream sphere. Ingolstadt hosted "eine deftige Freak-Schau ... Typen, Trottel, Tunten, Bilderbogen, Comic-Strip"[101] (November 1986), directed by Ernst Seittgen, that encountered difficulties when it came to portraying the more serious themes of the drama – Susanne Oechsner played a consciously ironic Käthchen from the very outset. The Luisenburger Festspiele initiated their season in July 1987 with Herbert Kreppel's open-air version which, according to Leo Fremgen (*Deutsche Wochen-Zeitung*, 31 July 1987), demonstrated, in this warmly applauded staging, the degree to which "Kleist's Dichtung und Sprache ... für eine Freilicht-Aufführung wie geschaffen [sind]." A Städtebundtheater production in Biel/Solothurn (September 1987), for which guest director Neidhardt Nordmann was responsible, took as its focal point Käthchen's fate and achieved a noteworthy success through Katharina von Arx's capable and believable characterization of the titular heroine: "Schöner, intensiver und richtiger läßt sich das Käthchen wohl kaum spielen."[102] And finally, another guest director, Edwin Noël, had to contend with less favourable reactions in Ulm (October 1987) when he failed to exploit fully or effectively either *Käthchen's* comic or tragic potential. Damning with faint praise, Barbara Miller described his accomplishment as "[eine] biedere Stadttheateraufführung, mehr kam nicht über die Rampe."[103]

Kleist enthusiasts owe a considerable debt of gratitude to *Das Käthchen von Heilbronn* for having kept the dramatist's work alive on stage throughout the nineteenth century, albeit more often than not in the perverted form of an adaptation (Holbein). It was one of the very few of his dramas performed in his lifetime, in fact the only one to be performed with some success, and it was greatly admired by writers of such different literary and philosophical persuasions as E.T.A. Hoffmann, Friedrich Hebbel, or Theodor Fontane. The strong appeal of the poetic or fantastic as embodied in the heroine, "eine echtgeborene Tochter der Poesie," to quote Hebbel,[104] provided the main source for its popularity which reached a highpoint in the spectacles of the Meininger in the 1870s, a tendency carried over into the present century with Reinhardt's 1905 production. In the second half of the twentieth century, its previous asset, the romantic, poetic dimension, has frequently become a liability in view of the more cynical, prosaic approach to life after the Second World War and the influence of Brecht's epic theatre. The "märchenhafte Anschaulichkeit" of Rohmer's 1979 staging was found to be "trop étrangère aux goûts du jour." In an age where democratic principles may be said to prevail, there is some irony in the fact that *Käthchen*, a play written by a renegade *Junker* and based on a value system derived almost exclusively from an autocratic, aristocratic tradition, should continue to inspire even left-wing directors to interpret it on stage. If the efforts of Peymann (1975), Flimm (1979), or Beauvais (1981) are a reliable indication, *Das Käthchen von Heilbronn* will continue to fill theatres, although not with the regularity now more characteristic of *Der zerbrochene Krug*.

## CHAPTER SIX

# Die Hermannsschlacht

Written with a scarcely concealed political goal in mind and conceived of with typically Kleistean enthusiasm and total commitment,
*Die Hermannsschlacht* has been accorded a warm or cool reception
almost entirely in relation to the German political situation. Kleist's
promoter, Heinrich von Collin, submitted it for consideration to a
group of aristocrats in control of Vienna's Burgtheater, but because
of their continual procrastination and the Austrian defeat at Wagram,
the drama could not be performed. A production was also impossible
during the Restoration (1815–1848), since the attitudes of the times
such as moderation and political non-involvement could not be
brought into harmony with the play's excesses. Commenting upon
the stage history of *Die Hermannsschlacht* from a chauvinistic point
of view common to several intellectuals after Germany's defeat in the
First World War, Otto Fraude characterized it as "eine Illustration zu
den Worten Bismarcks von der Blutarmut der Deutschen in Hinsicht
auf nationales Empfinden."[1]

The turning point in acquainting the public with Kleist's play
occurred in 1858 when the noted historian and German nationalist,
Heinrich von Treitschke, recommended in an essay for the *Preußische
Jahrbücher* that Kleist's version of the tale be performed.

Schon die Mehrzahl der modernen Männer steht dem Staate fremd und
gleichgültig gegenüber; ein Dichter, in dessen stolzem Geiste die Vaterlandsliebe zur persönlichen Leidenschaft geworden, ein so rein politischer Held
wie dieser Hermann wird nur allzu vielen Männern unverständlich bleiben;
unsre Frauen werden ganz bestimmt ratlos vor dem Rätsel stehn. Trotzdem
sollte man die Aufführung der Hermannsschlacht versuchen, auf den
zwei oder drei Bühnen mindestens, welche noch ein erträgliches Ensemble
zu Stande bringen. ... Und dieses Werk mit der tiefen Wahrheit seiner

Charaktere, mit der gedrungenen Kraft seiner Sprache, wo selbst "die See, des Landes Rippen schlagend, Freiheit brüllt" – dies Werk sollte nicht einmal des Versuchens werth sein, ob es auch von der Bühne herab zündend wirken könne?[2]

At approximately the same time as Treitschke's article appeared, Feodor Wehl had begun to adapt the play, whose patriotic content, he felt, was especially suited "das Publikum mit Enthusiasmus für das Vaterland und seine Unantastbarkeit zu erfüllen."[3] Since he recognized that it could not be mounted in its original form, he made cuts, alterations, and additions. Varus took on greater significance as Hermann's opponent: now the main dramatic interest centred on a clash between two male protagonists, culminating in their final duel in which Hermann cut down his valiant foe. In the interest of middle-class moral sensivities, the bear episode disappeared completely; Thusnelda was reduced to a run-of-the-mill housewife kept totally in the dark about her husband's plans; and Hally, no longer dumb, begged for death, a request which her father reluctantly fulfilled. Wehl also shortened some scenes, eliminated several of the minor roles, and changed many speeches to make them conform to the spirit of his times. Assessing the final product, Fraude noted: "Zusammenfassend müssen wir sagen, daß durch die Bearbeitung Wehls so viele fremde Elemente in das Original hineingebracht wurden, daß von dem Stil, der elementaren Kraft des ursprünglichen Werkes nur noch wenig zu spüren war."[4] After Wehl published his version in the *Deutsche Schaubühne* (March-June edition 1860), it met with an enthusiastic response from a large number of directors and producers. If anything, many felt that the adapter had preserved too much of the primary text. In 1863, subsequent to his staging of *Die Hermannsschlacht*, Eduard Devrient wrote to Wehl: "Was Ihre Hand an dem Gedicht getan, ist der Aufführung sehr zustatten gekommen: die Handlung gruppiert sich anschaulich und die einzelnen großen dichterischen Schönheiten, der große politische Geist, der durch den wilden Haß des Autors leuchtet, kommen frei zur Geltung."[5] Despite the fact that Wehl's adaptation did serious damage to the dramatist's intent, it still provided the incentive and an acceptable form for production of the play.

The *première*, directed by Friedrich Schwemer, took place on 18 October 1860 in the Stadttheater in Breslau.[6] "Das Haus war leer, die Aufnahme lau, die Inszenierung nach der gewöhnlichen Komödian-tenmanier ohne Anstrengung" (*Breslauer Theater-Nachrichten*).[7] The audience proved generally indifferent and even laughed at inappropriate points, while the actors were "über den verborgenen Inhalt und das, was sie eigentlich darzustellen hätten, noch nicht recht über sich einig" (*Schlesische Zeitung*). Ludwig von Ernst, who played Hermann, succeeded in suggesting the latter's violent hatred of the Romans, but failed to display any human warmth in his scenes with Thusnelda. The critic of the *Theater Nachrichten*, commenting upon Ernst's tendency to bellow, remarked facetiously that "aus den uns zu Gebote stehenden Geschichtsbüchern wenigstens nicht zu ersehen ist, daß Thusnelda taub gewesen sei." The reviewers unanimously praised Joseph Weilenbeck's Varus, an admirable, obedient soldier of his emperor, but found serious fault with Agnes Schäffer's Thusnelda and with the total lack of regard for historical accuracy both in the anachronistic costumes and in the sets. After one further performance, the production had to be withdrawn.

*Die Hermannsschlacht* enjoyed its first limited success in Dresden's Hoftheater on 1 January 1861, largely because of a suitable political atmosphere – the question of German unity had come to the fore with the Schleswig-Holstein affair – and the availability of one of the leading male actors of the day, Bogumil Dawison, whose spontaneous interpretation of the title role won overwhelming public acclaim. Interestingly enough, this staging illustrated the rivalry between two conflicting and competing styles of acting: most of the performers utilized the Weimar classical approach, while Dawison, with his more energetic, realistic mode based on the Hamburg tradition – "Die Wahrheit ist das höchste Gesetz der Kunst, nur was wahr ist, ist schön"[8] – rejected gratuitous rhetoric and intentionally showed up his colleagues by his example. The production received enthusiastic reviews, most of which dealt with the lead's exceptional interpretation. As Dawison later commented to Wehl: "Das Stück ging meisterhaft, das überfüllte Haus horchte atemlos – ich selbst aber wurde siebenmal gerufen, für Dresden eine Seltenheit."[9] Unfortunately, racial prejudice is evident in the evaluation of one theatrical historian, published after the First World War: "Aber eins fehlte Dawison zu seinem Hermann: germanisches Blut." "Wie keine Hamburger und keine Pariser Schule seiner Sprache den slawischen Klang nehmen konnte, so wenig konnten sie aus dem polnischen Juden einen germanischen Heerführer machen."[10] Although many commended the modified Hally episode for its excellent acting, it was cut completely in the third performance out of deference to certain aristocratic female patrons, and the fourth evening was cancelled at the insistence of the king, Johann von Sachsen, in order to avoid adding fuel to the growing demand for German unity.

Several other productions were offered in 1861, such as that in Leipzig's Stadttheater which stirred up the audience by appending the key words "ein freies, einiges Deutschland" to the end of almost every act. Popular taste, which apparently preferred second-rate French drama, was largely responsible for the failure of the play in Hamburg's Stadttheater (21 January 1861), while the Stuttgart Hoftheater's production (4 December 1861), lacking the support of both the court and general public that preferred French and Italian opera, saw only two performances. In Berlin the authorities repudiated the play on the grounds that it would encourage an audience to see in the cunning, deceptive Hermann a symbolic dramatization of the Hohenzollern family.

To commemorate the fiftieth anniversary of the battle of Leipzig, the Hoftheater of Karlsruhe and of Kassel presented *Die Hermannsschlacht* in a production directed by the celebrated Eduard Devrient, noted for his espousal of the idealized Weimar style of acting. Although the principle behind this staging could not be said to accommodate Kleist's realism in either language or content, the interpretation came, according to Fraude, closer to the dramatist's goal than any previous attempt, largely on account of the well-disciplined ensemble acting, the hallmark of the company's director. For the first time Johanna Lange managed to convey both the naive, ostensibly harmless housewife Thusnelda and the cruel avenging princess. The reviewer of the *Schaubühne* (1863) found very little to criticize in Devrient's production: "Gespielt wurde vorzüglich. Herr Schneider [Hermann] war bis auf eine Szene mit Thusnelda, in welcher er in einen allzu bürgerlichmodernen Ton verfiel, ein würdiger Repräsentant. Frau Lange erschöpfte ihre schwierige Aufgabe vollständig und gab uns dadurch wiederholt eine Probe ihrer so reichen Begabung durch Adel des Ausdrucks und würdevolle Haltung ... und so gereicht die Darstellung der *Hermannsschlacht* ... unserem Kunstpersonal zur Ehre, das sich mit aller Liebe dieser nicht leichten Aufgabe gewidmet hatte."[11] Unhappily, the audience, unaccustomed to such strong fare, did not appreciate the significance of the achievement.

After these initial, generally unsuccessful attempts had been made to acquaint the public with Kleist's political play, it disappeared from the German stage until the Franco-Prussian War of 1870–71 rekindled interest in it. Writing for the *National Zeitung* (21 January 1875), Karl Frenzel claimed: "[Hermann] ist doch unser Held, der Deutschen Stolz und Ehre. Wir teilen mit ihm die Siegerfreude." Suddenly, no work in the whole of German literature seemed more topical or modern, as critics pointed to the parallel between the Romans and the French, and to Kleist's anticipation of the Wars of Liberation against Napoleon and the formation of the second "Reich" after the victory over France in 1871. Whereas Hermann's victory-at-all-cost philosophy had previously been dismissed as unacceptable radicalism, Frenzel stressed that the needs of the fatherland rendered any means to defeat an enemy permissible. The reviewer of the *Berliner Tageblatt* (18 April 1875) promoted Joseph von Eichendorff's assessment of the play as "eine großartige Poesie des Hasses, ... der endlich auch einmal in blutroten Flammen aufschlägt." Although Theodor Fontane feared the excesses of German nationalism, he nevertheless praised the drama for the "Gewalt seiner *Gefühls*-Wahrheit" (Fontane's emphasis), "die Einheit des Tones," and above all "die großartige Unsentimentalität, die Schlichtheit des Ausdrucks, auch da noch, wo sich Unerhörtes vollzieht." Calling the work, "im besten Sinn *nationales Tendenzstück*" (Fontane's emphasis), he expressed the wish "daß das Stück dem Repertoire erhalten bleiben möge."[12]

In the 1870s, the Wehl version was discarded in favour of a new one provided by Rudolf Genée who, although he retained more of the original, still tampered with the text quite extensively. He not only removed many of the realistic images, especially from the lighter, more intimate scenes, thus toning down considerably the great vitality of Kleist's poetic language, but he also wrote his own patriotic verses to conclude each act. This adaptation was first used in a Munich production on 6 January 1871, on which occasion the interpolated final lines with their obvious allusion to the contemporary political situation released a storm of enthusiastic applause. However, a theatrical contest in Berlin between a local production at the Schauspielhaus *premièred* on 19 January 1875 and that offered by the Meiningen troupe (10 March 1875), created even more interest. Since the director of the Meininger was a strong believer in preserving the author's text and intent, his version, despite its indebtedness to the Genée adaptation, endeavoured to keep as close as possible to the original, and hence several of the traditionally eliminated scenes or lines reappeared. In addition, *Die Hermannsschlacht* profited extensively from the Meininger's fully earned reputation for the skilful manipulation of mass scenes and the effective use of authentic décor. One of the sets depicting a village scene around a flourishing linden tree in the second act, had a tremendous impact when it returned in the last act, a picture of desolation dominated by the silhouette of the burned linden tree. Historical colour was respected and adhered to even in the least significant detail. Indeed, some critics expressed the opinion that with the emphasis upon magnificent display and authenticity, the staging ran the risk of concentrating upon matters of secondary importance to the detriment of the play's universal message (*Kreuz Zeitung*, 23 April 1875). But for the first time the audience had the distinct impression that the stage extras, especially during the Hally episode or the march of the Romans into the Teutoburg Forest, formed an integral part of a living performance. Again dissent was voiced by a few Berlin critics, perhaps out of loyalty to the obviously overshadowed effort of the Königliches Schauspielhaus; they felt that the excessive activity of the crowds detracted from the main concern of the drama. Notwithstanding these reservations, the Meininger not only scored a triumph comparable to that enjoyed by their *Käthchen von Heilbronn* production – eighty-three performances in all of *Die Hermannsschlacht* – but they also ensured its inclusion in the German theatrical repertoire.

Despite the revival of interest engendered by the Meininger in the 1870s, the fortunes of the drama remained closely linked to the political climate. When in November 1912 the Königliches Schauspielhaus again produced *Die Hermannsschlacht*, this time to commemorate the hundredth anniversary of the Wars of Liberation, the emperor, the empress, and their daughter were in attendance, underlining the tendency to regard the work as a vehicle to induce patriotic sentiment. Not surprisingly, several of the critics saw in the titular hero, "der so klug wie rücksichtslos ist,"[13] a prefiguration of Bismarck: "Hermann der Cherusker hatte sich inzwischen in Otto v. Bismarck verwandelt. Ahnungslos und ahnungsvoll hatte Kleist in seinem Helden ... den Vollender der deutschen Schicksale vorgezeichnet." Out of deference to public sensitivities, director Albert Patry endeavoured to eliminate or at least dilute "das Krankhaft-Dämonische" element, so that he deleted the bear episode. With the same purpose in mind, Otto Sommerstorff played Hermann more in the tradition of the noble hero than the less sympathetic, unscrupulous, barbaric German prince. Since Louise Willig managed to convey only the naive submissiveness of Thusnelda's character, all the commentators felt that she was unable to make credible the vengeful fury of a woman scorned. Hans Mühlhofer's Varus impressed one reviewer with the immense strength of his voice and decisiveness of expression, while Karl von Ledebur's Marbod provided an excellent mixture of "Mißtrauen und Glauben, Instinkt und Gefühl." The only major criticism levelled against this production concerned the night scene in the Teutoburg Forest: the whole set was shrouded in such darkness that the audience remained at a loss as to what was happening on stage.

At no time in the stage history of *Die Hermannsschlacht* has its theatrical fate been more intimately connected with a political regime than during the National Socialist years. Anxious to establish links with older traditions and to gain greater respectability by laying claim to recognized historical predecessors, the party promoted Kleist as the "Verkünder" of Nazi Germany,[14] and *the* classical writer of the Third Reich, a policy which grew out of the movement's own cultural poverty. Most of the leading writers, such as Thomas Mann or Bertolt Brecht, chose exile after Hitler's ascension to power in 1933, and not a single work of note can be directly attributed to pro-Nazi inspiration. Official veneration for Kleist even inspired a radio drama entitled "Kleist. Ein vaterländisches Spiel," written by Hans Franck and broadcast nationwide on the "Stunde der Nation" in April 1933. In this piece of overt propaganda, Franck transformed Kleist's suicide into a sacrificial death so that he might one day rise, "um die Fanfare in dem Endkampf gegen die undeutschen Mächte ... zu blasen."[15] November of the same year witnessed the *première* of *Michael Kohlhaas* in the Württembergisches Staatstheater, an opera in four acts with text and music by Paul von Klenau, based upon Kleist's narrative of the same name.[16] The extent to which Kleist's *Hermannsschlacht* was exploited as an instrument of indoctrination is exemplified by the following sample of suggested essay topics for school students:

13. Welchen Kardinalfehler der Deutschen bekämpft Kleist in seiner *Hermannsschlacht*?
14. *Die Hermannsschlacht* als politisches Bekenntnis Kleists
15. Nicht die Zahl gibt den Ausschlag, sondern der Wille (Adolf Hitler). Weise die Richtigkeit dieses Ausspruches an Kleists *Hermannsschlacht* nach!
    ...
18. Die Menschen sind nichts; ein Mann ist alles. – Nachgewiesen an Kleists *Hermannsschlacht*.[17]

This propaganda was not limited to Germany's schools, for the Kleist-Gesellschaft, led by its president, Professor Minde-Pouet, became a voluntary extension of the Nazi cultural apparatus and remained the only important literary organization which actively supported the National Socialist program for the arts.

Compared to the four theatrical seasons before the Nazi assumption of power, the number of productions and performances of Kleist plays more than doubled. The most popular works were *Der zerbrochene Krug* and *Das Käthchen von Heilbronn* (almost double the stagings), *Prinz Friedrich von Homburg* (three times), and above all *Die Hermannsschlacht* (almost ten times!), with 146 performances in the 1933–34 season the most often produced play in Germany. Kleist's popularity reached its peak during the Bochum Kleist-Woche (1936) held to commemorate the 125th anniversary of his death. For the first time, all of his dramas were mounted with the official blessing and cooperation of both the Kleist-Gesellschaft and the state. A great deal of publicity went into promoting this event through press statements and public speeches which interpreted Kleist in the framework of Nazi ideology. The effort to introduce the cultic aspects so dear to the National Socialists and their glorification of "Blut und Boden" resulted in the extensive utilization of open-air theatres, especially for *Die Hermannsschlacht*, in order to celebrate a "Thingspiel," a festive national assembly complete with party-sponsored parades and youth choirs.

During the imperial period preceding the First World War, Hermann, as previously noted, was frequently paralleled with Bismarck, and it required very little imagination to extend the identification to a far more unscrupulous politician, Adolf Hitler. "Hermann ist im echten Sinn ein Führer, und das bedeutet in einem besonders eigentümlichen Sinne, daß ihm eine Gefolgschaft zugeordnet ist. ... Hermann ist der aus dem Volk, der Rasse herausgewachsene Heros, der die politische Norm gibt. Durch ihn wird somit aus einer Anzahl von Stämmen das Volk, aus dem Volk der Staat."[18]

In addition to justifying the doctrine of the chosen leader, *Die Hermannsschlacht* reinforced and upheld the Nazi concept of total war[19] and readily lent itself to the propagation of the "Volksgemeinschaft" ideology, the nation as one common people. "[Kleist] suchte das Gemeinschaftserlebnis und fand es in Rassebewußtsein und Vaterlandsliebe, und hier glühten in seiner Gestaltungskraft die großen Visionen seiner Dramen auf. Er findet den scharfen Trennungsstrich zwischen romantischer und germanischer Kultur, zwischen der Geistesäußerung nordischer und südlicher Art. Er wurde Künder des deutschen Volksbewußtseins und des heroischen Gedankens, der sich eine neue Ethik schafft."[20] It is true that *Die Hermannsschlacht* does advocate the necessity of doing evil to achieve ultimate good,[21] but the Nazis conveniently overlooked the following lines from the drama spoken by the titular hero:

> Wenn sich der Barden Lied erfüllt,
> Und, unter *einem* [Kleist's emphasis] Königsszepter,
> Jemals die ganze Menschheit sich vereint,
> So läßt, daß es ein Deutscher führt, sich denken,
> Ein Britt', ein Gallier [i.e. a Frenchman!] oder wer ihr wollt;
> Doch nimmer jener Latier, beim Himmel!
> Der keine andre Volksnatur
> Verstehen kann und ehren, als nur seine. (307–14)

Even before Hitler gained political control in 1933, the extreme right made several attempts to infiltrate the theatre and to stir up hatred in the local press for Jewish directors, especially those active in Berlin, such as Max Reinhardt called the "Juden Goldmann," or Leopold Jessner, who was verbally attacked on numerous occasions. This antisemitism surfaced in a review of the production of *Die Hermannsschlacht* for Munich's Prinzregententheater in October 1927, to celebrate the 150th anniversary of Kleist's birth. Written by Alfred Rosenberg, since 1921 the chief editor of the official Nazi paper, *Der Völkische Beobachter*, the article sought to arouse a revolutionary enthusiasm in imitation of the example set by "Hermann unser Weggefährte"[22] and in its invective appealed to the most blatantly racist and chauvinistic prejudices of its readers by quoting or paraphrasing the drama out of context: "Wir wissen, daß heute Juden, Polen und Franzosen die 'ganze Brut ist, die in den Leib Germaniens sich eingefilzt wie ein Insektenschwarm.' Wir wissen, daß ein Ende sein muß mit der Liebespredigt für unsere Feinde, daß heute noch viel mehr als vor 1000 Jahren Haß 'unser Amt ist und unsere Tugend Rache.' Wir wissen auch, was wir zu sagen haben, wenn Angstmänner ihre Feigheit mit der Bemerkung bemänteln wollen, 'es gäbe doch auch gute Juden': dasselbe, was Kleist den Hermann sagen ließ, als seine Gattin ihn um das Leben der 'besten Römer' bat: 'Die Besten, das sind die Schlechtesten.' Denn diese machen uns mürbe im Kampf gegen die andern." Rosenberg felt that the Munich staging had its strong moments, but lacked the passionate fervour which Kleist imparted to the drama. While Armand Zaepfel and Max Nadler gave solid performances as Varus and Marbod respectively, Friedrich Ulmer's well-rounded portrayal of Hermann still neglected to suggest his "magische Eindringlichkeit." The major drawback amounted to an at times ludicrous attempt to realize historical authenticity. "Muß man die Sueven denn wirklich wie die Eskimos vermummt herumlaufen lassen?"

According to Carl Weichardt, Lothar Müthel's new staging of *Die Hermannsschlacht* for Berlin's Schauspielhaus am Gendarmenmarkt, *premièred* on 23 October 1934 (with Prussian prime minister Göring and propaganda minister Goebbels in the audience) was intended to celebrate "ein kultisches Weihespiel unserer Vorfahren ... de[n] ganze[n] Mythos unseres Volksschicksals."[23] The propaganda was fully evident in Weichardt's review: "[U]nsere (heute endlich überwundene) zweitausendjährige Uneinigkeit, unser Haß und unsere Liebe, unsere alles überwindende Kraft, wenn wir eins sind [liegen in dieser Dichtung]. Wir wissen wahrhaftig keinen größeren Helden in der deutschen dramatischen Literatur als Kleists Hermann." As part of the general campaign to bring "die urgermanische Welt in all ihrer Großartigkeit" onto the stage, Traugott Müller designed monumental sets which excessively darkened the scene, interfered with

Müthel's aim of emphasizing the language, and conflicted with the quick dramatic tempo demanded by the plot. The outstanding performer of the evening turned out to be Paul Hartmann who, according to several reports, gave a brilliant portrayal of Hermann: "Wie helle Schwerthiebe klingt es, wenn er Freiheit ruft. ... Am größten aber, Held und Christ zugleich, ist er, wenn er vor der Schlacht gegen Varus den Deutschen zuruft: 'Vergebt, vergeßt, versöhnt, umarmt und liebt euch!'" Eugen Klöpfer played Marbod as "ein vom Mythos umwehter Weiser," especially when he knelt down before Hermann. Whereas the critics generally approved of the male cast, Hilde Weissner as Thusnelda was censured for her inability to suggest the violent potential of her female vanity. "Eine denkwürdige Aufführung, ein unvergeßlicher Abend, das deutscheste Drama. Heinrich von Kleist feierte seinen Einzug ins Dritte Reich, das er vorausgeahnt hatte."[24]

Needless to say, the tremendous popularity enjoyed by *Die Hermannsschlacht* during the National Socialist regime did serious damage to its post-Second-World-War reputation. Ironically, the first production since the war took place in the socialist state of the German Democratic Republic. Just as the Nazis promoted Kleist's patriotic drama as a natural cult celebration performed in predominantly rural areas in open-air theatres, so now, "[im] Staat der Arbeiter und Bauern wurde es zum großen Volkstheater unter freiem Himmel."[25] The staging directed by Rudolf Thieme was presented at the festival of the Harzer Bergtheater zu Thale, first established in 1903 by Dr Ernst Machler to encourage "eine 'von nationaler Eigenart durchtränkte Dramatik'." The alleged association of "das schönste Naturtheater Deutschlands" with its reputation as a witches' dance locale reinforced the connection with the past pagan tradition. The mere decision to produce the play created such a stir in East German theatrical circles that the management felt obliged to seek support from leading artists and intellectuals (Helmuth Holtzhauer, Lion Feuchtwanger), and to justify its choice by the inclusion of a thirty-six page program outlining the pros and cons. The official stance was to regard the play as "Kleists großes Befreiungsdrama," not Prussian but rather German, directed against an army of occupation. However, Till Hoffmann, who played Dagobert in this production, later reported: "Motto der Aufführung war: Die Römer sind die Amerikaner, der Aristan ist Adenauer."[26] Kleist, who saw the contradictions inherent in the German people at the beginning of the nineteenth century, expressed himself in a very extreme fashion. Being ahead of his times, he sensed the problem but failed to see the solution: "Ihm fehlte die Ausgeglichenheit, die die Verbindung mit dem Volk hätte schaffen können; daher blieb er zeit seines Lebens bis zum selbstmörderischen Ende ein isolierter Individualist. Ihm fehlte der Blick, der ihm die verborgenen Qualitäten der Volksmassen erschlossen hätte. Hier zeigt sich die einzige Schwäche der *Hermannsschlacht*." Having little confidence in the people whom he regarded as a mere tool, Kleist longed for a great single leader as Germany's sole source of hope. Hermann Stövesand's acting ability and natural vitality served him well in his rendering of a Hermann who seemed at times to carry the whole performance: "Aber auch seine verhaltenen Szenen mit der ebenfalls sehr ausdrucksstarken Gudrun Neumann [Thusnelda] sind mit faszinierendem Leben erfüllt." The main drawback of the production seems to have been the crowd scenes. During the emotion-packed episode where Teuthold strikes down his own daughter Hally, frequently the highpoint of a production, the Germans, played by upper-year students, came across as being "zu verhalten und unscheinbar." Despite these difficulties in the ensemble acting, the production as a whole earned Victor Weimer's endorsement.

"Hochgestimmter, ungeteilter Beifall und ein Regen von Blumensträußen feierte am Mittwochabend (November, 1982) am Schauspiel Bochum die Premiere der *Hermannsschlacht*".[27] This turned out to be only the beginning of one of the most successful and influential stagings of any of Kleist's dramas, comparable only to Vilar's courageous post-Second-World-War production of *Prinz Friedrich*. In view of the *Hermannsschlacht*'s prominence at the Bochum Kleist Festival in 1936, where it was used to promote a right-wing political ideology, it is surely one of history's ironies that the man largely responsible for both the theatrical and the literary reassessment of this political play was Claus Peymann, "der als linksanarchischer Flügelmann unter Deutschlands Theaterleitern gehandelt wird."[28] The critical reevaluation is evident in the wealth of reviews, a veritable *embarras de richesses*, the majority of which endeavoured to come to terms, aesthetically and intellectually, with the work itself as brought to the reviewer's attention by Peymann's stage triumph. As was confirmed by many commentators, the director achieved his objectives by taking Kleist at his word: "Alles das steht – man glaubt es kaum – wörtlich bei Kleist, dessen Text Peymann nicht antastet";[29] "Kleists Sprache – als kompliziert und unzugänglich geltend – erweist sich in [Hermann's and Thusnelda's] Gesprächen als glasklar, von erstaunlicher Modernität und Aktualität."[30]

Although there appeared to be some confusion as to what constituted the thematic focus of the interpretation, a consensus nevertheless emerged from the reviews, supported by the program notes: "In einem solchen Kampf ...," wrote Peymann, "kann es keine Moral geben. Vielleicht sind unsere Werte von Anstand, Hilfsbereitschaft, Gerechtigkeit nur Privilegien, die mit dem Blut der Völker in der dritten Welt bezahlt werden."[31] Hermann, sporting Che Guevara's "Baskenmütze," has become the archetypical guerilla: "Im Verlauf der Bochumer Aufführung summieren sich bei Hermann, dem Cherusker, die Kennzeichen des modernen Guerilleros: Die utopische Paradies-Perspektive, die Hoffnung auf einen Sieg der Kinder oder Kindes-Kinder. Der finstere Haß, der sich die Skrupellosigkeit der Kampfmittel gestattet, den Vertrauensbruch, die Greuelpropaganda, den ruchlosen Einsatz von Liebe, Lüge und Leichen. Der trotz seiner Aussichtslosigkeit geführte Kampf gegen einen Superstaat. Die Todesbereitschaft und die Todessehnsucht."[32] These tactics and attitudes find their justification in the demands made by wars of liberation "gegen die Kolonialmächte."[33] Whereas Peymann's reading obviously sought to establish a direct link between an historical play and the current political scenario – "Wir haben auf den Proben Mao Tse-tung gelesen"[34] – it still managed to suggest an external, universal message, underlined by costumes (Ursula Renzenbrink) ranging from primitive, horned war-helmets, through Biedermeier top hats and white dress uniforms, to the colonial sun hats worn by the invaders: "Man sah Römer weder als Franzosen noch als Bolivianer, Germanen weder als Sandinisten noch Afghanen, man sah Konstellationen" (Kurasek). Having singled out the extent to which Hermann cunningly manipulates both friend and foe to achieve his goal, Sabine Rauh (*Mannheimer Morgen*, 25 November 1982) designated Peymann's version as "ein psychologisches Stück." Winfried Roesner (*Basler Zeitung*, 19 November 1982) pointed to "die Ambivalenz, die Doppelbödigkeit von Werten" such as unity, justice, freedom, and love, demonstrating how easily force can destroy these values; and Sonja Luyken explained the staging as an attempt, "das Pathos, mit dem aus Hermanns Haß und Grausamkeit eine frühe Einigung deutscher Stämme zur Nation betrieben wird, lächerlich zu machen – und zu zeigen, zu welch schrecklichem Ende nationalistisch drapierte Barbarei führen kann, ja geführt hat" (*Weser-Kurier*, 13/14 November 1982).

The extremely sparse set designed by Vincent Callara consisted of a wide, sloping acting surface with a few dried-out oak leaves and the stage hung with black drapes. The necessary props were provided when required as, for example, in the opening scene where the slaughtered aurochs, dragged down the incline, vomited a considerable quantity of blood. The scenic poverty served to concentrate the spectator's attention on the roles, especially those of Hermann and Thusnelda, played by Gert Voss and Kirsten Dene to enthusiastic acclaim. Indeed, as many commentators observed, "Den Mittelpunkt der Inszenierung und ihren nachhaltigsten Eindruck bilden die Gespräche zwischen Hermann und seiner Königin Thusnelda";[35] these conversations illustrated, to use Georg Hensel's apt formulation, "die beiden Pole der Inszenierung: Gewalt und Gelächter." Peymann simply allowed the implied humour in these *petit-bourgeois*, domestic interludes to realize its full potential, so that "Thuschen" came across as Kleist once described her to Friedrich Christoph Dahlmann: "[M]eine Thusnelda ist brav, aber ein wenig einfältig und eitel, wie heute die Mädchen sind, denen die Franzosen imponieren."[36] The "Gewalt" enters the picture when one bears in mind that the husband is cunningly exploiting his mate as yet another tool to advance his political aspirations.[37]

Several other episodes attracted critical attention primarily for their visual effectiveness and their general applicability, i.e., they did not come across as gags merely for the sake of gags. The potentially repulsive Hally incident Peymann transformed into a ritual complete with ceremonial masks. Once the participants had picked up long ropes tied to various parts of the body and prepared to tear it to pieces, the curtain mercifully fell to signal the intermission. The same ropes resurfaced as a net to entangle the Romans lured into the swamp. For the traditionally most repugnant scene featuring Thusnelda's vicarious avenger, the she-bear, the production offered a cardboard décor with a painted moon and played the sequence as "ein burleskes Märchen": "Der Römer [Ventidius] wird zum Todesopfer eines schwarzen Humors, der die Leiche irreal und belachbar macht" (Hensel). No doubt taking his cue from Komar's description in act five – "Zerschellt ward nun das ganze Römerheer, / Gleich einem Schiff, gewiegt in Klippen, / Und nur die Scheitern hülflos irren / Noch, auf dem Ozean des Siegs, umher!" (2455–58) – Peymann had the defeat of the Roman forces played in slow-motion[38] in an attempt to dramatize Kleist's simile: "[Der] Untergang der römischen Kohorten, deren erhobene Lanzen hin und her schwanken wie Schiffsmasten in schwerer See, findet in wuchtig choreographierter Stilisierung statt."[39] But the most discussed and memorable image concluded the staging: Hermann appeared alone at the front of the stage wearing a Viking helmet, raising his sword aloft with his right arm, a shield in his left hand, while a spotlight cast his silhouette in gigantic proportions onto another projected picture at the back of the stage, depicting the ruins of a bombed-out city to the accompaniment of warlike sound effects. The now dominant heroic shadow reproduced the outline of the famous "Hermannsdenkmal" at the recognition of which the audience broke into laughter. Then Hermann, having examined his monumental likeness, proceeded to cast aside his sword and helmet, thus reverting to the normal dimensions of the partisan with his wife at his side, threatening Rome with eventual and inevitable annihilation. The various critical approaches to this symbolic finale again underline the intellectual stimulus and challenging originality of Peymann's production. Hannes Schmidt interpreted the final visual motif as the destruction of the stereotypical heroic myth and the failure of the new folk hero; Jochen Schmitt-Sasse, as the end of Hermann's identity as a liberator and the beginning of his being exploited as a figure to justify chauvinistic national expansion; Peter Iden, as a warning that those who have evoked the national liberator in the past have only plunged Germany into the catastrophe of war.

While the extensive coverage of this staging was overwhelmingly positive, there was nevertheless one recurring criticism: the marked tendency to play down the irrational, dionysiac element in the text, either by seeking to objectify the horror through distancing the audience from its consequences (the Hally and the "Bärin" episodes), or by minimizing its terrifying presence through humour. Voss's intellectual Hermann could not convey "die Dämonie des Volksführers, der zum Volksverführer wird, der Völkerhaß und Völkermord predigt" (Grack), or as Jörg Johnen expressed it: "Der leidenschaftliche Text von Kleist schwebt wie eine Fata Morgana über einem intellektuellen Ensemble, unnahbar, fern."[40] However, despite these reservations, Ingeborg Schader's general assessment gave credit where credit was due: "Trotz Ent-Heroisierung bleibt als Gesamteindruck, daß Peymann die wegen mangelnder Vergeistigung und Differenzierung vielorts als 'nicht kleistisch' eingestufte *Hermannsschlacht* für unsere Zeit entdeckt hat."

I have described the reaction to the Bochum version at some length, because it not only constituted the first genuine recognition of *Die Hermannsschlacht* as a viable stage work rather than as a piece of theatrical propaganda, but it also made an important contribution to a wider, receptive awareness of Kleist. As Karin Kathrein noted in a review of a 1987 revival of essentially the same production for the Burgtheater, "[zählt] *Die Hermannsschlacht* Peymanns, 1982 in Bochum herausgekommen und seither in aller Welt vorgeführt, ... gewiß zu den hervorragendsten Inszenierungen der letzten Jahre" (*Die Presse*, 23 February 1987). In fact, the further history of the drama consists of numerous guest performances of Peymann's celebrated production beginning with the Jahrhunderthalle in Höchst in the spring of 1983. The same year the staging travelled to Berlin as the final presentation of the Berliner Theatertreffen. Notwithstanding some isolated boos, "obsiegten der Humor, der Witz des Regisseurs im Verein mit vor allem zwei schauspielerischen Leistungen: Kirstin Denes als Germanenkönigin Thusnelda mit dem Ausdruck einer erotisch aus dem Gleis geratenen Hausfrau und Gert Voss, der Hermann dem Cherusker die Züge kleinbürgerlicher Verschlagenheit verleiht."[41] In the context of the "Progetto Germania" (Project Germania) (November 1983), the audience of Rome's Teatro Argentina especially enjoyed the humorous aspects of the *Battaglia di Arminio*, while one reviewer saw in the "müden Helden, der den Krieg läßt, einen Bruder Hamlets" (*La Repubblica*), and another spoke of the drama's "existenziell[e] Paradoxie" (*Corriere della Sera*).[42] *Le Figaro* critic Pierre Marcabru (1 March 1984), in his analysis of *La Bataille d'Armenius* as performed in German at the Théâtre de l'Odéon in Paris, also felt obliged to stress the philosophical aspect by singling out "ces limites [théâtrales] que Claus Peymann a brutalement transgressées, forçant la pièce, la durcissant, jusqu'à en faire une sorte de drame existentiel, sanglant et triste, couleur de nuit et de boue." In Budapest, where *Die Hermannsschlacht* was also warmly welcomed, Tamás Ungvári decried Kleist's play as being an unhealthy symptom of "die deutsche Misere," but still extolled Peymann's production for serving "einer richtigen historischen Tendenz. Jener Tendenz, die der Meister des neuen deutschen Theaters, Brecht, auf seiner eigenen Bühne heimisch gemacht hat und deren Wirkung ... bis nach Bochum reicht."[43] The work's popularity under Peymann's direction would seem to have reached a climax in May 1984 when the ZDF network aired it as part of the series, "Die aktuelle Inszenierung," the first of four televised segments dealing with Kleist. But in March of the next year, in the context of the Europäische Kulturtage, Rüdiger Krohn proclaimed "ein[en] strahlend[en] Triumph phantasievollen, intelligenten Theaters über die Literatur, der nun bei einem Gastspiel in Karlsruhe zu bestaunen ist" in one of the most glowing notices ever: "Wie da am Text herumgefeilt worden ist, wie feinste Nuancen herausgearbeitet, Bezüge im Dialog unterstrichen, ironische Brechungen, Schattierungen des Ausdrucks und charakteristische Momente hörbar gemacht wurden – das war ein Vergnügen besonderer Art."[44] And finally, having been called to assume the directorship of the German-speaking world's oldest classical theatre, the Burgtheater, Peymann mounted his production in May 1987 for the second time in Vienna, again with Dene and Voss[45] in the key roles.

The eighties witnessed a remarkable resurgence of interest in the least popular of Kleist's works, not only on the stage but in literary criticism as well. The latter development began with Jeffrey

Sammons's suitably entitled article, "Rethinking Kleist's *Hermanns-schlacht*,"[46] and continued with several books that aimed at re-evaluating Kleist's second-last play.[47] Peymann's new approach which, as many reviewers pointed out, kept close to the original and based its innovations on hints or images contained within the text, has undoubtedly provided an equally productive incentive for the literary critic to examine the drama from a different perspective. The following passage cited from the "Vorwort" to Wolf Kittler's important and meticulously documented scholarly study, *Die Geburt des Partisanen aus dem Geist der Poesie*, fully exemplifies the mutually beneficial relationship that could and should exist between the theatrical director and the academic critic:

Von faschistischen Ideologen vereinnahmt, danach strikt abgelehnt von einer Literaturkritik, die die zarten psychischen Valeurs und die Subtilitäten von Kleists Sprachskepsis ins Zentrum des philologischen Interesses rückte und die die *Hermannsschlacht* nicht nur aus ideellen, sondern auch aus ästhetischen Gründen für mißlungen hielt, dann aber im Jahre 1982 von Claus Peymann in einer Inszenierung vorgeführt, die bewies, daß man das Stück nur beim Wort zu nehmen braucht, um ein theatralisches Meisterwerk zu produzieren. Der Grund für diese sensationelle Neuentdeckung ist unschwer zu erkennen. *Die Hermannsschlacht* braucht man nicht zu aktualisieren. Als "größte Partisanendichtung aller Zeiten" [Carl Schmitt] gehört sie zu den Zeichen einer Zeit, in der Guerillakampf und internationaler Terrorismus im Schatten der atomaren Bedrohung zu höchster Perfektion getrieben werden.[48]

## CHAPTER SEVEN

# Prinz Friedrich
# von Homburg

Although in more recent times *Prinz Friedrich von Homburg* has rightfully come to be appreciated as Kleist's greatest masterpiece by virtue of its language, its evocative theatrical qualities, and its structure based on contrasts,[1] it was not so recognized throughout much of the nineteenth century. That which does not fit into society's preconceived pattern and which seems to fly in the face of convention is either rejected outright or obliged to conform. Consequently the titular hero was found to be totally unsympathetic, and early critics, such as Ludwig Tieck in his preface to the *Hinterlassene[n] Schriften*, interpreted the play as "ein echt vaterländisches Gedicht," in which "alles erklärt, rühmt und lobt auf angemessene Weise das teure Vaterland."[2] It naturally followed that the Elector, "ein kühner, hochstrebender, edelgebildeter Geist, ein wahrer Stolz des gesamten deutschen Vaterlandes,"[3] held the centre of attention, while the second choice fell to Kottwitz, again out of sentiments of national loyalty. The Prince's somnambulism and, above all, his most unPrussian fear of death – what has been called "the Achilles' heel of Homburg" – offended critics and audiences alike. In his preface, Tieck sought to rationalize the young man's behaviour as being dictated by hallucinations and dreams, i.e., as a temporary self-alienation, and many directors were to put Tieck's suggestion into practice. However, even as early as 4 November 1821 a commentator for the *Dresdner Abendzeitung* put his finger on the real problem: "Seyn wir übrigens billig gegen die, die unbekannt mit dem Stück, an dieser Stelle einen Anstoß finden, weil sie nun einmal gewohnt sind, die Theaterhelden das Leben wie einen Pappenstiel wegwerfen zu sehen."

On 19 March 1810, Kleist wrote to his sister Ulrike: "Jetzt wird ein Stück von mir, das aus der Brandenburgischen Geschichte genommen ist, auf dem Privattheater des Prinzen Radziwil [sic] gegeben, und soll nachher auf die Nationalbühne kommen, und wenn es gedruckt ist, der Königin übergeben werden."[4] Kleist obviously wrote *Prinz Friedrich* out of some sense of nationalistic feeling since he once characterized it to his publisher as "ein *vaterländisches* [Kleist's emphasis] (mit mancherlei Beziehungen),"[5] but unfortunately the "Todesfurcht" scene (III/5) proved to be too bitter a pill for the aristocracy to swallow and efforts to *première* the play in Berlin, including the private performance mentioned above, ended in failure. Naively, in an attempt to solicit support from the court, Kleist dedicated this, his final drama to a descendant of the titular protagonist, the wife of the king's brother, Amalie Marie Anne, Princess of Hessen-Homburg, but the woman in question did everything in her power to prevent the work from being performed. On 16 March 1822, Heinrich Heine wrote in the *Rheinisch-Westphälischer Anzeiger*: "Es ist jetzt bestimmt, daß das Kleistische Schauspiel *Der Prinz von Homburg oder Die Schlacht bei Fehrbellin* nicht auf unserer Bühne erscheinen wird, und zwar, wie ich höre, weil eine edle Dame glaubt, daß ihr Ahnherr in einer unedlen Gestalt darin erscheine. Dieses Stück ist noch immer ein Erisapfel in unsren ästhetischen Gesellschaften. Was mich betrifft, so stimme ich dafür, daß es gleichsam vom Genius der Poesie selbst geschrieben ist."

It was not until 1821, the year in which Tieck published *Prinz Friedrich*, that the innovative director of the Vienna Burgtheater, Joseph Schreyvogel, responsible for launching Austria's greatest dramatist Franz Grillparzer, first dared to produce and direct Kleist's controversial creation. Because censorship in the Danube monarchy was notoriously severe and since several officers in the army and a sovereign prince bore the main character's name, the title was changed to *Die Schlacht bei Fehrbellin*. Other alterations included the omission of all references to living families, the deletion of the political glorification of Brandenburg in the concluding line, and a revision designed by Schreyvogel to lessen the impact of Homburg's very human reactions in act III scene 5, so that it was not death itself, but rather the dread of an ignominious execution as a common criminal which motivated his unheroic behaviour. However, the Viennese public, accustomed to the popular theatre of August Wilhelm Iffland and August von Kotzebue, proved totally unprepared for and incapable of appreciating Kleist's unconventional view of life. A theatre scandal erupted. Early in the performance, at the point where Homburg collapses upon hearing his name, the audience broke out in laughter, while his later confrontation with death led to an uproar and hissing that did not cease until the final curtain. "Ich kann mich nicht erinnern, jemals über die Unverschämtheit irgend eines

Parterres so im Innern empört gewesen zu sein!" Carl Ludwig Costenoble reported, "Einmal, weil das Stück zu ehrenwert für solch eine barbarische Behandlung war, und zweitens, weil die Darsteller unverdient leiden mußten."[6] Despite Costenoble's defence of the actors, inappropriate casting evidently contributed to the overall poor reception. Joseph Koberwein, noted for comic roles, did not achieve or even suggest the dignity and depth of personality of the Elector, while the fifty-year old Maximilian Korn, whose main strength lay in the role of the elegant salon lover, interpreted the part of Homburg almost exclusively from the point of view of a love-stricken youth. The drama was performed four more times until prohibited by the censor at the insistence of Archduke Karl who feared that the prince's disgraceful example would ruin discipline in the army. Strangely enough, the critics defended the play, but the "Todesfurcht" sequence, repudiated by Grillparzer on account of its "Natürlichkeit, die man ausspeien müsse,"[7] alienated sympathy for Homburg's character, described by one critic as "neu und fremd"[8] to the Viennese. Writing in his diary on the night of the *première* (3 October 1821), Schreyvogel noted: "Kleists *Friedrich von Homburg*, das heute unter dem Titel *Die Schlacht von Fehrbellin* gegeben wurde, ist gänzlich (unter Lachen und Zischen) durchgefallen. Die Gemeinheit herrscht im Theater wie überall."[9]

In the hope of offsetting the lack of success in Vienna, Tieck went to considerable lengths to assure a more positive acceptance of *Prinz Friedrich* in Dresden where, after taking up residence, he exerted considerable artistic influence. As part of his program to prepare the public, he published an essay in the *Dresdner Abendzeitung* which sought to justify the prince's fear of death as psychologically true to life and hence demanded by the actual situation. Tieck not only attended the dress rehearsal, but also influenced the decision to follow the printed version as closely as possible, except for the cutting of five-and-one-half lines from the controversial scene. The actor Friedrich Julius, who assumed the title role after much hesitation, feeling that he was too old, directed the production which opened on 6 December 1821. The critics praised this carefully planned effort for its total effect as well as for individual achivements. Julius portrayed Homburg "zur Befriedigung aller Kenner," truly a theatrical *tour de force* if one considers that Tieck characterized the part as "eine der schwierigsten Rollen überhaupt, die noch auf der Bühne dargestellt sind."[10] Helwig, as the Elector, won acclaim for his acting in the concluding scenes, but was found lacking in dignity in the first act, while Friederike Schirmer played Natalie with nobility and sincerity. Since much thought went into the actual staging of group settings, the "Parole," the two garden, and the battle scenes were singled out for special praise, and an overture and interlude composed for the intermissions by Heinrich Marschner, the royal Saxon music director, also made a positive contribution. The Dresden production proved to be a notable event and a convincing demonstration of the drama's stageworthiness. As Tieck observed: "Die Aufführung war so korrekt und präcis, wie ich noch keine hier gesehen habe, so daß auch nichts in den Nebensachen stockte, zweckwidrig erschien oder störend in die Sinne fiel."[11]

The year 1821 witnessed several stagings with varying degrees of success in Breslau, Frankfurt am Main, Karlsruhe, Königsberg, Brünn, and Prague, but few of these had any lasting influence. In 1822, subsequent to his triumph with *Das Käthchen von Heilbronn*, Franz von Holbein endeavoured to rework *Prinz Friedrich* for the stage, but in the view of Tieck and most contemporary commentators, he only managed to distort and destroy Kleist's masterpiece. For example, Holbein's Homburg displays no fear of death, becoming a typical theatrical hero of the early nineteenth century. This butchered version, called a "Romantisches Schauspiel in 4 Abteilungen nach Heinrich von Kleist, für die Bühne bearbeitet von Franz von Holbein," was performed in 1822 in Munich, Stuttgart, Hannover, Würzburg, and Bremen. Still another adaptation appeared in the same year, that of Friedrich Ludwig Schmidt, the director of Hamburg's Stadttheater, who tried to revise the play to meet the particular needs of his playhouse and times. Leaning heavily upon Holbein and presenting the prince in a more positive light, Schmidt's production (8 March 1822) deserves mention for its realistic presentation, the main feature of the Hamburg theatrical school, which revealed itself to be more suitable for a Kleistian work than the idealizing tendencies of the Weimar tradition. Furthermore, the conscious attempt to achieve effective ensemble acting, a feature of the successful Dresden staging and the later Meininger approach, helps to explain the popularity enjoyed by Schmidt's interpretation.

Although Kleist wrote *Prinz Friedrich* for the Berlin stage, it had to wait seven years after its *première* in Vienna for a performance in the Prussian capital, and only then after a concerted campaign on the part of the liberal section of society attracted to the artistic merit of the work. Tieck, the brothers Grimm, Heine, Karl von Holtei, and above all Friedrich Ludwig Robert strongly promoted a Berlin production against the active opposition of the court and military circles. The difficulty was compounded through an arrangement whereby the royal court theatre had a monopoly on all historical dramas and hence, as Eckehard Catholy has pointed out: "In einer Hoftheater-

Aufführung hatte Kleists *Prinz von Homburg* dem Bilde zu genügen, das der Adel und das Militär von der preußischen Geschichte und ihrer eigenen Rolle in dieser Geschichte entworfen hatten und propagierten."[12] Robert wrote a series of articles for the *Morgenblatt* in support of the drama, and, to make it more acceptable to the court, he made two major revisions: he cut the first scene completely in order to avoid the risk of laughter – the crucial events were narrated later in the action – and he shortened the "Todesfurcht" scene by almost one half with the approval of the Berlin critics. As in the Viennese *première*, it is not so much the fear of death, but rather the despair at the prospect of suffering a dishonorable end before a firing squad which motivates the prince. Also, in deference to Berlin decorum, the Elector appeared at the beginning of the last act fully dressed, for a ruler of the house of Brandenburg could not in all decency be shown "*halbentkleidet*" (p. 691) as Kleist's stage directions dictate. To quote the reviewer of the *Vossische Zeitung*, "Mit geschicktem Sinn ist da gekürzt oder geglättet, wo Schroffheiten des hochpoetischen Werkes Anstoß erregten."[13]

The play finally came before the public in Berlin's Hoftheater on 26 July 1828, under the direction of Karl Stawinsky. The sets and costumes were designed with an eye towards historical accuracy, the parts well cast, and the acting adequate. Georg Wilhelm Krüger, noted for his interpretation of the young lover, was commended by all for his rendition of Homburg. Although the performance was widely acclaimed by the critics, the audience remained indifferent. This reaction may be in part explained by the fact that the staging depended heavily upon the Weimar tradition with its declamatory, rhetorical style, and out of respect for this school there was a conscious attempt to stylize the work and transform it into "ein monarchisch-höfisch[es] Repräsentationsstück"[14] along conservative lines. But the court, unable to deny its old prejudices, boycotted the theatre. Indeed, in August 1828, the king's privy councillor, Albrecht, wrote to Count Brühl who took over the directing from Stawinsky: "Des Königs Majestät [Friedrich Wilhelm III] haben befohlen, daß das gestern aufgeführte Stück *Prinz Friedrich von Homburg* niemals wieder gegeben werden soll, und ich beeile mich daher, dies Ew. Hochgeboren ganz ergebenst anzuzeigen."[15] Despite this setback, this court-theatre interpretation not only persisted in Berlin, but spread to many other stages. The custom arose of offering the drama or parts of it, especially the battle scenes, to commemorate great festive events from past history, so that *Prinz Friedrich* enjoyed tremendous popularity as a national poem celebrating the battle of Fehrbellin, the basis of Prussia's military fame. In keeping with this distorted view, the Elector, embodying the spirit of enlightened authority and reflecting the greatness of the Prussian royal family, became the uncontested central character, while Kottwitz, a popular, sought-after role, personified the Prussian fatherland. According to the *Neue Preußische Zeitung* (27 October 1848), when he spoke his lines beginning with "Als mich ein Eid an deine Krone band" (1606), his words found an echo "in jedem preußischen Herzen." Froben's sacrificial death, intended by Kleist as a contrasting episode, was now blown by directors out of all proportion into a major incident with pomp and fanfare. Needless to say, the figure of Homburg suffered severely from this patriotic bias, and directors came to see his role as an illustration of an educational process towards the majestic, self-effacing attitude of the supreme Prussian father figure, the Elector. Consequently, after the revolution of 1848, conservative circles tended to view the drama as advocating the triumph of law and order over arbitrary self-will, and for similar reasons the play was frequently offered after the German victory in the Franco-Prussian War of 1870–71.

From the 1820s until the advent of the Meininger, the German-speaking stages may be said to have reached their nadir in artistic terms. On the one hand the court theatre, as already noted, reflected the lack of discrimination of the ruling class, while the public theatres, concerned primarily with box-office receipts, pandered to public taste. The one truly bright light in this period of decline shone from a stage in Düsseldorf, which was under the very capable management of Karl Immermann. In seeking to revise Kleist's play, he made several cuts and a few additions, alterations determined largely by the physical limitations of a smaller playhouse. Whereas a concession to the court theatre may be ascertained in the cutting of two lines from the objectionable "Todesfurcht" scene, Immermann's adaptation still represented a noteworthy advance over those of his predecessors. The director devoted considerable time and study to making the production acceptable. As he himself remarked: "Gegeben wurde das Stück nicht eher, als bis Jeder, bis zum anmeldenden Bedienten hinab, seine Sache wenigstens so gut machte, wie Naturell und Fleiß es ihm nur irgend gestatteten."[16] The main emphasis upon a lively, carefully organized, dramatic cooperation between the actors, especially during the crowd scenes, drew great support and inspiration from the Düsseldorf painter, Professor Hildebrandt, who assumed responsibility for the artistic arrangement of groups on the stage. The effect thereby achieved exceeded everyone's expectations. Meisinger, who gave a well-rounded portrayal of Natalie, especially during her confrontation with the Electress (a dialogue applauded in mid-scene), provided the most outstanding individual effort. The production was in fact a triumph, a highpoint in Immermann's drive to reform the stage. Writing to his brother, he could justifiably claim: "Es war eine ganz allerliebste, geistvoll und abgerundet in sich zusammenhängende Darstellung, wo selbst das Schwierigste mit einer Leichtigkeit exekutiert wurde, daß ich selbst darüber erstaune."[17] This same production was used on 28 October 1834 for the opening of Düsseldorf's Aktientheater. Friedrich Schenk who played Homburg "war nahezu tadellos. Besonders die Sache zwischen ihm und Hohenzollern im III Akt war beinahe vollkommen."[18] Skilfully designed visual effects and ensemble acting ensured an enthusiastic reception. In what was for the times a daring departure, Karl Immermann, a writer and dramatist in his own right, revealed a true respect for Kleist's words and their intent and by fully exploiting the principle of ensemble performance, he anticipated the major direction the play would follow with distinction some forty years later.

After a long, drawn-out struggle with the censor, *Prinz Friedrich* returned on 5 October 1860 to the Burgtheater for the first time since its *première* there in 1821. The play again failed, and almost as badly as it had done in Schreyvogel's staging. The director, Heinrich Laube, who seems to have had a low regard for Kleist, showed little respect for the original text and miscast the production. The actor most out of place was Emil Franz who played the Elector, in the words of one critic, "mit geradezu beleidigender Nachlässigkeit,"[19] while Gebhardt (Natalie), a beginner, could not even pronounce Kleist's verses correctly. The audience reacted by laughing at the serious parts and by very rarely applauding.

After many years of decline, new blood was brought to the stage and concomitantly to the plays of Kleist with the phenomenal rise of the Meininger troupe as already noted in the chapters on *Käthchen* and *Die Hermannsschlacht*. The "Theaterherzog," turning his back on the court-theatre tradition, insisted on historical realism, aesthetic uniformity, and above all surrender to the poetic word, which he viewed as the soul of the performance.[20] Hence, for the first time the original text, including the "Todesfurcht" scene, was played in its entirety, except for a few cuts necessitated by purely practical considerations. The initial Meininger performance of *Prinz Friedrich* took place on 28 March 1878 in Meiningen. In the words of the critic of the *Grenzbote*: "In diesem Zusammenwirken von prächtiger Dekoration und historisch treuer Kostümierung, von malerisch schöner Gruppierung und präcisem Zusammenspiel steht nun einmal die Meininger Bühne einzig da."[21] In the eyes of some, the company executed the moonlight, battle, and Froben scenes to the point of dramatic perfection. More significantly, the Homburg of Josef Kainz, his most famous role, gained for this character the recognition hitherto accorded to the Elector: "Josef Kainz, dem Wiener, gelang es zum ersten Mal, den Prinzen vollständig von der Schablone des preußischen Offiziers wie von der Schablone des klassischen jungen Helden zu befreien und damit die Dichtung über die gesellschaftliche Bedingtheit des Hoftheaters hinaus zu heben."[22] Kainz, the foremost interpreter of this part in the nineteenth century, captivated his audience and forced it to empathize with Homburg as he passionately pleaded for his life, the episode which had been responsible for the drama's lack of public support and acceptance for more than half a century. Critics have pointed to the shortcomings of this company, mentioning among other things how historical accuracy, i.e., setting the play in seventeenth-century Prussia, detracts from its universal appeal and places matters of secondary concern on the same level with those of primary importance, or how preoccupation with the crowd sequences can obscure what the drama says about the fate of the individual. Nevertheless, the Meininger greatly encouraged the use of the original text and the expenditure of more time and money on ensemble acting, costumes, and sets; travelling widely with *Prinz Friedrich* they gained enthusiastic recognition for it in Prague (1879), Vienna (1879), Düsseldorf (1880), Leipzig (1880), and Budapest (1881).

Before passing on into the twentieth century, I should refer briefly to a celebrated interpretation of Homburg by Adalbert Matkowsky. Reviewing a Berlin performance of 22 October 1889, Theodor Fontane commented:

Herrn Matkowskys Prinz von Hessen-Homburg ist nicht sonderlich nach meinem Geschmack. ... Er spielte den Prinzen nicht schlechter und nicht besser, als er alle derartigen Rollen spielt. Seine Beziehungen zu Kunst (dem Schauspieler [Wilhelm Kunst,] gest. 1859) sind intimer als zur Kunst, aber daß er, als "Heldenspieler" älteren Datums, mit Mitteln wirkt, die heute nicht mehr recht gelten, darin müssen wir uns ergeben und haben nur an Abenden, wo's zu toll kommt, ein Recht zur Auflehnung. ... Es war die herkömmliche degagierte Haltung, der schöne Mann, das Kopfwerfen, die rollenden Molltöne, ... der bekannte Gegensatz von wild und weich, von Sturm und Ruhe – kurzum Matkowsky.[23]

Despite Matkowsky's attempt to achieve a realistic portrait of the prince, especially during his confrontation with death, and despite his efforts to avoid the excesses of Weimar-style histrionic mannerisms, Fontane's review makes it clear that most of the German-speaking stages, aside from that in Meiningen, were still groping their way towards a consistent dramatic approach.[24]

The growing recognition at the beginning of the twentieth century that each play possesses its own distinctive ethos and that this ethos determines the style of performance, from the acting down to the choice of sets, did much to encourage a uniform interpretation of *Prinz Friedrich*. The most innovative figure in this development which freed Kleist from the classical mould of the court theatre was the gifted director, Max Reinhardt, manager of Berlin's Deutsches Theater. More than anything else he sought to underline and, by so doing, to call into question the Prussian military tone commonly associated with this drama. Reinhardt confronted his audience in the very first scene of his production not with the usual rococo castle garden, but with an austere castle portal in the foreground with only a little space for some sand and a bench. He avoided all temptation to indulge in impressive display, even to the extent of ignoring Kleist's stage directions and eliminating the crowd around Froben's coffin, a situation which had traditionally been used as an excuse for a dramatic spectacle. Although Reinhardt was to become famous for his manipulation of crowd scenes, in this instance he staged them sparingly but with a precision and tempo in keeping with his concept of the work as containing a veiled criticism of the military world: "So weht durch das ganze Stück der Hauch echt preußisch-brandenburgischer Kargheit und Sparsamkeit, wobei Reinhardt doch geschickt den Eindruck des Primitiven vermied."[25] The production, directed by Reinhardt himself, had its *première* on 14 September 1907. Friedrich Kayssler portrayed Homburg as a heavy, melancholy prince, totally lacking in youthful spirit; Wilhelm Diegelmann's Elector received a mixed reaction, many finding him monotonous; Else Heins avoided the heroic in her presentation of Natalie but appeared reserved and distant; and Paul Wegener's Kottwitz was celebrated as "die einzige Meisterleistung der Aufführung."[26] Generally, the critics felt that in terms of total effect the Meininger were more successful, but historically Reinhardt's interpretation ultimately paved the way for a greater understanding and wider acceptance of the play.

"In dem Hause, wo vor dem Kriege Kleists dichterisch reifstes und menschlich reichstes Werk meist nur für Festgelegenheiten zweckhaft genug war (man hörte zuletzt nicht nur Kanonendonner, man sah auch Feuerschlünde blitzen), ist gestern das Herz der Dichtung ganz erschlossen worden. Kaum Reinhardt ist es gelungen, den menschlichen Kern so freizulegen, wie es Ludwig Berger in einer wundersam abgewogenen, musikalisch erfühlten, malerisch erschauten Aufführung restlos geglückt ist."[27] Whereas Reinhardt had imposed a militaristic slant upon his staging, Ludwig Berger opted in his production of 13 February 1925 for the Staatliches Schauspielhaus in Berlin, according to Herbert Ihering, to let the work speak for itself. He chose to underline, if anything, the musical themes which he felt were inherent within each of the scenes. This interpretation is of major significance, for director and commentators alike recognized the incontestable poetic merits of Kleist's masterpiece: "Man spürt überall, daß Berger diese Dichtung versteht und bewundert wie wenige, und daß er weder einzelne ihrer Teile noch einzelne ihrer Eigenschaften auf Kosten ihrer einzigartigen Einheitlichkeit herausheben will."[28] This same insistence upon full awareness of artistic quality dictated to a large extent the critical assessment of the acting, which was found to be generally satisfactory. Writing for the *Berliner Börsen-Courier* (14 February 1925), Ihering observed: "Die Harmonie des Werkes übertrug sich, obwohl Paul Hartmann gegen den Fall, gegen den Bau der Sätze spielte. Es gibt heute keinen Prinz von Homburg. Wahrscheinlich ist Hartmann der einzige, der ihn darstellen kann. Aber er spielt menschlich und künstlerisch Schiller."

On 15 September 1933, in an article for the National Socialist paper, *Der Völkische Beobachter*, Hans Christoph Kaergel proclaimed:

Die ersten Klassiker der nationalsozialistischen Literatur ... sind ohne Zweifel Schiller und Kleist. Vornehmlich Heinrich von Kleist. Er ist heute der wirkliche Prophet dieser neuen über uns gekommenen Welt; denn größer konnten die Pflichtgedanken und erhabener nicht dargestellt sein als in seinem *Prinz von Homburg*. Ich möchte unsere bisherige Literaturgeschichte mit ihren Klassikern und Nachklassikern und ihren seltsamen Einteilungen wirklich über den Haufen werfen und nur sagen, daß wir in unserer wesentlichen Literatur vor der Hitlerzeit nur die *Propheten* [Kaergel's emphasis] zu sehen haben, die auf dieses Weltereignis hinweisen. Sie sind deswegen nicht klein, aber sie erhalten eine viel größere und wesentlichere Beziehung zum Volkstum; denn letzten Endes war ihre Sehnsucht jenes Reich, das nun anfängt, durch den Gestaltungswillen Adolf Hitlers, Wirklichkeit zu werden.

The official Nazi view of *Prinz Friedrich* amounted to a throwback to the nationalistic patriotic concept common to the nineteenth century. Indeed several performances took on the distinct flavour of a political program designed to inspire in the Hitler Youth, or later on in young men about to be sent to the front, sentiments of devotion and sacrifice to the fatherland and unquestioned obedience to the supreme authority figure, Adolf Hitler. "Der Kurfürst erzieht den Prinzen zu dieser Haltung, ebenso wie das deutsche Volk seine Führer dazu einst und jetzt dazu zurückführen, wenn es sich selbst im Zweifel oder in der Schande zu verlieren scheint."[29] As an indication of the importance attached to the play, Nazi authorities encouraged and supported its being used to open the first theatre season of the National Socialist state in Krefeld in September 1933; and on the occasion of the German annexation of Austria, it was performed as a symbolic gesture with Hitler himself in the audience. A good example of the extent to which even well established and respected directors had to compromise their artistic integrity can be seen in Jürgen Fehling's 1938 "ecstatic" production. The actors declaimed the final patriotic lines directly to the audience from the front of the stage.

It is not surprising that at the conclusion of the Second World War a certain Nazi stigma should cling to Kleist's masterpiece, thus seriously affecting its public appeal. As François Mauriac noted in an article written for *Le Figaro*, it required no small amount of courage for someone to introduce Kleist to the French public for the very first time so soon after hostilities. The individual who dared to do this at the Festival d'Avignon in the summer of 1951 was no ordinary man of the theatre, but Jean Vilar, the imaginative director of the Théâtre National Populaire, who revitalized the French stage and whom many considered to be one of France's most brilliant directors. Since Vilar believed that one should renounce decorative stage settings that detract from the inherent merits of the work itself, he presented the drama in the courtyard of the Palais des Papes on a bare, sloping surface open to the sky. Nevertheless, effective use of lighting, combined with colourful, contrasting costumes and canons fired from the walls of the castle, provided striking theatrical effects and offset the stark economy of the scenery. Maurice Jarre composed some rather sombre music for the event. The enthusiastic reception enjoyed by this production, called "[une] révélation décisive: celle du chef-d'oeuvre inconnu en France, de Kleist,"[30] can be attributed in part to the popular young screen and stage actor Gérard Philipe who gave a sensitive portrayal of Homburg. "Gérard Philipe succeeded where no other actor of the last one hundred years could have," wrote Morvan Carrefour. "The brilliance of his success was indescribable. Those who saw Gérard Philipe in Avignon would talk of it the rest of their lives."[31] Vilar himself played the Elector as a pragmatic, contrasting figure to the somnambulistic, isolated prince. Although critics did not agree about the message of the production, one point was clear: Vilar sought to downplay the glorification of the state or authority and to focus upon the intimate, personal tragedy. One may therefore view his version as a statement of both "the misery and glory of the human condition."[32] To confirm further Homburg's existential isolation, the final nationalistic outburst simply does not reach him because it has become totally meaningless.

Vilar's Théâtre National Populaire brought essentially the same staging to the Théâtre des Champs-Elysées in Paris, in February 1952, and again it proved to be an unqualified triumph, an even more spectacular one than that achieved by Vilar with Georg Büchner's *Dantons Tod*.[33] Robert Kemp of *Le Monde* (24/25 February 1952) enthused about this "spectacle de majesté et de beauté. ... Comme la pièce de Heinrich von Kleist ... est puissante, généreuse, taillée dans une pierre dure; voilà une réconfortante et excitante soirée!" The production, called the best of the season, ran for forty performances, alternating with Corneille's *Le Cid*, and it was taken on tour to other parts of France, Switzerland, and Germany, notably to the Deutsches Schauspielhaus in Hamburg, where "die Ovationen am Schluß ... nach einer Viertelstunde noch keinen Abschluß gefunden [hatten]."[34] Despite reservations about the ability of Jean Curtis's translation to convey the original, many German critics have acknowledged the great debt owed to Vilar for having instilled new life into and aroused interest in *Prinz Friedrich*. Indeed, the Kleist renaissance on the European stage has been directly attributed to his being rediscovered in post-war France, "ein[em] Frankreich, das aus dem Inferno des zweiten Weltkrieges, der Besetzung, der Verfolgung, des geheimen Widerstandes sich eine Lebensphilosophie zurechtlegen mußte, die ihm eine Existenz trotz eines offenbar sinnlosen Weiterlebens bestätigte, und die sich gerade aus dem Willen, dem Leben einen Sinn zu geben, ergab."[35]

Vilar's influence can be readily ascertained in a version offered as a parting gesture in April 1958 by manager-director Helmut Heinrichs of the Wuppertaler Bühnen before leaving for Munich, where he also produced the play for Munich's Residenztheater in 1963. In this competent effort, which endeavoured to do justice to the text but appears to have lacked the necessary supporting cast, one actor stood out from all the rest, the youthful Werner Meissner. "Daß er – gemessen an Gérard Philipe – in dieser anspruchsvoll somnambulen Rolle noch manche 'Lücken' offenbart," observed the critic of the *Frankfurter Allgemeine Zeitung* (10 April 1958), "sei ihm nicht zu scharf angerechnet." Clearly the model for the interpretation of Homburg's role remained Meissner's French predecessor. Perhaps the austere staging of the drama by Hans Reinhard Müller for Freiburg's Stadttheater in November 1960 also looked to Vilar's example, for Toni Businger's sets consisted solely of a flight of stairs leading into the dark and a bare minimum of stage props. There was no room for displays of military grandeur and hence Müller "konzentrierte das Spiel behutsam auf den Kurfürsten und den Prinzen."[36]

Increasing interest in the drama was further confirmed by the televised Cologne production of Fritz Umgelter which, broadcast on 2 April 1961, received very conflicting reviews. The critic of the *Stuttgarter Zeitung* (7 April 1961) maintained that the dark sets by Theo Zwierski and Helmut Gassner only served to conceal the dream play, that the acting (Thomas Holtzmann as Homburg, Ewald Balser as the Elector) lacked vitality, and that Umgelter had misunderstood Kleist. In contrast, the report of the *Stuttgarter Nachrichten* (4 April 1961) referred to the scenery as having been conceived and constructed "mit großer Intelligenz," complimented both male leads for the interpretations of their respective roles, and praised the performance as "ein spontanes, begeisterndes Erlebnis": "Die Inszenierung betonte sehr schön das Unrealistische, Legendenhafte jenes seltsamen märkischen Sommernachtstraumes unter dem strengen Gestirn Kants durch kunstvolle Gruppierungen und Bildkompositionen, durch schwebendes Lichtspiel."[37]

The tendency to set up Vilar's staging as the ideal continued well into the sixties, as exemplified by Kurt Honolka's review of an interpretation by Heinz Schirk for the opening of the new season in das Kleine Haus der Württembergischen Staatstheater in September 1966: "Wenn Schirk Kleist, so wie er ist, als antiquitiert, als 'zu preußisch' empfindet, warum inszeniert er ihn dann? Jean Vilars [sic], der mit einem französischen *Prinz Friedrich von Homburg* vor etwa zehn Jahren durch Europa reiste und Triumphe für den wahren Kleist erfocht, hatte viel weniger Skrupel – offenbar darf man kein Deutscher sein, um dem Dichter gerecht zu werden."[38] The performance led to what another critic characterized as the Staatstheater's "ersten kleinen Skandal,"[39] since the audience booed the director when he appeared before the curtain at the conclusion of the evening. The general critical consensus deplored the overall poor casting (Ulrich Mötschoß played the Elector with marked indifference and Peter Roggisch proved incapable of suggesting the psychological complexity of Homburg's personality), the inadequate management of the crowd scenes ("Das Schlachtstück vor Fehrbellin spielt sich unsäglich komisch ab"[40]), and Schirk's failure to appreciate the artistic idiom and inner structure of the drama and hence his inability to convey its poetic message: "Der glühende Atem Kleistischer Sprache und szenischer Visionen war penibel gebändigt."[41]

Despite the difficulties in casting and staging Kleist's last play, there were signs that the drama now possessed more than a strictly

West-German appeal. *Die Welt* briefly noted on 27 December 1961 a highly acclaimed Portuguese production in Lisbon's Trinidade-Theater, which went on tour to Brazil, its South-American *première*; and in the summer of 1967 at the Paris Théâtre des Nations Festival, the Düsseldorf Schauspielhaus performed *Prinz Friedrich* and *Tango* by Mrożek, which, according to *The Times* (21 July 1967), "had a tepid welcome, which they deserved." But a noteworthy breakthrough occurred in September 1969 as the play, hitherto banned for political reasons, finally appeared in the German Democratic Republic's Leipzig Schauspielhaus in a staging by Karl Kayser. According to the East Berlin newspaper *Junge Welt*, the performance maintained the "nötige Distanz vor der Ausmalung einer preußisch-militärischen Geschichtsepoche," so that an "erregend[e] Entdeckung des Dramatikers Heinrich von Kleist"[42] could be made. In order to encourage a uniform interpretation of this drama, which takes place "in der Sphäre der reaktionären feudalen Aristokratie und ihrer Offizierskaste,"[43] the weekly paper of the National People's Army published a fictitious literary dialogue between an NCO and a producer, the latter expounding the party line. Consequently, what was once one of the most popular classics of the Third Reich was vindicated for public consumption in a socialist state as "ein poetisches, utopisches Gleichnis auf die Frage der Disziplin, der Staatsraison, auf das Verhältnis zwischen engagiertem Individuum und Staat. ... Ein Modellbild für eine Harmonisierung dieses Verhältnisses auf der Basis der Einsicht in die objektiven Notwendigkeiten." However, this tendency to politicize Kleist was not limited to the GDR. Before Heinz Dietrick Kenter's Heidelberg production of 1971 began, a Goethe quotation was displayed on the back of the set. Three actors then stepped to the apron of the stage and read aloud from Rousseau, Hegel, Bakunin, Brecht, and Adorno. The all-important personal dimension apparently suffered severely through this political-philosophical orientation which became even more blatant as the spectators were greeted after the intermission with a quotation from Mao. "Der Prinz, der im Massenrausch der Schlacht den Tod nicht gescheut hatte, verzweifelte im Todeskerker – hier, im Mitleiden Kleists mit dem Menschen, liegt die Bedeutung dieses Werkes. Die Heidelberger Aufführung konnte das nicht verdeutlichen."[44]

The year 1972 witnessed an exceptional number of attempts to produce *Prinz Friedrich*, for example, in Bad Hersfeld, Kassel, Essling, Marbach, and especially in Berlin, where two stagings vied for the attention of the theatre-going public. The productions in Berlin received extensive coverage, and critics could not resist the temptation to compare the different approaches. Peter Stein's version, mounted for the Schaubühne am Halleschen Ufer and entitled "Kleists Traum vom Prinzen von Homburg," strove above all to abandon the historical situation and to create a fantasy attributed to Kleist: the characters were treated as combining simultaneously a real form (the dramatist's experience of reality) and an ideal form (the poetic realization of a wish-fulfillment). "It was Homburg the somnambulist, the dreamer," to quote Donald Crosby, "rather than Homburg the Prussian General who fascinated Stein."[45] Hans Lietzau of the Schiller Theater offered his interpretation with a reduced cast but in a setting of large proportions. At the back of the vast stage hung two menacing Prussian eagles, and a giant marble statue of a naked, kneeling youth stood in the middle of the floor throughout the performance. As a result the actors seemed small im comparison to the overwhelming set. In contrast, Karl Hermann's décor for the Schaubühne suggested the intimacy of a peep-show with both the stage and the auditorium draped in black cloth.

Refusing to conceal any of the contradictions within the play and hence rejecting Stein's uniformity, Lietzau avoided creating any one dominant impression. Roland Wiegenstein felt, however, that Homburg and Natalie, on whom this performance was centred, held the production together. "Am Schiller-Theater ist der Prinz kein der Tradition entlaufener und dann in sie integrierter preußischer Obrist, den Jugendlichkeit verführt, sondern eher ein später Bruder des Tasso, ein hemmungslos egozentrischer, traumwandlerischer, von sich überzeugter Ekstatiker, dem mehr zufällig die brandenburgische Reiterei anvertraut ist. ... Dem entsprach in einer großen Festigkeit, die aus Allüre und Unschuld zugleich erwuchs, die Natalie der Heidemarie Theobald."[46] In keeping with his limited interpretation and in accordance with the dream logic Stein felt justified in taking considerable liberties with the text. The battle was slowed down; group scenes were exploited to create beautiful, pleasing pictures; the lovers conducted their courtship over the unconscious figure of the Electress; and Homburg (Bruno Ganz) was actually shown his grave. In the final scene, officers, exclaiming the final line, carried an unconscious puppet-prince off the stage, while the prince, appearing suddenly out of a dark corner, displayed the same attitude and trance-like state of mind evident in the opening sequence. The strength of the Schiller-Theater interpretation lay with the excellent cast; the appeal of the production at the Schaubühne rested more upon its offering a feast for the eyes. Although Roland Wiegenstein concluded "Mir scheint, beim Vergleich beider Inszenierungen, die normalere, traditionellere von Lietzau am Ende 'richtiger' als die riskante, auf einen rigorosen Kunstwillen programmierte von Peter

Stein,"[47] the former received a generally bad press, while the latter, heralded as the most significant theatrical event of the 1972/3 season, enjoyed almost unparallelled success and praise. Typical is the following comment by Gerd Vielhaber for the *Nationale Zeitung* (5 December 1972): "Traumverlorenheit und Traumerfüllung zugleich – wann wird dies schon einmal Ereignis? Peter Steins hinreißend schöne Inszenierung von Kleists letztem Stück, dem schwierigsten und größten Drama deutscher Sprache, schenkte in der Berliner Schaubühne am Halle'schen Ufer dies Glück. Seit Jean Vilars unvergessener französischer Adaption mit Gérard Philipe vor zwei Jahrzehnten erlebte man keine vergleichbare szenische Vision mehr dieses hart an die Ufer der Tragödie schwingenden Schauspiels. Eine Mozart-Partitur der Sprache – intoniert als märkisches Nocturno." According to Crosby, a great deal of the success enjoyed by this staging could be attributed to the very capable interpretation of the title role: "[Bruno] Ganz ... portrayed a Homburg whose naiveté and fine nerved sensibility made just those scenes – the opening 'sleep-walking' scene, its inverted pendant at the play's close, and, above all, the notorious 'fear of death' scene in Act III – just the scenes which strain the reader's (or the spectator's) credulity – into the most believable of the play."[48] Not only was the Stein production taken on a successful tour to such cities as Zürich, Vienna, or Stuttgart, but it was transmitted over television (ARD, November 1973; Hessen 3, May 1982), revived for a guest performance at the Warsaw Theatre of the Nations, and even made commercially available as a recording on the DGG label (Deutsche Grammophon Gesellschaft).

A third version of *Prinz Friedrich* had been planned for Berlin in 1972, but at the last moment and without explanation the East German offering was withdrawn. Three years later, the Deutsches Theater in East Berlin performed on the same evening both *Prinz Friedrich* and *Der zerbrochene Krug* in less than three hours. Günther Grack of *Der Tagesspiegel* (22 May 1975) commended director Adolf Dresen's "sportlich[e] Leistung," maintaining that the exacting tempo avoided a modern tendency to drag out the play in search of hidden meaning, but Sibylle Wirsing (*Frankfurter Allgemeine Zeitung*, 5 June 1975) felt that while the swift pace conformed to the needs of the comedy, it did serious damage to the message of *Prinz Friedrich*. Both critics, however, agreed in underlining the basically unproblematic impression left by this "historische Anekdote, die uns nichts mehr angeht, die uns nur noch angenehm unterhält."[49] "Am Ende ist Kleists strittiges Schauspiel ein präzises Lehrstück, das junge Reitergeneräle ermahnt, nicht nachts im Garten zu schwärmen, wenn es anderentags gegen die Schweden geht."[50] The Deutsches Theater subsequently took this double production to Moscow.

After Vilar's great triumph of 1951, only provincial stages in France ventured to produce *Le Prince de Hombourg* (Guy Parigot with the Comédie de l'Ouest in Rennes in 1963, or Raymond Paquet with the Compagnie dramatique d'Aquitaine in Bordeaux in 1968). Unfortunately, when in 1976 Jean Negroni, who took part in Vilar's staging, mounted the drama again for Paris in the Maison des Arts de Créteil, his production left the distinct impression of being presented in homage to the successes of 1951–52: "In den wesentlichen Punkten scheint es eine Rekonstruktion von Vilars Regie, aber ohne ihren Schwung, ihre Inspiration, ihre szenische Poesie und ihr vorzügliches Ensemble."[51] The only variations from the model consisted of an attempt to update the drama with nineteenth-century costumes replacing the more historically accurate Louis XIV style, the use of music borrowed from Gustav Mahler to accompany the prince's dream, a Kafkaesque or Freudian accent tacked on to Bernard Giraudeau's interpretation of Homburg, and finally a very scholarly program note sixty-five pages in length!

In September 1976, Sir Laurence Olivier stepped onto the stage of Manchester's newly constructed Royal Exchange Theatre and formally declared it open. For the inaugural production in this new theatre-in-the-round Caspar Wrede selected Kleist's *Prinz Friedrich* because of the work's continuing relevance (its treatment of the opposition between blind obedience and individual consciousness) and because of his desire to acquaint an English audience with a German drama of high literary merit in a translation by Jonathan Griffin. Although the British *première* generally found enthusiastic endorsements such as that of the *Daily Telegraph*, which referred to it as "exciting entertainment" and a means to provide "new insights into the moral complexity of the most important European nation," J.W. Lambert in his column for *The Sunday Times* (19 September 1976) exhibited little appreciation or enthusiasm either for the work itself, calling it "no more than a standard bit of high Romantic twaddle complete with the 'Is it all a dream?' bit," or for the English production. He laid the blame largely at the feet of the dramatist: "Mr. [Tom] Courtenay, required to project a poetic dreamer who is also an insubordinate soldier and Gilbertian Slave of Duty, gets little help from the text ... until, that is, Homburg (nothing to do with hats) is made to break down at the thought of being executed, and burst out into pitiful appeals for help from otherwise superfluous womanfolk. This is supposed to show that he is a real human being, not just a moral show-off, but it is ill-prepared for by Kleist, and quickly dropped, and there's little Mr. Courtenay can do but act it for what it is worth." This rather uninformed, insensitive assessment contrasts drastically with the opinion held by Alfred Starkmann of *Die Welt* (22 September 1976): "Selten nur kann man einen Schauspieler beobachten, der sich so unbedingt wie er mit seiner Rolle identifiziert, ohne dabei das Maß für den poetischen Text und die erforderte Strenge der Gestik zu verlieren. Selbst in der prekären Szene, da er im Staub um sein Leben fleht, bleibt er trotz seiner Erniedrigung im Bild des Charakters." From all accounts the drama captivated the audience until the very end in spite of Lambert's concluding lament: "If only Verdi had made an opera out of it!"

"The Prince of Homburg was Heinrich von Kleist's last play, completed in 1811, the year the author committed suicide. Although the play has come to be accepted as a classic, the production of the Chelsea Theater Center which opened last night [30 October 1976] at the Brooklyn Academy of Music, is the professional American premiere. That it should take 165 years for the work to be produced here is astonishing and it is characteristic of Chelsea's daring that it should be the first to attempt it." The above comment was made by the *The New York Times*'s drama critic Mel Gussow (1 November 1976) in his review of a production which required more than a year to prepare and which owed its existence largely to the efforts of artistic director Robert Kalfin. It was indeed a "daring achievement," for Kalfin had neither a suitably large theatre nor a cast familiar with Kleist. At best, a few New Yorkers may have been aware of Kleist's name through the showing of Eric Rohmer's film "The Countess of O," based on one of his short narratives. Taking a clue from the play itself, Kalfin opted, as the German producer Peter Stein had done, to treat the drama as a dream experience: "In this interpretation the prince becomes an enchanted child, caught up in an approximation of a fairy tale."[52] However, Gussow went on to point out that the rest of the performance failed to sustain this illusion. Although Gussow and Walter Kerr (*New York Times*, 7 November 1976) found fault with Frank Langella's at times melodramatic portrayal of the Prince, Gerard H. Wilk of *Der Tagesspiegel* (30 November 1976) praised his acting as "überzeugend und oft mitreißend." Patricia Elliot as Natalie conveyed grace and dignity in her role but, according to Gussow, came dangerously close to self-parody. The concluding sequences – again recalling to mind Stein's "Kleists Traum vom Prinzen von Homburg" – saw the officers carry what seemed to be Homburg into the castle, while a second incarnation of the prince dreamily wound a victory wreath. "Dann tritt Frank Langella vor das Publikum, stumm, verwundert, mit leisem Lächeln – war alles nur ein Traum?" (Wilk). Although the New York critics generally found the production, to quote Walter Kerr "irrelevant and at best inconsistent," it nevertheless engendered sufficient interest and enthusiasm to warrant a television version co-directed by Kalfin and Kirk Browning, filmed at Biltmore House, an historical landmark in Asheville, NC. It was aired on WNET, Public Broadcasting System, in April 1977, as part of the Theater in America series.[53]

In March of 1978, Hamburg's Deutsches Schauspielhaus furnished the means for the realization of an experiment conceived of and prepared for in East Berlin. The idea was to perform "zwei politische Stücke, zwei Beiträge zur 'deutschen Misere'" (*Süddeutsche Zeitung*, 23/24 March 1978) – *Prinz Friedrich* and Brecht's *Fatzer Fragment* – on the same day with the same actors and directors, separated by a two-hour intermission (an unlikely combination of plays if one considers Brecht's dislike for Kleist's drama).[54] In an interview conducted by *Der Spiegel*, 6 March 1978, the young directors from the German Democratic Republic, Manfred Karge and Matthias Langhoff, who were unable to find a sympathetic ear for their project amongst the East German authorities, enlarged upon the common perspective from which they had endeavoured to view the dramas – the fear and hysteria associated with terrorism. "Karge: Ich glaube ..., ganz richtig verstanden, daß in diesem jungen Burschen [Homburg] etwas ungeheuer Anarchistisches ist, was mit aller Gewalt zerstört werden soll. Ich finde eigentlich das Interessante an dem Stück, daß der Homburg wirklich dadurch, daß er am Schluß weiterleben muß, umgebracht wird." In keeping with Brecht's concept that only the "Materialwert" of the classics should be emphasized and exploited by the modern stage, Karge and Langhoff took great liberties with Kleist's drama, beginning with the language which was whispered, shouted, and generally abused in an effort to achieve maximum emotional impact to the detriment of its poetic content. Other startling innovations included an evil, bald-headed Elector (Christoph Quest) who bellowed at his officers, a prison cage which could be quickly lowered or raised, an effective stylization of the battle reports, the appearance of a naked Homburg (Heinrich Giskes) in the final garden sequence, the prince's frustrated attempt at suicide at the conclusion, and the omnipresent potatoes: "In allen Szenen, ob nun im altfranzösischen Schloßgarten oder bei Fehrbellin, ob im Gefängnis oder im Damengemach, liegen in dieser Inszenierung Kartoffeln herum, und bei der Schlußapotheose bringt Stranz dem Prinzen statt Nelken und Levkojen ebenfalls nichts als Kartoffeln, obwohl es zur Zeit des Großen Kurfürsten noch gar keine Kartoffeln in Preußen gab."[55] This novel *Homburg/Fatzer* double production met with a mixed reaction on the part of the critics, ranging from "Radikales Theater – extrem spannend und extrem schwierig dazu"[56] to "Am Ende dieses peinvollen, sechs Stunden langen Theatertages fragten sich die meisten Hamburger verwundert, wie eine seriöse Agentur dazu kommt, derartigen Stuß zu vermitteln, und noch dazu ins 'kapitalistische Ausland', wo man doch immer besonders guten Eindruck machen will."[57] This same staging was brought to West Berlin only a few months later where, according to Karin Kathrein, it provided a "Skandalaufführung, der eine wilde, suggestive, gewalttätige Wirkung nicht abzusprechen ist."[58]

"Das Reiterstandbild eines Fürsten, auf den Vorhang projiziert. Schicht um Schicht heben sich Schleier, und aus dem Schatten tritt eine Gestalt auf uns zu – *Prinz Friedrich von Homburg*. Kleists geniales Werk wird für uns Heutige lebendig. In einer sehr klaren, kargen, etwas spröden Burgtheaterinszenierung, die nichts aufzwingt, nur die Sicht einstellt auf ein Schauspiel, dessen Faszination über das Dichterische, Theatralische hinaus in der unvergänglich eingewebten Tragödie eines Menschen, der Tragödie eines Volkes liegt."[59] With these words Karin Kathrein began her enthusiastic article, describing a unique production directed by the manager of the East German Berliner Ensemble, Manfred Wekwerth, for Austria's most traditional theatre. This production may well be characterized as a middle-of-the-road approach, avoiding the extreme aestheticism of Peter Stein's "Traum vom Prinzen von Homburg" or the down-to-earth terror of Karge and Langhoff's nightmare. Influenced by Brecht, Wekwerth regarded the drama as a demonstration of how "die Helden eines präzise funktionierenden Militärapparates geschaffen [werden]," but fortunately, since he also elected to respect the original text, the audience could draw its own conclusions. The cast handled the acting in a very capable manner: Elisabeth Augustin as Natalie was "kraftvoll und zugleich mädchenhaft," Heinz Reincke put forward "eine beeindruckende Figur" as Kottwitz, and Heinz Moog's Elector was "weniger imposant und ehrfurchtgebietend als klug die Situation durchschauend." Helmut Lohner, however, supplied the dramatic highlight of the evening, "einen hinreißenden, frischen Jüngling, träumerisch und frech, arglos und sorglos, ein freier Vogel in seiner Umgebung, von dem es nicht wundert, daß ihm ausnahmslos alle Herzen zufliegen." This interpretation, called "klassisch und modern zugleich"[60] and "packendes Theater, nicht immer ganz staubfrei, aber doch zeitgemäß im Gesamteindruck,"[61] turned out to be a great success with both reviewers and public. Back on 4 December 1821, at the *première* of *Prinz Friedrich*, the critic of the

*Dresdner Abendzeitung* had lamented: "Der Charakter [des Prinzen] war [den Wienern] neu und fremd." The response now had come full circle. What had once been considered foreign was now recognized as a perceptive symbol of the German-speaking people "nach den Erfahrungen von zwei Weltkriegen";[62] what had once been greeted with boos and hisses was now celebrated "mit stürmischem Beifall, mit Bravo- und Jubelrufen."[63]

The militaristic bias of Karge/Langhoff which saw Prussian discipline as an anticipation of Nazi mentality,[64] can also be detected in Pétrika Ionesco's production for the Festival de Carcassonne in the summer of 1979. Taking full advantage of the open-air stage before the local castle, Bradu Boruzescu designed "au centre des murailles, tout un territoire fantastique et baroque, avec arcs de triomphe, obélisques, fabriques, parc à l'allemande,"[65] a conglomerate of props intended to underscore "la Prusse militariste que Kleist croyait célébrer et qu'en réalité il condamne à travers son prince."[66] In this romantic operatic version, accompanied by melodies from Verdi and Wagner and by the spectacles of torch-lit parades, flying doves, horses, and special lighting effects, Ionesco set the senseless devotion to duty demanded of the soldier against the solitude and the desire to live of the individual, Homburg, played by Marcel Bozonnet. (According to Mathilde La Bardonnie, Bozonnet stole the show.[67]) Goose-stepping soldiers buried Froben, the epitome of self-sacrifice to the state; but nowhere did the director's intent become more evident than in the revised conclusion. A firing squad, having executed the prince, dragged his body before an obelisk to the accompaniment of cries of victory and the thunder of cannons: "Tous les autres personnages du drame, bannières levées, défilent devant le cadavre. Sans même un regard: ce Prince n'était qu'un fou."[68]

Karge and Langhoff were not the only directors to pursue greater artistic freedom in the Federal Republic, when denied an opportunity to perform their own particular version in the German Democratic Republic. Jürgen Gosch, originally from East Berlin, accepted an invitation to visit the Staatsschauspiel in Hannover, where he chose to direct *Prinz Friedrich* in March 1980 for his Federal Republic début. As the curtain rose, the audience observed Homburg (Wolfgang Ransmayer) "in Unterwäsche am hinteren Teil der Bühne, mit dem Rücken zu den Betrachtern, als ginge er einer ganz anderen Verrichtung nach."[69] The courtiers – the men in tails, the ladies in long silk gowns – made their entrance with champagne glasses in hand and obviously under the influence. Emotional shock was not limited, however, to the somnambulistic prince, for he seized in turn the members of the party, embraced them violently and left them all gasping for breath. At the conclusion of the evening, once Homburg had received the laurel wreath (he was crowned seated on a chair bolted to the floor), he withdrew a dress suit from a cupboard and dragged it across the stage, while an insignificant old lady-in-waiting exclaimed in a very conventional fashion: "In Staub mit allen Feinden Brandenburgs!" As one critic observed, "Daß Homburg nun in die Gesellschaft aufgenommen ist, erscheint in diesem Moment tödlicher als der Tod."[70] The chair fastened to the floor was part of Gosch's overall "pedagogical" interpretation. On the basis of the Elector's query to his officers in the fifth act – "Die Schule dieser Tage durchgegangen, / Wollt ihrs zum vierten Male mit ihm [Homburg] wagen?" (1822–3) – he decided, according to Andreas Roßmann, to interpret the play as depicting "[die] Schule (der Nation) ... Prinz Friedrich von Homburg – eine Erziehung in Preußen."[71] As an extension of the unifying theme, the "Parole" scene looked like a dancing lesson, the officers were grouped like a school class for the battle of Fehrbellin, and Homburg performed gymnastic exercises in his cell: "Die Schule, die als Unterdrückungsinstrument des Staates das Dasein fast völlig durchdringt, ... ist das Motiv, das Gosch schon dadurch mannigfaltig variiert, daß er lauter ich-schwache, abgerichtete, gedemütigte und sich demütigende junge Menschen vorstellt." These "junge Menschen" included Natalie, who, in the scene where she pleads for her cousin's life, rubbed her uncle's thighs in a fawning manner. Whereas Roßmann congratulated the city of Hannover for having made possible the theatrical realization of Gosch's historical, anti-idealistic approach, Ursula Bunk recorded the negative reaction on the part of the audience – some left before the final curtain, while others expressed their disapproval through catcalls and boos – and took issue with the lack of respect for the author's intent: "Kleist meinte es wohl anders."

A further sign of the renaissance of Kleist's dramas both in and outside the German-speaking countries, was László Márton's production of Prinz Friedrich in May 1980 in Budapest. (The official Hungarian première took place in 1973 in Kaposvár.) An effective exploitation of space and projected images proved to be the most memorable aspect of this Budapest staging. Against a dark background were set three large walls which could be easily moved to create continually varied scenes, and onto which were projected larger-than-life paintings of soldiers, horses, or dream images as demanded by the plot. "Doch daß diese ganze bunte Kavalkade an sich großartiger Ideen nicht immer eine funktionelle Berechtigung hatte, sondern eher zu einer falschen Übertönung führte, lag vor allem an den Schauspielern."[72] In the view of Agnes Tasnádi, only Géza D. Hegedüs was convincing as the prince.

In the year 1982, Kleist's reputation outside Germany continued to grow. In France, Patrick Guinand staged for the Théâtre de l'Odéon a *Prince de Hombourg*, which focussed on "conflits d'examens de conscience à propos du droit de désobéissance militaire."[73] Across the channel, a London *première* occasioned considerable critical interest as John Burgess in April 1982 offered on the smallest stage of the National Theatre, the Cottesloe, a "schlichte, doch saubere und zügige Inszenierung," on which the director imposed no particular point of view, "um den unbekannten Klassiker für sich selber sprechen zu lassen."[74] This analysis by Julian Exner was supported by Benedict Nightingale's judgment: "It is so drab and plodding, so lacking in any variety of excitement or any variety of variety, that it must surely have been deliberate."[75] Despite the omission of "any strong directorial viewpoint,"[76] one can deduce from the notices a tendency in the production to regard Kleist's final work as a manifestation of the military mentality that the public commonly associates with Germany's Prussian heritage. "The young Prince of Homburg," observed Stephen Spender, "... is perhaps not so much the portrait of a Romantic dreamer as the persona of the poet imprisoned in his world of the Prussian aristocratic military hierarchy ...,"[77] an impression sustained by the presence of a "gun-metal sky cloth" throughout the staging and the transfer of the action to the war-torn Napoleonic era. Patrick Drury did not project the emotional intensity which Tom Courtenay had brought to Homburg's character in the Manchester version of 1976, while "Robert Urquhart as the Elector [gave] what [was] probably the best performance here as an authoritarian who is capable of feeling and imagination."[78] The major drawback of the London *première*, singled out by German and English critics alike, was translator John James's inability to "convey either the powerful rhythmic unity of Kleist or his hard, severe, clean-cut imagery. ... Perhaps that is too much to ask, but the weakness of the Cottesloe production is probably to be traced mostly to the English text."

Ivo Chiesa, general director of the Stabile in Genoa, announced in July 1982 that its new theatrical season, dedicated to the rehabilitation of Kleist, would include *Prinz Friedrich*, *Der zerbrochene Krug* and *Amphitryon* and that a debate about Kleist's contribution to drama, involving directors, actors, set designers, etc. would take place in December. This program had evolved out of an even more ambitious scheme, the mounting of those plays by Kleist, Schiller, Goethe,

Büchner, Lenz, Tieck, and Grabbe, which mirrored the important changes occurring at the end of the eighteenth and the beginning of the nineteenth centuries. Since the project turned out to be impracticable, the organizers resolved to limit their project to Kleist, because his dramas, more than any others, demonstrated the contradictions inherent in an age in which Romanticism and Classicism existed side by side. The first offering, *Principe di Homburg*, opened in October 1982 in the Politeama di Genova under the direction of one of Giorgio Strehler's students, Walter Pagliaro. In an interpretation reminiscent of Peter Stein's reading, Pagliaro viewed the play as "un viaggio onerico" (a dream voyage),[79] as a fable told in a dream against a background of veils and curtains, "fluidi e fantomatici" (flowing and ghostlike),[80] arranged by Pier Luigi Pizzi. The actors made extensive use of candles to move about the dark set, and this device had the added advantage of casting large, ominous shadows and creating an atmosphere described by Roberto De Monticelli as "prevalenti penombre" (predominantly shadowy). This reviewer censored the production for having "[t]roppo sogno e poca realtà" (too much dream and little reality), but in an article in which Pagliaro defended his position, the latter argued that it is difficult to define the boundaries separating illusion from reality in *Prinz Friedrich*, and that other characters, not just Homburg, share some aspects of the improbable associated with dreams. Conceding, for example, that the Elector represents order and Prussian authority, the director nevertheless asked rhetorically: "E' così, ma si può immaginare realmente un Grande Elettore di Brandenburgo impelagarsi in uno 'scherzo ambiguo' alla vigilia di una battaglia importante?" (It is so, but can one really imagine a Grand Elector of Brandenburg getting involved in an 'ambiguous joke' on the eve of an important battle?), and he proposed as a solution to the many other contradictions within the play the general model of "un sonno infantile" (a childlike sleep).[81]

Ferrara hosted the second Italian version of *Il Principe di Homburg* in November 1982, one directed by and starring Gabriele Lavia. He elected to present a popular and fiery spectacle, "un dramma di conquista e di gloria, una lotta tra la legge e la coscienza (a drama of conquest and glory, a struggle between law and conscience)."[82] While attempting to capture the historical Romantic flavour of a work distanced by some two hundred years from our own times, and refusing to modernize its essential themes, Lavia realized on stage, in the opinion of Guido Davico Bonino (*La Stampa*, 13 November 1982); "'chiarezza' dello spettacolo: la sua gradualità e sistematicità, persin didattica, di segni (the 'clarity' of the spectacle: the gradual and systematic, even didactic, use of signs)." Some of these signs were colours: green, the illusion of hope; dark red, the blood of the battlefield; black, conflict and military repression; and a surrealistic white suggesting the harmony of existence. The performance proceeded at a very fast pace in order to produce "quasi una frenesia della finzione" (almost a frenzy of make-believe), especially in the group scenes; and the rhythm only slackened to a slower tempo during the long monologues or duologues. Lavia's portrayal of Homburg's fear of death and of his repudiation of Natalie represented for Bonino the highpoint of the evening "grazie alla finezza dell'interprete" (thanks to the finesse of the interpreter). In the same article for the *Corriere della Sera* (14 November 1982) in which Pagliaro outlined his views, Lavia insisted, "In Kleist poeta e drammaturgo si fondono in un'anima sola" (In Kleist poet and dramatist are fused into one single soul). For this reason one should respect the poetic dimension and at the same time resist the temptation to overemphasize one aspect of a subplot: the director should strive to "raccontare una storia densa di significati" (narrate a story filled with meanings). Lavia, who has earned for himself a reputation as the most notable interpreter of Kleist in Italy, brought his production to Rome in the same year.

There were three major productions of *Prinz Friedrich* in Germany in 1982, the most novel of which was the return of Hans Werner Henze's opera to the Staatstheater in Darmstadt, twelve years after its first performance in Hamburg's Staatsoper. After its *première*, the original staging went on tour to Spoleto, Paris, Frankfurt, London, Münster, Gelsenkirchen, Düsseldorf, Augsburg, Lyon, and finally Graz in 1967. The opera then disappeared from the repertoire until director Kurt Horres decided to revive it as part of his effort to promote significant contributions to modern musical theatre. Lucchino Visconti had drawn Henze's attention to Kleist's play as a suitable subject and Ingeborg Bachmann had supplied an adaptation that abridged but respected the original text. Because Henze felt particularly drawn to the figure of Homburg, "der nun, als ein vom Realitätsprinzip unberührter Anti-Held, fremd und unintegrierbar seine Innenwelt gegen die brandenburgische Außenwelt setzt,"[83] the subjective dream world of the titular protagonist dominates over the objective "real" world of the state; and in this sense, as Gerhard Koch pointed out, Henze's perspective – "das Ganze ein Traum"[84] – anticipated Peter Stein's dream version for Berlin's Schaubühne. Consequently, the action between the introductory and concluding garden scenes comes across as a series of stages in an extended dream sequence, tragically shattered in the final segment. "Homburg ist auch in der letzten Szene eingehüllt in seine somnambule, irreale

Klangsphäre, aus der sich der hymnische Abgang zu den Worten 'In Staub mit allen Feinden Brandenburgs' brüchig und grell heraushebt, ein jähes Erwachen in eine Wirklichkeit hinein, die nicht die des traumhaften Prinzen ist. Die Handlung hat kein Happy-End."[85] The music, dedicated to Stravinsky, owes much to its acknowledged inspiration: "Strawinskysche Blechbläser-Vereisung kennzeichnet vor allem die Sphäre des Kurfürsten." Horre's staging remained basically true to the composer's interpretation – the sets conveyed the unreality and only the costumes suggested the Prussian milieu – and achieved the underlying objective, the creation of "ein ästhetisches Ereignis."[86] The orchestra, under conductor Hans Drewanz, and the cast, including baritone Thomas Hampson (Homburg) and tenor George Maran (Elector), received generally positive but not enthusiastic reviews. "Die Darmstädter Aufführung ist allemal verdienstvoll," Koch wrote in summary, "nicht zuletzt, weil sie das Werk überhaupt wieder einmal zur Diskussion stellt. Aber allzu beredte Fürsprache für das Stück leistet sie nun auch nicht gerade. Fast gewinnt man den Eindruck einer Pflichtübung."

In September of the same year Germany witnessed two productions of the stage play, one in the Democratic Republic and the other in the Federal Republic, and these tended to reflect the political and social differences between East and West. Günter Rüger's presentation for Potsdam's Hans-Otto-Theater highlighted the "Staatspragmatismus des Kurfürsten" at the expense of "die ideale Traumwelt des Prinzen." "Man sieht einen Jüngling, der manipulierbereit ist und manipuliert wird. Das Schlußbild sagt's, wenn die Offiziere ihn hinten wegtragen als einen im Grunde eher vom Leben Gefoppten als zum Leben Begnadigten, dieweil der Kurfürst, den breiten Rücken zur Rampe, breitbeinig als Denkmal steht, den schweren Stock demonstrativ in Händen."[87] Rainer Kerndl attributed the dominance of the Elector in part to the "darstellerischen Glanzleistung" of Hansjürgen Hürrig who easily won the full support and admiration of the audience. In a different approach, Valentin Jeker, noted for his theatrical experiments (he staged a dramatization of Anna Seghers's novel *Transit* in Freiburg's Alter Wiehre-Bahnhof) saw in *Prinz Friedrich* a "Staats- und Familiendrama zugleich. Die staatstragende Familie, das ist hier der Offiziers-Clan; Despot und Gesetzgeber: der patriarchalische Kurfürst. Und dem stellt der Prinz die Frage nach der Autorität, nach Legitimität."[88] In this version for Freiburg's Großes Haus, Homburg (Karsten Gaul) embodied in his "Sinnlichkeit" und "Humanität" a serious challenge to the pragmatism, the cold rationalism of the state father. Part of the originality of this interpretation derived from the attempt to realize Kleist's poetic images visually in the expressionistic tradition. Taking a cue from Hohenzollern's comment: "Daß hier kein Spiegel in der Nähe ist! / Er würd ihm eitel, wie ein Mädchen nahn" (61–2), Jeker had Homburg in the opening scene preen himself before a full-length mirror in narcissistic self-indulgence. A ladder, no doubt inspired by the prince's exclamation: "O Cäsar Divus! / Die Leiter setz ich an, an deinen Stern!" (713–4) led from a dark cloth depicting the hind quarters of some Prussian war horses up to a "Neonkasten": "Da oben, im hellen Neonquader steht immer wieder, starr, zum Denkmal versteinert, der Kurfürst."[89] But the most memorable dramatization of a metaphor occurred in the introductory sequence when Homburg, having climbed a few steps up the ladder, tried to fly and crashed to the floor, a feat attempted later on in the evening by Natalie as well: "Das Experiment, die Schwerkraft der Realität im Gefühlssturm zu überwinden scheitert." Although both the East and West German stagings refused to go along with Kleist's bid to cover up the play's irreconcilable conflicts with a contrived conciliatory conclusion, Rüger left his audience with the positive impression of a triumphant Elector, while Jeker, borrowing from the dramatist's biography, had Homburg, once the warmongering officers had exited, remain alone on the stage and place a pistol to his temple as the curtain fell.

Except for Oskar Werner's poorly received "Paraphrase auf Kleist"[90] for the Wachau-Festival in the Brauhofsaal in Krems, the only other major production of 1983, one attracting considerable attention, was that presented by Hansgünther Heyme in Stuttgart's Altes Schauspielhaus. The critical response was frequently contradictory: "Eine Sprechtechnik von so außerordentlicher Klarheit und Nuanciertheit, wie man das in Deutschland seit Jahrzehnten nicht mehr erlebt hat";[91] "Kaum war, der schlechten Artikulation wegen, dem Gesprochenen zu folgen, der Sinn flog am Gehör vorüber, von Schönheit ... keine Rede."[92] It ranged from unqualified endorsement – "Ein Wunder von einer Inszenierung. Ein Höhepunkt im Schaffen des Regisseurs Hansgünther Heyme"[93] – to sarcastic rejection – "Mit dieser Aufführung allerdings scheint [Heyme] vor der häufigen Abweisung, die ihm im Publikum begegnete, kapituliert zu haben, um sie mit Unfreundlichkeit und mit der Schlampigkeit eines stark gekürzten Spiels voll schnoddriger Reden, motziger Mienen und wegwerfender Gesten beantwortet zu haben."[94] The latter negative review, reflecting the majority, cites two of the main criticisms levelled at the Stuttgart production: Heyme's reduction of the playing time to two hours by cutting approximately one quarter of the lines (a stratagem to which several directors have resorted since the war) and his alleged "capitulation" to public pressure. As if to contradict his previous reputation as "ein heftiger Zertrümmerer von Stücken,"[95] Heyme reportedly took the position that with the failure of the current educational system to acquaint students with the works of the classical German authors, he, as director, would have to assume this responsibility and allow the text to speak for itself.[96] Such an aim led no doubt to the often reiterated objection, "[Es] war nicht auszumachen, was Heyme wollte,"[97] and it may explain the varied claims as to what his staging was intended to portray: a nonpolemic analysis of authority and obedience,[98] an anti-war statement,[99] a dream fantasy,[100] or an exposure of the relationship between physical well-being and spiritual decay.[101] Wolf Münzner's décor did, however, provide some visual sense of unity, because the production, intended to reflect the year 1675 and the battle of Fehrbellin, set the baroque (the men wore colourful historical uniforms, while the ladies were clothed in white wigs and long, flowing black capes) against a stage that was bare, except for two rows of period chairs lined up opposite one another in groupings of three and eight. Departures from a strict adherence to the text entailed Homburg's attempted rape of Natalie (Inge Anderson) in the opening dream sequence, a noisy emphasis on "die preußisch zuchtvolle Männerwelt,"[102] and the half-naked Volker Lippmann's pantomimic portrayal of Homburg's *Todesangst* scene. Despite the low critical opinion of this version, it sparked a debate in the press and earned the spectators' stamp of approval: "Das Publikum dankte für diese Abfertigung mit eifrigem Beifall."[103]

When Jean Vilar brought his famous staging of *Le Prince de Hombourg* to the Berlin Festspiele in 1952, the eleven-year old Matthias Langhoff sat in the audience. In 1984 Langhoff and his collaborator Manfred Karge returned the favour by presenting a new interpretation[104] for Vilar's Théâtre National Populaire de Lyon-Villeurbanne after a short guest appearance in the Paris Odéon. The result, heralded as "une superproduction européenne: deux metteurs en scène-stars, une distribution prestigieuse, et une traduction commandée à Henri Thomas, poète incontesté,"[105] encouraged the critics to compare the two versions separated by more than thirty years. The introductory paragraph of Pierre Marcabru's review for *Le Figaro* (7 June 1984) typifies this tendency: "Le traitement de choc que Manfred Karge et Matthias Langhoff, metteurs en scène prussiens et anarchistes, font subir à Heinrich von Kleist, poète prussien et nationaliste, risque fort de surprendre, sinon de désarçonner, tous ceux qui ont imaginé *Le Prince de Hombourg* sous les traits charmeurs et romantiques de Gérard Philipe, plus proche, à l'évidence, de Musset que d'un junker." The desire to strike terror into the audience was apparent from the opening scene, as the stage presented the spectator with the shattered remnants of a baroque theatre, a cement wall with gates of rusty metal, a blood-red curtain that later fell with the finality of a guillotine to separate the scenes, and (reminiscent of the 1978 Hamburg production) quantities of sand. The desolation was designed to recall cultural and human destruction from the Thirty Years War to the Second World War represented by a bombed-out Berlin. This neo-Brechtian antiwar approach, which sought to undermine the idealizing glorification of the military tradition through a naturalistic portrayal, furnished the unifying element: "Toute la première partie est une farce militaire noire, une sorte de MASH sans bonne humeur. Le rire vient des situations absurdes, et l'absurde des excès d'une vérité brutale."[106] Gérard Désarthe, playing Homburg as an antihero, a clown in a carrot-top wig, appeared before the Elector to plead for his life in a ballerina's costume. At the conclusion, he stood unprotected in pouring rain with his head concealed in a cowl, surrounded by umbrella-bearing soldiers and members of the court. After a repetition of the pantomime with the laurel wreath, Homburg screamed and collapsed. He was then carried off by the military, as if he were being committed to an insane asylum. When Mörner announced the Elector's death, he made his entry held by two cavaliers to form "la figure d'un groupe de moribonds sanglants après la bataille."[107] The brutal background of disfigured, bleeding human cadavers and a severed head strewn upon the battlefield rendered the foreground heroic stances of the main characters meaningless, if not absurd.

On the whole, Karge's and Langhoff's French experiment garnered positive notices from the press: "Malgré les distorsions qu'ils font subir à l'idée qu'on peut avoir de Kleist, Karge et Langhoff construisent un édifice solide, poursuivent inexorablement leur but, qui n'est pas de faire rêver mais de râper, de labourer, de secouer, le [sic] montrer le risible, le grandiose, l'humain."[108] However, of particular historical interest is the reappearance of a predilection, beginning with Mme de Staël in her essay on suicide, to see in Kleist a laying bare of the dark German soul. For example, Brigitte Salino claimed: "[Les] thèmes [de ce *Prince*] – l'armée, la nation, l'État, l'autorité – collent comme une peau de chagrin au temps et à la maudite histoire de l'Allemagne." Another critic, Guy Dumur, even went as far as to explain Germany's recent fascination with Kleist as displaying the phenomena of association and expiation: "Les metteurs en scène allemands actuels semblent faits pour exprimer la culpabilité d'un peuple, ses hantises et ses angoisses secrètes, que dissimule la prospérité. Ils se reconnaissent en un auteur maudit tel que Kleist et veulent résumer, chaque fois, en une seule soirée, leur histoire, comme pour se la faire pardonner."[109] But whatever may be said of the two Karge and Langhoff versions, they stand in distinct opposition to both Jean Vilar's and Peter Stein's interpretation and have therefore established a more realistic yardstick against which to measure future treatments of the drama.

Subsequent productions of *Prinz Friedrich* have so far failed to attract the press coverage given to the T.N.P. staging. Walter Ruch, the "Oberspielleiter" of the Landestheater Schwaben, selected Kleist's final play to open the new theatrical season in Memmingen (September 1985). By deleting the two concluding patriotic, nationalistic verses: "Ins Feld! Ins Feld! Zur Schlacht! Zum Sieg! Zum Sieg! / In Staub mit allen Feinden Brandenburgs!" (1857–8) and by ending the evening with the dialogue "DER PRINZ VON HOMBURG. Nein, sagt! Ist es ein Traum? / KOTTWITZ. Ein Traum, was sonst?" (1856), Ruch gave a clear indication of the thrust of his interpretation. As Rolf Lehnhardt succinctly put it in his report for the *Schwäbische Zeitung* (24 September 1985): "Facit: ein preußischer Sommernachtstraum sozusagen, den man freilich auch als Alptraum verstehen kann." Interlude music from Schönberg's "Verklärte Nacht" and Richard Strauß's "Tod und Verklärung" suitably reinforced this impression. While Ruch stressed the dream content, Jaroslav Chundela avoided any hint of a one-sided interpretation when he presented an even-handed production for Wiesbaden in October 1986. "Weder will [die Inszenierung] den schrecklich-schönen Traum des Prinzen (wie Stein) noch die politische Realität der Kurmark Brandenburg von 1675 und Preußens um 1810 [an allusion to Karge/Langhoff] ... besonders nachdrücklich akzentuieren."[110] This balancing act between past extremes was evidently intended to illustrate the continual play or tension between the inevitable instability and fallibility of all social institutions and the equally unavoidable realization that these institutions, however imperfect and transitory, are necessary for community living. The pendulum swung again, however, to "die politische Realität der Kurmark Brandenburg" in Vera Oelschlegel's staging for the East-Berlin Theater im Palast. The final visual image left here with the audience suggested that Kleist's utopian dream of a Prussian state which successfully reconciled "[d]as Kriegsgesetz" and "die lieblichen Gefühle" (1129–30) was not achieved: the Elector transformed the prince into a monument to which the ruler himself paid homage. "Solch radikales theatralisches Verfahren," observed Gerhart Ebert, "löst die Kleistsche Utopie unübersehbar in der militanten Erbarmungslosigkeit preußischer Geschichte auf."[111] This staging aroused little interest or support in East Germany.[112] The touring production of Zürich's Schauspieltruppe shared a similar fate when it came to Lindau in October 1987. Rolf Lehnhardt found fault with the directing of Robert Freitag – "ein ganz unangebrachter Lustspielton fließt ein"[113] – with the acting except for Hans Otto Ball's Kottwitz, and with the arrangement of the players on stage: "Die Teichoskopie mit der 'Einheitsfront' der aufgeregten Feldherren zum Parkett hin war sogar von leichter Albernheit."

Throughout the nineteenth century, with only a few exceptions (Immermann), Tieck's evaluation of *Prinz Friedrich von Homburg* as "ein echt vaterländisches Gedicht" proved to be the only interpretation acceptable to the ruling aristocracy, the military hierarchy, and the general public. The Elector became the main character who, out of paternal love, sought to educate his nephew towards a more responsible patriotic attitude. Even with the Meiningen troupe's greater fidelity to the text after the Franco-Prussian War, one can still detect the same bias at work in their dramatic extravaganza, glorifying Prussia's militaristic past. Except for Reinhardt's only modestly successful staging in 1907, with its down-to-earth, implied anti-militaristic perspective, the patriotic tendency persisted and culminated during the Nazi period. The turning point in the drama's stage history, a new emphasis, arrived in 1951 with Vilar's courageous production for the Festival d'Avignon, significantly after the war and under the growing influence of existential thought. Now Homburg was the centre of interest, as the French director, fortunate to have at his disposal the talent of Gérard Philipe, focused on the intimate, personal tragedy while downplaying the role of the state. The Théâtre National Populaire's overwhelming triumph with *Le Prince de Hombourg* contributed substantially to a postwar Kleist renaissance both on the stage and in academic circles. Vilar's interpretation remained as an ideal model into the sixties and seventies and increased international awareness of a dramatist generally ignored outside the German-speaking countries. Even "Kleists Traum vom Prinzen von Homburg," the most acclaimed modern German version to date, owed some of its inspiration to Vilar's innovative approach, since Peter Stein endeavoured to present a dream fantasy attributable to Kleist himself, while minimizing the importance of the historical situation. And finally, in more recent times, Karge and Langhoff with their theatrical and political terrorism placed the play in a more universal, timeless framework, in which the despotic state eliminates the anarchist Homburg. In other words, all the theatrical highpoints in the constantly changing fortunes of *Prinz Friedrich von Homburg* are, as one would expect, a direct or indirect reflection of the socio-political context in which they originated.

## CHAPTER EIGHT

# Conclusion

Unfortunately for Kleist in terms of his own career and the fate of his works, he grew up without any real contact with the theatre, and although he often sought to establish a link to it, he was never to find any beneficial rapport with the dramatic trends of his day. Not surprisingly then, Kleist's plays did not adhere to prevailing conventions in either content or style, but rather to his own subjective vision, and when he later sought to win public approval and support, he received very little. Only six performances of his dramas took place during his lifetime, none of which he attended. As early as November 1800, before the so-called Kant crisis, he expressed to his fiancée a general sense of being out of place, of not being able to adapt himself to contemporary society: "[Wenn] ich auch auf dieser Erde nirgends meinen Platz finden sollte, so finde ich vielleicht auf einem andern Sterne einen um so bessern" (2: 586). This theme would recur several times throughout his correspondence up until his admission on the day of his suicide: "[Die] Wahrheit ist, daß mir auf Erden nicht zu helfen war" (2: 887). Writing to Marie von Kleist in the late fall of 1807, he commented in reference to *Penthesilea*: "Ob es, bei den Forderungen, die das Publikum an die Bühne macht, gegeben werden wird, ist eine Frage, die die Zeit entscheiden muß. Ich glaube es nicht, und wünsche es auch nicht, so lange die Kräfte unserer Schauspieler auf nichts geübt, als Naturen wie die Kotzebueschen und Ifflandschen sind, nachzuahmen" (2: 796). With the exception of *Das Käthchen von Heilbronn*, Kleist elected not to take into consideration the then accepted theatrical standards and paid the penalty. But even in the second half of the twentieth century, commentators and directors constantly underscored the linguistic and technical difficulties of mounting a Kleistian work. Because of the unique nature of his poetic idiom, a disjointed, often alienating syntax that mirrors the disharmonious nature of his world, his dramas have been largely restricted to German-speaking playhouses. Whereas Büchner's plays, written in prose, readily lend themselves to English translation and have thus had an extensive and successful stage history in North America,[1] Kleist's dramas have enjoyed at best a *succès d'estime* in the English-speaking world. The almost total isolation of the main protagonists is reflected in their propensity to live out their inner life, incapable of communicating with one another, with the result that the language used not only resists an accurate rendering by the English translator, but even poses a major obstacle for the German-speaking actor or theatre-goer. However, the stage histories of Kleist's dramas clearly demonstrate how imagination, if combined with sensitivity and respect for Kleist's text, can produce a memorable and meaningful evening, for few nineteenth-century authors speak so directly to our contemporary understanding of the human condition.

As noted in the introduction, there remains a noticeable discrepancy between the academic approach to a Kleistian play and the attitude of someone trained in the theatrical tradition. In the midst of the tremendous popularity enjoyed by Claus Peymann's Bochum production of *Die Hermannsschlacht*, a staging that closely adhered to the original text, a spirited debate, published in the *Kleist-Jahrbuch 1984*,[2] took place between Peymann and the president of the Heinrich-von-Kleist-Gesellschaft, Hans Joachim Kreutzer. It served to re-affirm the old controversy between the literary historian's goal of determining the dramatist's intent and the director's right to re-interpret the drama in terms of his/her contemporary perception:

PEYMANN  Darum geht's Kleist überhaupt nicht, sondern es geht ...
KREUTZER  Verzeihung, wem geht es: Kleist oder Peymann? Das ist nämlich die Frage, aber lassen wir sie für jetzt ...
PEYMANN  So wie ich den Kleist halt verstehe ...
KREUTZER  ... halt offen.[3]

Even though my academic colleague may have had the final say in this particular exchange, his last word "offen" possesses a particular appropriateness, for it makes allowances for a potentially advantageous tension between theoretician and practitioner. *Open*-mindedness can only expand our appreciation of Kleist the dramatist and help to assure another two hundred years of exploring the seemingly inexhaustible potential and continuing relevance of his plays.

# Notes

INTRODUCTION

1 Kleist, *Sämtliche Werke*, 2: 805. All subsequent references to Kleist's works will be drawn from this edition. I shall include in my text verse lines for the dramas and page numbers for the letters or narratives.

2 I have borrowed the phrase from Walter Müller-Seidel's 1961 assessment of the play: "Nur mit immer erneut auszusprechenden Vorbehalten wird man dieses Stück [*Die Hermannsschlacht*] in das dichterische Werk Kleists einbeziehen dürfen" (*Versehen und Erkennen*, 53).

3 Hering, quoted in Michaelis, *Kleist*, 85.

4 Rudolf Krämer-Badoni, *Die Welt*, 30 December 1983.

5 Michael Skasa, *Süddeutsche Zeitung*, 24/25 December 1983.

6 Peter Eschberg's Bonn production of *Penthesilea* in 1981 gave rise to this controversy which I shall describe in detail in the chapter on *Penthesilea*.

7 In reference to *Käthchen*, Kleist wrote to Marie von Kleist: "Es war von Anfang herein eine ganz treffliche Erfindung, und nur die Absicht, es für die Bühne passend zu machen, hat mich zu Mißgriffen verführt, die ich jetzt beweinen möchte" (2: 874), and in his effort to have *Die Hermannsschlacht* performed in Vienna, he confessed to Heinrich von Collin: "Sie können leicht denken, wie sehr mir die Aufführung dieses Stücks, das einzig und allein auf diesen Augenblick berechnet war, am Herzen liegt' (2: 824). Both references contain an allusion to intent, but couched in the most general of terms.

8 As a classic example, one could point to Brecht's vain efforts to alienate the audience's sympathy for Mutter Courage.

9 Joachim Schmitt-Sasse, *Deutsche Volkszeitung/die tat*, 31 May 1985.

CHAPTER ONE

1 Kleist, *Sämtliche Werke*, 2: 731. Unless otherwise indicated, italics will denote stage directions or my own emphases.
2 Ludwig Tieck, from the introduction to Kleist's *Gesammelte Schriften*, quoted in Sauer, "Kleists *Familie Schroffenstein*," 19.
3 Quoted in Sauer, "Kleists *Familie Schroffenstein*," 21.
4 Bauerles, *Theaterzeitung*, Vienna, 1824, quoted in Sauer, "Kleists *Familie Schroffenstein*," 45.
5 Küstner, quoted in Sauer, "Kleists *Familie Schroffenstein*," 51.
6 Cf Schmidinger, "Kleist und das Burgtheater," 23.
7 Holbein, quoted in Sauer, "Kleists *Familie Schroffenstein*," 58.
8 Sauer, "Kleists *Familie Schroffenstein*," 64.
9 *Privilegierte, wöchentliche, gemeinnützige Nachrichten von und für Hamburg*, 4 August 1836, quoted in Sauer, "Kleists *Familie Schroffenstein*," 77.
10 Friedrich Ludwig Schmidt, quoted in Sauer, "Kleists *Familie Schroffenstein*," 79.
11 *Vossische Zeitung*, 20 March 1849, quoted in Sauer, "Kleists *Familie Schroffenstein*," 99.
12 *Allgemeine Theater Chronik*, Leipzig, 22 March 1849, quoted in Kühn, *Kleist*, 269.
13 Sauer, "Kleists *Familie Schroffenstein*," 113.
14 *Berliner Tageblatt*, 22 January 1888, quoted in Sauer, "Kleists *Familie Schroffenstein*," 153.
15 Sauer, "Kleists *Familie Schroffenstein*," 176.
16 *Meininger Tageblatt*, 23 November 1910, quoted in Sauer, "Kleists *Familie Schroffenstein*," 181.
17 Kilian, quoted in Sauer, "Kleists *Familie Schroffenstein*," 194.
18 *Münchener Neueste Nachrichten*, 23 September 1911, quoted in Sauer, "Kleists *Familie Schroffenstein*," 196.
19 Sauer, "Kleists *Familie Schroffenstein*," 199.
20 *Dresdner Neueste Nachrichten*, 4 October 1924.
21 Michaelis, *Heinrich von Kleist*, 86.
22 Günther Rühle, *Frankfurter Allgemeine Zeitung*, 21 March 1962. The next two quotations are also drawn from this review.
23 Ivan Nagel, *Deutsche Zeitung*, 22 March 1962.
24 Gerd Klepzig, *Die Welt*, 13 September 1974. Klepzig is referring to Heinrich Zschokke's report: "Als Kleist eines Tages sein Trauerspiel vorlas, ward im letzten Akt das allseitige Gelächter der Zuhörerschaft, wie auch des Dichters, so stürmisch und endlos, daß bis zu seiner letzten Mordszene zu gelangen Unmöglichkeit wurde" (Kleist, *Sämtliche Werke*, 1: 919).

25 Heinz Ludwig Arnold, *Frankfurter Rundschau*, 11 September 1974.

26 Klepzig, *Die Welt*, 13 September 1974.

27 Eo Plunier, *Die Welt*, 14 April 1977.

28 *Frankfurter Rundschau*, 10 May 1977.

29 Roland H. Wiegenstein, *Frankfurter Rundschau*, 20 March 1982.

30 "Wichtiger ist die Frage, ob es eigentlich angeht, ein so lange nicht gespieltes, gleichwohl wichtiges, neu zu entdeckendes Stück derart aufzuführen, daß damit alle Gerüchte, die über es in Umlauf sind, nur bestätigt werden, während es doch darauf ankäme nachzuweisen, wie genau, betreffend und intelligent es von Regungen und psychischen Befindlichkeiten handelt, die gar nicht von gestern sind" (Wiegenstein).

31 *Der Bund*, 16 March 1983.

32 Quoted in a review by Wilfried Mommert, *Ludwigsburger Kreiszeitung*, 27 March 1984.

33 Quoted in a review by Günther Schloß, first printed in the *Stuttgarter Zeitung*, 12 April 1985, but also appearing in the *Basler Zeitung*, 16 April 1985. For a more detailed account of Neuenfels's film, see Irmela Schneider, "Aktualität," 113–19.

34 Jens Frederiksen, *Die Welt*, 22 April 1985. Eckhard Franke also noted Jendryko's "strenge[n] realistische[n] Ansatz," *Badische Zeitung*, 30 April/1 May 1985.

35 Peter Iden, *Frankfurter Rundschau*, dated Ostern 1985. Another critic, Fritz Bajorat of the *Rhein-Neckar-Zeitung* (11 April 1985), felt that Jendryko's interpretation failed to suggest the uncanny, incalculable aspect of the tragedy: "Kleists zweideutige Realität leidet darunter. Seine Menschen sind in Unordnung, ihr Bewußtsein ist in Unordnung. Das ist ganz und gar modern, existentiell zu verstehen. Das Absurde scheint vorweggenommen."

36 Eckhard Franke, *Badische Zeitung*, 30 April/1 May 1985.

37 Günther Schloß, *Stuttgarter Zeitung*, 10 May 1985.

38 Heike Kühn, *Frankfurter Rundschau*, 27 April 1985.

39 Verena Auffermann, *Süddeutsche Zeitung*, 17 May 1985.

40 Günther Schloß, *Stuttgarter Zeitung*, 10 May 1985. As a further indication of increased awareness, director Rolf P. Parchwitz chose *Die Familie Schroffenstein* to inaugurate the new Badische Landesbühne in Bruchsal in December 1987. To emphasize the parallel attitudes in the two branches of the Schroffenstein family, this staging saw Albert Frank and Eva Behrmann play Rupert and Eustache and Sylvester and Gertrude, respectively, using different wigs and costumes to suggest the change from Rossitz to Warwand: "Die Aufführung, in der der Ernst der Lage nicht immer sichtbar wurde ..., glich zuweilen einem Schauerdrama, bei dem man auf Anhieb gewiß nicht Heinrich von

Kleist als Autor vermutet hätte!" (Dieter Schnabel, *Schwäbische Zeitung*, 8 December 1987).

CHAPTER TWO

1 *Goethes Briefe*, 3: 53.
2 Quoted in Kleist, *Sämtliche Werke*, 1: 926.
3 Quoted in Federn, *Das Leben*, 215.
4 Sembdner, "Der 'zerbrochene Krug,'" 57–67. The first Adam also has his defender: "Da Goethe nicht allzuviel Verständnis für Kleists Wesen und Dichtung hatte, muß allerdings gefragt werden, ob nicht der Darsteller, Becker, das Stück richtiger verstanden hat. ... Hat nicht Becker, dem ein anderer Kritiker bescheinigt, er sei 'vortrefflich' gewesen, mit seinem 'Zerren und Dehnen' vielleicht das Sträuben Adams ausdrücken wollen, der den Augenblick der Entlarvung so lang wie möglich hinausschieben möchte?" (Michaelis, *Heinrich von Kleist*, 85–6.)
5 Quoted in Federn, *Das Leben*, 216.
6 Quoted in Buchtenkirch, *Kleists Lustspiel*, 25.
7 Buchtenkirch, *Kleists Lustspiel*, 38.
8 Friedrich Ludwig Schmidt, quoted in Buchtenkirch, *Kleists Lustspiel*, 28.
9 *Abend Zeitung*, 18 August 1832.
10 *Allgemeine Preussische Zeitung*, 3 May 1844, quoted in H. Ziegelski, "Kleist im Spiegel," 283.
11 Quoted in Buchtenkirch, *Kleists Lustspiel*, 83.
12 Ziegelski, "Kleist im Spiegel," 107.
13 Cf Schmidinger, "Kleist und das Burgtheater," 34.
14 Theodor Fontane, quoted in Goldammer, *Schriftsteller über Kleist*, 415.
15 Brahm, *Theater*, 373.
16 Ibid., 373.
17 Bab, *Über den Tag hinaus*, 196.
18 Richardson, *Kleist in France*, 64.
19 Quoted in Richardson, *Kleist in France*, 64.
20 Jacobsohn, *Jahre der Bühne*, 170. The next two quotations are also drawn from this review.
21 Hilpert, *Liebe zum Theater*, 33.
22 Richardson, *Kleist in France*, 154.
23 Jean-Paul Fauré, *Théâtre de France*, 1955, quoted by Richardson, *Kleist in France*, 154.
24 Hermann Missenharter, *Stuttgarter Nachrichten*, 18 November 1957.
25 Brooks Atkinson, *New York Times*, 2 April 1958. All subsequent references are taken from this article.
26 *Stuttgarter Zeitung*, 25 August 1959.

27 *The Times*, 8 December 1961.
28 Quoted in Goldammer, *Schriftsteller über Kleist*, 406.
29 *Rheinischer Merkur*, 18 March 1966.
30 Hans Bayer, *Stuttgarter Nachrichten*, 24 February 1968.
31 Richard Biedrzynski, *Stuttgarter Zeitung*, 24 February 1968.
32 E. Hennemann-Bayer, *Schwarzwälder Bote*, 26 February 1968.
33 Hans Bayer, *Stuttgarter Nachrichten*, 24 February 1968. The next two quotations are also taken from this article.
34 *Neue Zürcher Zeitung*, 25 February 1969. Subsequent quotations are also from this review.
35 Gotthard Böhm, *Die Presse*, 13 December 1971.
36 *Frankfurter Allgemeine Zeitung*, 16 February 1971.
37 *Frankfurter Rundschau*, 30 October 1972. All references to this staging are drawn from this review.
38 *Frankfurter Allgemeine Zeitung*, 5 January 1973.
39 *Mannheimer Morgen*, 28/29 June 1975.
40 Friedrich Luft, *Die Welt*, 13 April 1974.
41 Jost Nolte, *Deutsche Zeitung*, 19 April 1974.
42 Dieter Schnabel, *Schwäbische Zeitung*, 29 July 1977.
43 Wilhelm Ringelband, *Badische Neueste Nachrichten*, 29 July 1977.
44 *Badische Neueste Nachrichten*, 19 November 1977.
45 *Badische Zeitung* 24 October 1977. The next two quotations are also drawn from this article.
46 These statistics were widely reported in several newspapers, for example, in the *Frankfurter Allgemeine Zeitung*, 28 December 1978.
47 Gertrud Waldecker, *Badische Neueste Nachrichten*, 14 February 1978. This positive review has its negative counterpart in that of Andreas Roßmann for the *Stuttgarter Nachrichten*, 20 May 1978: "Doch diese zweite Karlsruher Inszenierung Bödys ist nicht nur flach, sie ist auch unsorgfältig."
48 Sigi Fastus, *Stuttgarter Nachrichten*, 19 September 1978.
49 Dieter Bachmann, *Frankfurter Allgemeine Zeitung*, 27 September 1978.
50 Rolf Lehnhardt, *Schwäbische Zeitung*, 16 September 1978.
51 Heinrich Domes, *Schwäbisches Tagblatt*, 11 May 1979.
52 Quoted in a review by Dieter Schnabel for the *Schwäbische Zeitung*, 27 February 1979.
53 Schnabel. Hans-Joachim Köhler went much further, criticizing the "Vergröberung der Kleistschen Vorlage bis hin zur Posse" (*Ludwigsburger Kreiszeitung*, 28 February 1979).
54 H. Lehmann, *Badische Neueste Nachrichten*, 28 April 1979.
55 Rosemarie Borngässer, *Bayernkurier*, 28 April 1979.
56 Wilhelm Ringelband, *Badische Neueste Nachrichten*, 4 August 1979. Joachim Kaiser (*Süddeutsche Zeitung*, 8 April 1979) called into question

Haughs's inclusion of the first variant, seeing it as possible "Interessantmacherei."

57 Quoted in Ringelband's review.

58 K., *Budapester Rundschau*, Nr. 2, January 1980.

59 Sabine Heymann, *Frankfurter Rundschau*, 24 January 1980.

60 Heinz Ritter, *Frankfurter Rundschau*, 30 January 1980.

61 Annemarie Weber, *Die Presse*, 29 January 1980.

62 Günther Grack, *Der Tagesspiegel*, 25 January 1980.

63 Hellmut Kotschenreuther, *Mannheimer Morgen*, 30 January 1980.

64 Cf also "Der in anderen Aufgaben durchaus bewährte Helmut Wildt ist mit dem Adam überfordert" (Ritter).

65 *Badische Neueste Nachrichten*, 6 September 1980.

66 Hellmut Butterweck, *Die Furche*, 15 September 1982.

67 Karin Kathrein, *Die Presse*, 13 September 1982.

68 Heinrich Domes, *Schwäbisches Tagblatt*, 22 February 1983; Ulrich Staehle (*Stuttgarter Zeitung*, 18 February 1983) rejected Heydenreich's attempt to justify his interpretation by appealing to "Texttreue": "Es stimmt hinten und vorne nicht bei dieser Inszenierung."

69 Simon Neubauer, *Weser-Kurier*, 17 March 1983.

70 Werner Burkhardt, *Süddeutsche Zeitung*, 11 March 1983.

71 Benjamin Henrichs, *Die Zeit*, 18 March 1983. In this same context, Lothar Schmidt-Mühlisch wrote in his review for *Die Welt* (11 March 1983): "Entsprechend gewinnt die Hamburger Version ein neues, zusätzliches Motiv für Eves Schweigen. Sie (Therese Affolter) nimmt Adams Liebe ernst."

72 Guy Dumur, *New Statesman*, 27 January 1984. The reference to whispering alludes to a dramatic technique whereby the actors largely whispered their lines, often rendering them inaudible to the audience.

73 Hans Göhl, *Bayern Kurier*, 28 January 1984.

74 ct, *Schwäbisches Tagblatt*, 15 February 1985.

75 *Der Bund*, 4 February 1985. The anonymous reviewer is quoting from the director's program notes.

76 *Neue Zürcher Zeitung*, 6 February 1985.

77 Martin Cropper, *The Times*, 5 June 1986.

78 Friedrich Luft, *Die Welt*, 6 October 1986.

79 This adaptation was first performed in 1975.

80 Günter Grack, *Der Tagesspiegel*, 7 October 1986.

81 Friedrich Luft, *Die Welt*, 6 October 1986.

82 Agnes Baltsa was scheduled to sing the title role but withdrew at the last minute allegedly because of tracheobronchitis, but according to the "grape-vine" because of irreconcilable differences between conductor and singer.

83 *Die Welt*, 28 July 1986.

84 Quoted in *Die Presse*, 26/27 July 1986.

85 Hans Lehmann, *Rhein-Neckar-Zeitung*, 28 July 1986.

86 Karin Kathrein, *Die Presse*, 28 July 1986. The one major dissenting voice was that of the critic signing him or herself as "egw" of *Die Welt* (28 July 1986): "Überhaupt wird mehr gekreischt und gebrüllt als gesprochen, was dem doch im Stil recht interessanten Text keineswegs bekommt."

87 *Süddeutsche Zeitung*, 28 July 1986. Joachim Kaiser, writing for the *Süddeutsche Zeitung* (16 October 1986), interpreted this kiss in a much more optimistic vein: "Am Schluß aber, wenn der strenge und strafende Gerichtsrat Walter, dessen Züge für Eve *Menschlichkeit* 'vom Antlitz strahlen', eben das Vertrauen, auf das Eve vorher gepocht hat, nun auch für sich und seinen König einklagt, dann besiegelt ein keineswegs Treulosigkeit signalisierender Kuß des Staatsbeamten, daß Eve nun wieder der Welt vertraut." This view, based on a performance in Munich, runs counter to that expressed by the critics of the Salzburg version.

88 Lothar Sträter, *Badische Neueste Nachrichten*, 29 July 1986.

89 Dorothee Hammerstein, *Badische Zeitung*, 2 January 1987.

90 Christoph Schneider, *Basler Zeitung*, 19 December 1986.

### CHAPTER THREE

1 Quoted in David, *Kleist und Frankreich*, 9.

2 *Journal de Paris*, July-September 1807. See also Richardson, *Kleist in France*, 10–11.

3 Cf Wittkowski, "The New Prometheus," 109–24.

4 David, *Kleist und Frankreich*, 10.

5 Wolfgang Kirchbach, *Bühne und Welt*, 1 December edition, 1899, quoted in Dorr, *Kleist's [sic] Amphitryon*, 82.

6 Dr G. Mauz, *Tägliche Rundschau*, 11 April 1899.

7 *Bühne und Welt*, 11. Jahrgang, October 1899–March 1900, 477.

8 Summarizing his analysis of this adaptation, Dorr maintained, "daß Henzen dem Kleist'schen Drama nur geschadet hat, ja, daß vom Kleist'schen Geiste so gut wie nichts übrig geblieben ist" (*Kleist's Amphitryon*, 62).

9 Schmidinger, "Kleist und das Burgtheater," 57. See also Dorr, *Kleist's Amphitryon*, 86f.

10 Ibid., 58.

11 Quoted in Schmidinger, "Kleist und das Burgtheater," 59.

12 *Berliner Börsen Courier*, 3 July 1910.

13 Jacobsohn, *Jahre der Bühne*, 133.

14 Ibid., 134.

15 *Leipziger Tageblatt und Anzeiger*, 6 September 1910.

16 The Jessner staging was first performed on 19 June 1926 in the Lauchstädter Goethe Theater.

17 Dorr, *Kleist's Amphitryon*, 122.

18 Ibid., 77.

19 Ruppel, *Großes Berliner Theater*, 8.

20 Ibid., 8.

21 Ibid., 125. Subsequent references to this staging will be drawn from this article.

22 Ibid., 127. Further quotations relating to this production are taken from this review.

23 Hilpert, *Gedanken zum Theater*, 135.

24 Ruppel, *Großes Berliner Theater*, 128.

25 Hilpert, *Gedanken zum Theater*, 136.

26 Ibid., 136.

27 Ruppel, *Großes Berliner Theater*, 129.

28 Norbert Hampel, *Nordwest Zeitung*, 29 October 1956. The next quotation is also taken from this article.

29 Winfried Wild, *Stuttgarter Nachrichten*, 21 April 1961.

30 *Stuttgarter Zeitung*, 21 April 1961.

31 Michaelis, *Heinrich von Kleist*, 92.

32 Ibid., 93.

33 Alf Brustellin, *Süddeutsche Zeitung*, 17 May 1968.

34 Howard Thompson, *New York Times*, 18 November 1970. Subsequent quotations referring to the Brücke production are also drawn from this review.

35 Wolfgang Ignée, *Stuttgarter Zeitung*, 6 November 1971.

36 Joachim Kaiser, *Süddeutsche Zeitung*, 6/7 November 1971. The next two quotations are also taken from this review.

37 Kurt Honolka, *Stuttgarter Nachrichten*, 6 November 1971.

38 Clara Menck, *Frankfurter Allgemeine Zeitung*, 10 November 1971.

39 Valentin Polcuch, *Die Welt*, 28 October 1975. The next quotation is also taken from this review.

40 Georg Hensel, *Frankfurter Allgemeine Zeitung*, 28 October 1975.

41 Rudolf Krämer-Badoni, *Die Welt*, 27 June 1973.

42 *Neue Zürcher Zeitung*, 29/30 November 1975. All subsequent references to this production are drawn from this article.

43 Erich Thanner, *Die Furche*, 15 July 1977.

44 *Die Welt*, 14 December 1977.

45 Peter Burri, *Basler Zeitung*, 29 April 1977. The next two quotations are also taken from this review.

46 Lothar Schmidt-Mühlisch, *Die Welt*, 28 April 1977.

47 use., *Neue Zürcher Zeitung*, 13 May 1977.

48 Rainer Stephan, *Badische Zeitung*, 29 April 1977.

49 Monika von Zitzewitz, *Die Welt*, 28 August 1979. All subsequent quotations referring to the Lavia productions are taken from this review.

50 Renato Palazzi, *Corriere della Sera*, 20 July 1979. Cf also: "[E] lascia intravedere con un secolo almeno di anticipio su Pirandello, la scissione lacerante fra l'interiorità del sentimento e l'esteriorità della maschera" (He allows one to glimpse, at least a century before Pirandello, the tearing split between the interior realm of feeling and the exterior realm of the mask).

51 *Berliner Rundschau*, 24 September 1981.

52 Karena Niehoff, *Süddeutsche Zeitung*, 11 September 1981.

53 Günther Grack, *Der Tagesspiegel*, 6 September 1981.

54 Andreas Roßmann, *Badische Neueste Nachrichten*, 1 October 1981.

55 Roland H. Wiegenstein, *Frankfurter Rundschau*, 10 September 1981.

56 Friedrich Luft, *Die Welt*, 7 September 1981.

57 "Die Buh-Rufe am Schluß hatte [Jürgen] Flimm dennoch nicht verdient." Lothar Schmidt-Mühlisch, *Die Welt*, 8 March 1982.

58 Heinz Klunker, *Deutsches Allgemeines Sonntagsblatt*, 18 April 1982.

59 Rolf Michaelis, *Die Zeit*, 12 March 1982.

60 Paul F. Reitze, *Rheinischer Merkur*, 12 March 1982.

61 Ulrich Schreiber, *Frankfurter Rundschau*, 12 March 1982.

62 Jochen Schmidt, *Frankfurter Allgemeine Zeitung*, 12 March 1982.

63 Heinrich Vormweg, *Süddeutsche Zeitung*, 9 March 1982.

64 Karin Kathrein, *Die Presse* 17 May 1982. Cornelia Krauß expressed an equally high opinion of Sylvia Lukan's interpretation: "Vor allem der Alkmene Sylvia Lukans gelingt es dann, mit ihrer zwischen dem Mädchen und dem Weibchen vermittelnden Natürlichkeit jene Heiterkeit ins Spiel zu bringen, die man sich eigentlich für den ganzen Abend wünschte" (*Stuttgarter Zeitung*, 22 May 1982).

65 Rudolf Krämer-Badoni, *Die Welt*, 13 September 1982.

66 Günter Schloß, *Stuttgarter Zeitung*, 21 September 1982. Most critics panned her performance with one exception: "Almut Zilcher spielt die emotionale Hochspannung ihrer Rolle in einigen intensiven Szenen voll aus und gibt damit eine Ahnung von den explosiven Fragen, die in diesem Text ruhen" (Gregor Paul, *die tat*, 15 October 1982).

67 Georg Hensel, *Frankfurter Allgemeine Zeitung*, 13 September 1982.

68 Joachim Kaiser, *Süddeutsche Zeitung*, 23 December 1982.

69 Cf "Es ist ... nicht ganz einfach, herauszufinden, wo der zentrale Ansatz seiner lebhaften und einfallsreichen Einstudierung des vertrackt-erdhaften wie vertrackt-mysteriösen Zauberstücks lag" (Hans Schwab-Felisch, *Frankfurter Allgemeine Zeitung*, 4 January 1983).

70 Quoted in an article by Charlotte Nennecke, *Süddeutsche Zeitung*, 27/28 November 1982.

71 Helmut Voith, *Schwäbische Zeitung*, 28 February 1983.

72 Hans Chiout, *Frankfurter Rundschau*, 21 January 1984. This is a devastatingly negative review: "Da lenkt nichts ab, weder der Text noch die Bewegung auf der Bühne; man kann sich voll auf die Versuche seines Nachbarn konzentrieren, eine angenehmere Sitzposition zu finden."

73 Isabelle von Neumann-Cosel-Nebe, *Rhein-Neckar-Zeitung*, 22 May 1986.

74 Christel Heybrock, *Mannheimer Morgen*, 22 May 1986.

75 Cf "['Ach'] zieht sich sozusagen leitmotivisch durch das ganze Stück" (Christoph Müller, *Schwäbisches Tagblatt*, 23 May 1986).

76 Doris M. Trauth-Marx, *Die Rheinpfalz*, 22 May 1986.

77 Renate Braunschweig-Ullmann, *Badische Neueste Nachrichten*, 17 February 1987.

78 Rüdiger Krohn, *Stuttgarter Zeitung*, 8 January 1987.

79 Gerhard Jörder, *Badische Zeitung*, 16 February 1987. Cf also: "Die Verlegenheit muß grenzenlos gewesen sein. Sie war vorprogrammiert – Alkmene, Jupiter, Amphitryon, die Protagonisten immerhin, glichen mehr Opernhelden als Schauspielern, sie hätten ebenso gut ihren Text singen können" (Reinhardt Stumm, *Basler Zeitung*, 16 February 1987).

80 Reinhardt Stumm, *Basler Zeitung*, 16 May 1987.

81 Th. T., *Der Bund*, 19 May 1987.

82 m.v., *Neue Zürcher Zeitung*, 16 May 1987.

83 "Die Marquise von O," 2: 126.

84 From an essay entitled, "*Amphitryon* – Eine Wiedereroberung," 51.

CHAPTER FOUR

1 *Goethes Briefe*, 3: 64.

2 Quoted in Lowien, "Die Bühnengeschichte," 3.

3 *Stuttgarter Morgenblatt*, 28 May 1811.

4 Ludwig Tieck, quoted in Lowien, "Die Bühnengeschichte," 12.

5 Quoted in Lowien, "Die Bühnengeschichte," 16.

6 *Shakespeare Jahrbuch* 47 (1911), 209f, quoted in Lowien, "Die Bühnengeschichte," 14.

7 Quoted in Lowien, "Die Bühnengeschichte," 25.

8 Ziegelski, "Kleist im Spiegel," 99.

9 *Allgemeine Zeitung*, Munich, 17 June 1892.

10 *Mecklenburger Tageblatt*, 28 November 1893.

11 *Weimarische Zeitung*, 18 October 1908.

12 Ernst Stern, quoted in Lowien, "Die Bühnengeschichte," 55.

13 Lowien, "Die Bühnengeschichte," 56.

14 Ibid., 58.

15 Schmidinger, "Kleist und das Burgtheater," 74. The following quotation is also drawn from this work.

16 Johannes Jacobi, from a review which unfortunately does not indicate either the date or the newspaper. The next two quotations are also drawn from this review.

17 Quoted in Richardson, *Kleist in France*, 151.

18 Richardson, *Kleist in France*, 152.

19 Quoted in Michaelis, *Heinrich von Kleist*, 93.

20 Michaelis, *Heinrich von Kleist*, 94.

21 Kurt Honolka, *Stuttgarter Nachrichten*, 9 November 1970.

22 Günter Schloz, *Deutsche Zeitung*, 13 November 1970.

23 *Stuttgarter Nachrichten*, 9 November 1970. The next reference is also drawn from this article.

24 *Deutsche Zeitung*, 13 November 1970.

25 *Le Figaro*, 4 August 1973. This review is also the source of the following quotation.

26 Richard Strauß, quoted in a review by Klaus Adam for the *Schwäbisches Tageblatt*, 20 August 1982.

27 Gabor Halasz, *Badische Zeitung*, 13/14 March 1976.

28 Klaus Adam, *Schwäbisches Tagblatt*, 20 August 1982.

29 Franz Endler, *Die Presse*, 19 August 1982.

30 Emil Staiger, quoted in a review by Lothar Sträter for the *Badische Neueste Nachrichten*, 21 August 1982.

31 Othmar Schoeck, quoted in Halasz's review.

32 Hans-Klaus Jungheinrich, *Frankfurter Rundschau*, 11 September 1973. All subsequent references to the Lucerne performance belong to this article.

33 Michael Cournot, *Le Monde*, 16 November 1977.

34 Anne Surgers, *Les Nouvelles littéraires*, 16/23 December 1976.

35 Ruth Henry, *Frankfurter Rundschau*, 1 February 1977. The next two quotations are also taken from this review.

36 Irving Wardle, *The Times*, 9 February 1977. Subsequent quotations referring to this production are also drawn from this review.

37 *Frankfurter Rundschau*, 11 March 1978. The next quotation also comes from this article.

38 Peter Iden, *Frankfurter Rundschau*, 14 March 1978. This commentary is also the source for the next quotation.

39 Peter Iden.

40 Rudolf Krämer-Badoni, *Die Welt*, 14 March 1978.

41 Christoph Müller, *Schwäbisches Tagblatt*, 17 March 1978.

42 "A Statement by Eric Bentley," from the program notes kindly supplied to me by Professor Saul Elkin. Bentley's feminist slant, however much it may fly in the face of Kleist's view, finds ample support in other recent interpretations. As Hellmuth Karasek noted in an article for *Der Spiegel* (29 December 1979): "*Penthesilea* ist sicherlich das Lieblings-lesedrama der Frauenbewegung."

43 Bentley, *The Fall of the Amazons*, 42.

44 Saul Elkin, from the program notes.

45 Quoted from a letter which Saul Elkin wrote to me on 14 February 1989.

46 Peter Iden, *Frankfurter Rundschau*, 8 December 1980.

47 Georg Hensel, *Frankfurter Allgemeine Zeitung*, 8 December 1980.

48 *Die Welt*, 8 December 1980.

49 *Badische Neueste Nachrichten*, 15 December 1980.

50 Gerhard Stadelmeier, *Stuttgarter Zeitung*, 8 December 1980.

51 Benjamin Heinrichs, *Die Zeit*, 12 December 1980.

52 Ihe, *Mannheimer Morgen*, 12 December 1980.

53 Jens Wendland, *Süddeutsche Zeitung*, 12 December 1980.

54 *Berliner Rundschau*, 30 July 1981.

55 I have examined twenty reviews of this Berlin production which obviously aroused considerable critical interest not only in all parts of Germany, but also in Austria (*Die Presse*, 2 July 1981) and Switzerland (*Neue Zürcher Zeitung*, 11 July 1981).

56 Günter Grack, *Der Tagesspiegel* / "Feuilleton", 30 June 1981. The major exception to this overall sympathetic reception was Rolf Michaelis's rather cutting commentary for *Die Zeit* (3 July 1981): "Kein Gedanke verschwendet an Kleist: Wer sein kurzes, ihm am Ende lang dünkendes Leben so tapfer überstanden hat wie Heinrich von Kleist, der übersteht auch eine Inszenierung von Hans Neuenfels."

57 Michael Stone, *Schwäbische Zeitung*, 13 July 1981.

58 Hedwig Rohde, *Rhein-Neckar-Zeitung*, 30 June 1981.

59 Sibylle Wirsing, *Frankfurter Allgemeine Zeitung*, 29 June 1981.

60 Andreas Roßmann, *Badische Neueste Nachrichten*, 3 July 1981.

61 Annemarie Weber, *Die Presse*, 2 July 1981.

62 Joachim Kramarz, *Berliner Rundschau*, 30 July 1981.

63 Hellmuth Karasek, *Der Spiegel*, 13 July 1981. Neuenfels later interpreted *Penthesilea* again, but this time he used the film medium. For a detailed account of this cinematic treatment entitled "Heinrich Penthesilea von Kleist," see Schneider, "Aktualitat," 105–13.

64 *Le Nouvel Observateur*, 22 June 1981.

65 Rudolf Hohlweg, *Süddeutsche Zeitung*, 13 July 1981.

66 Colette Godard, *Manchester Guardian*, 23 May 1982.

67 *Saarbrücker Zeitung*, 9 July 1981. Schlocker's same review also appeared in the *Stuttgarter Zeitung*, 9 July 1981 and the *Basler Zeitung*, 15 July 1981.

68 Pierre Marcabru, *Le Figaro*, 24/25 April 1982.

69 *Schwäbisches Tagblatt*, 16 April 1982.

70 Günter Engelhard, *Rheinischer Merkur*, 2 October 1981.

71 Lothar Schmidt-Mühlisch, *Die Welt*, 29 September 1981. Stefan Odry, in a review for the *Mannheimer Morgen*, 1 October 1981, reached essentially the same conclusion.

72 Klu., *Deutsches Allgemeines Sonntagsblatt*, 23 January 1983.

73 Quoted in an article by Ute Naumann, *Die Zeit*, 14 January 1983.

74 *Süddeutsche Zeitung*, 15/16 May 1982.

75 Rolf Urs Ringger gave an informative and well attended talk about the tragedy on the day of the performance at the University of Salzburg.

76 *Neue Zürcher Zeitung*, 21 August 1982.

77 Sabine Heymann, *Frankfurter Rundschau*, 7 June 1983. All subsequent quotations referring to the two Italian stagings have been drawn from this review.

78 Michael Hofmann, *The Times Literary Supplement*, 9 December 1983.

79 Hofmann, for example, showed his awareness of the "Schmerz" vs "Schmutz" controversy from Kleist's famous pronouncement on *Penthesilea*.

80 Wolfgang Ignee, *Stuttgarter Zeitung*, 12 December 1984.

81 Martin Schaub, *Frankfurter Rundschau*, 14 December 1984.

82 "[S]tatt der geballten Sprache Kleists gibt es nur die gebellte Sprache Hollmanns" (*Der kleine Bund*, 15 December 1984).

83 Gerda Benesch, *Wiener Zeitung*, 3 January 1985.

84 Reinhardt Stumm, *Basler Zeitung*, 10 December 1984.

85 Klara Obermüller, *Die Weltwoche*, 13 December 1984.

86 Thomas Thieringer, *Süddeutsche Zeitung*, 15 February 1985.

87 rur., *Neue Zürcher Zeitung*, 10/11 November 1985.

88 Ulrich Schreiber, *Frankfurter Rundschau*, 1 February 1986. In the same review he wrote, "Und doch transportiert [die Aufführung] Schoecks Genialität: über die Musik."

89 Quoted in an article by Peter Iden for the *Frankfurter Rundschau*, 2 January 1986.

90 Hans Berndt, *Mannheimer Morgen*, 14/15 December 1985.

91 Kläre Warnecke, *Die Welt*, 9 December 1985.

92 Werner Burkhardt, *Süddeutsche Zeitung*, 10 December 1985.

93 Ino, *Kieler Nachrichten*, 9 December 1985.

94 Herbert Glossner, *Deutsches Allgemeines Sonntagsblatt*, 15 December 1985. Cf also: "Dem Regisseur aber ist zu danken für eine passable Lösung einer fast unlösbaren Aufgabe" (*Kieler Nachrichten*, 9 December 1985).

95 Gerhard Stadelmaier, *Stuttgarter Zeitung*, 9 December 1985.

96 *Der Spiegel*, 6 April 1987.

97 Charlotte Nennecke, *Süddeutsche Zeitung*, 28/29 March 1987.

98 Wolfgang Höbel, *Badische Zeitung*, 31 March 1987.

99 C. Bernd Sucher, *Süddeutsche Zeitung*, 31 March 1987.
100 Roland H. Wiegenstein, *Rheinischer Merkur*, 3 April 1987.
101 Rolf Michaelis, *Die Zeit*, 7 August 1987.
102 Dirk Grathoff, *Wilhelmshavener Zeitung*, 4 December 1987.
103 Quoted in a review of *Penthesilea* for the *Gießener Allgemeine*, 29 January 1987, signed "aw."
104 A collection of black and white photographs depicting Edith Clever's performance is available in book form: Syberger, *Kleist. Penthesilea.* "Die Aufnahmen entstanden während der Proben zur *Penthesilea*-Aufführung im Bouffes du Nord, Paris, Herbst 87 und anläßlich des Films, der dort anschließlich gedreht wurde, von Hans Jürgen Syberberg, mit Edith Clever, im Auftrag des Festival D'Automne, Paris."
105 Sibylle Wirsing, *Frankfurter Allgemeine Zeitung*, 29 June 1981.
106 Kläre Warnecke, *Die Welt*, 9 December 1985.
107 *Wilhelmshavener Zeitung*, 4 December 1987.

CHAPTER FIVE

1 Kleist, *Sämtliche Werke*, 2: 806.
2 Kleist, *Sämtliche Werke*, 2: 818.
3 Kleist asserted in a letter to August Wilhelm Iffland that the première occurred "bei Gelegenheit der Vermählungsfeierlichkeiten" (2: 836), i.e., Napoleon's marriage to Marie Luise von Österreich, but this claim has been refuted. See Kleist, *Sämtliche Werke*, 2: 939.
4 Quoted in Stolze, *Kleists Käthchen*, 12. See also Schmidinger, "Kleist und das Burgtheater," 16–17.
5 Quoted in Stolze, *Kleists Käthchen*, 12.
6 Stolze, *Kleists Käthchen*, 15–16. Stolze is my major source for the descriptions of the various *Käthchen* adaptations up to the year 1920.
7 Quoted by Stolze from a review published in 1818 in Frankfurt, *Kleists Käthchen*, 27.
8 Stolze, *Kleists Käthchen*, 20.
9 Quoted from a review by Ludwig Börne (Stolze, *Kleists Käthchen*, 32).
10 *Vossische Zeitung*, 29 April 1824. Cf also: "Diese Schauspielerin war als Käthchen-Darstellerin so berühmt, daß selbst im Brockhaus-Lexikon verzeichnet wurde, sie sei 'namentlich als Käthchen von Heilbronn unübertroffen'" (Grathoff, *Erläuterungen*, 122).
11 Quoted in Stolze, *Kleists Käthchen*, 44.
12 *Dresdner Abendzeitung*, 23 October 1817.
13 *Der Sammler*, 8 December 1821.
14 Stolze, *Kleists Käthchen*, 49.
15 Ludwig Tieck, quoted in Goldammer, *Schriftsteller über Kleist*, 644.
16 Cf Stolze, *Kleists Käthchen*, 51.

17 Cf Kleist, *Sämtliche Werke*, 1: 939.

18 Quoted in Goldammer, *Schriftsteller über Kleist*, 646. Fontane reviewed two productions of *Käthchen* in Berlin for the *Vossische Zeitung*, 13 May 1873 and 17 December 1875.

19 Paul Lindau as quoted in Stolze, *Kleists Käthchen*, 84.

20 Otto Brahm, *Deutsche Illustrierte Zeitung*, 16 January 1886, reprinted in Brahm, *Theater*, 265.

21 Ibid., 265.

22 Quoted in Harden, "The Genius of Max Reinhardt," 223.

23 Stolze, *Kleists Käthchen*, 106.

24 Ibid., 107.

25 Jacobsohn, *Jahre der Bühne*, 19. In contrast Jacobsohn maintains: "Das Dichterwort war den Meiningern heilig."

26 Harden, "The Genius of Max Reinhardt," 222.

27 Ibid., 223.

28 Ibid., 223.

29 Ibid., 223.

30 Jacobsohn, *Jahre der Bühne*, 20.

31 Harden, "The Genius of Max Reinhardt," 223.

32 Ibid., 223.

33 Rühle, *Theater für die Republik*, 426.

34 Jacobsohn, *Jahre der Bühne*, 218.

35 Ibid., 218.

36 Paul Wiegler, from a review quoted in Rühle, *Theater für die Republik*, 427.

37 Jacobsohn, *Jahre der Bühne*, 218.

38 Wiegler, from a review quoted in Rühle, *Theater für die Republik*, 428.

39 Jacobsohn, *Jahre der Bühne*, 218.

40 Ruppel, *Großes Berliner Theater*, 114. All references to the 1937 Fehling production are drawn from this review.

41 Hensel, *Kritiken*, 53–5.

42 Luft, *Berliner Theater*, 307–9.

43 Sabina Lietzmann, *Frankfurter Allgemeine Zeitung*, 28 November 1957.

44 Quoted in Richardson, *Kleist in France*, 23.

45 Guy Dumur, "Concours des jeunes compagnies," *Théâtre populaire*, 39, fall 1960. Also in Richardson, *Kleist in France*, 176.

46 USE., *Stuttgarter Nachrichten*, 29 November 1961.

47 Edgar Schall, *Die Tat*, 15 October 1966. All quotations related to the Anouilh production are taken from this review.

48 Kleist, *Sämtliche Werke*, 2: 730.

49 *Frankfurter Allgemeine Zeitung*, 28 March 1967.

50 Karl Schumann, *Süddeutsche Zeitung*, 24 June 1968.

51 For a review of this production, see *Stuttgarter Zeitung*, 18 October 1968.

52 This staging received several reviews: *Schwäbische Zeitung*, 10 August 1973; *Frankfurter Rundschau*, 12 July 1972; *Stuttgarter Nachrichten*, 4 July 1972, etc.

53 Ulrich Seelmann-Eggebert, *Schwäbische Zeitung*, 17 August 1972. The next quotation is also taken from this article.

54 Georges Schlocker, *Deutsches Allgemeines Sonntagsblatt*, 27 August 1972.

55 Ulrich Seelmann-Eggebert, *Schwäbische Zeitung*, 17 August 1972.

56 Dietmar Grieser, *Frankfurter Rundschau*, 30 January 1974.

57 Erik B. Wickenburg, *Die Welt*, 28 January 1974.

58 Lothar Sträter, *Schwäbische Zeitung*, 30 January 1974.

59 *Der Spiegel*, 24 November 1975.

60 Hellmuth Karasek, *Der Spiegel*, 24 November 1975.

61 Hans Bayer, *Mannheimer Morgen*, 18 November 1975.

62 Crosby, "Regie as Interpretation," 248.

63 Karasek. The next quotation is taken from the same review.

64 Crosby, "Regie as Interpretation," 249.

65 *The Times*, 28 August 1977. This production created interest as late as June 1979 as a guest performance in the context of the Holland-Festival. Cf *Bayern Kurier*, 30 June 1979.

66 Cf *Mannheimer Morgen*, 3/4 December 1977.

67 These words have been attributed to Goethe in a famous anecdote recorded by Ernst Wilhelm Weber. It has been reproduced in Grathoff, *Erläuterungen*, 144–5.

68 *Neues Deutschland*, 15 February 1978.

69 Jochen Schmidt, *Frankfurter Allgemeine Zeitung*, 14 March 1979.

70 Gerd Vielhaber, *Der Tagesspiegel*, 13 April 1979.

71 Heinz Klunker, *Deutsches Allgemeines Sonntagsblatt*, 7 January 1979.

72 Werner Schulze-Reimpell, *Stuttgarter Zeitung*, 19 March 1979.

73 Horst Ziermann, *Die Welt*, 13 March 1979.

74 Jochen Schmidt, *Frankfurter Allgemeine Zeitung*, 14 March 1979.

75 The production did have its defenders, notably Peter Iden: "Seine [Schaaf's] Kleist-Inszenierung ist die sinnreichste Aufführung eines alten Textes in dieser Spielzeit" (*Frankfurter Rundschau*, 14 March 1979) and Gerd Vielhaber: "In dieser schönsten Käthchen-Inszenierung, deren ich mich erinnere, atmet der ganze Kleist" (*Der Tagesspiegel*, 13 April 1979).

76 Rolf Michaelis, *Die Zeit*, 16 March 1979.

77 Cf "Eric Wonder … baute für Kleists großes historisches Ritterstück … so ausladende … Szenerie, daß das Spiel sich darin kümmerlich verlor" (Günter Schloz, *Deutsche Zeitung*, 16 March 1979).

78 Cf "Peymanns Stuttgarter Arbeit gilt [Flimm] als vorbildlich" (Heinz Klunker, *Deutsches Allgemeines Sonntagsblatt*, 4 November 1979).

79 Quoted in a review by Otto F. Riewoldt, *Vorwärts*, 25 October 1979.

80 Horst Ziermann, *Die Welt*, 8 October 1979.

81 "Flimm stellt alle Wirkung ganz auf die Sprache ab" (Ziermann). "Zum erstenmal in einer Klassikeraufführung seit langem hört man den Sinn der Worte und ihren Klang, ihre Intelligenz und ihre Musikalität" (Benjamin Heinrichs, *Die Zeit*, 12 October 1979).

82 Heinrich Vormweg, *Süddeutsche Zeitung*, 11 October 1979.

83 Clara Menck, *Frankfurter Allgemeine Zeitung*, 18 November 1980.

84 Peter Iden, *Frankfurter Rundschau*, 14 November 1979.

85 Eric Rohmer, quoted in a review by Georg Hensel, *Frankfurter Allgemeine Zeitung*, 17 November 1979.

86 P.M., *Le Figaro*, 16 November 1979. Cf "Sa [Rohmer's] mise en scène est d'un amateurisme d'autant plus déconcertant qu'il se perd dans le beau et dans le luxe" (Colette Godard, *Le Monde*, 13 November 1979).

87 H. Lehmann, *Badische Neueste Nachrichten*, 18 December 1979. Rather than following the usual practice of cutting sections to render the drama more stageworthy, Wendt lengthened *Käthchen* by adding Kunigunde's "Putzmonolog" from the *Phöbus* fragment (1: 900–3). Cf Charlotte Nennecke, *Süddeutsche Zeitung*, 15/16 December 1979.

88 Ernst Wendt, quoted by Charlotte Nennecke.

89 Quoted in a review by Georg Hensel for the *Frankfurter Allgemeine Zeitung*, 18 December 1979.

90 Peter Iden, *Frankfurter Rundschau*, 20 December 1979. Cf also: "Ja, das Wunder dieser Begegnung [dream experience] wurde in Wendts Inszenierung glaubhaft" (Klaus Colberg, *Mannheimer Morgen*, 20 December 1979).

91 Dietmar N. Schmidt, *Stuttgarter Nachrichten*, 19 December 1979.

92 Roberto De Monticelli, *Corriere della Sera*, 30 April 1981. All subsequent references to Castri's Milan staging I shall draw from this review.

93 Gertrud Waldecker, *Badische Neueste Nachrichten*, 20 October 1981.

94 Albrecht Götze, *Zeitmagazin*, 18 December 1981.

95 Rolf Michaelis, *Die Zeit*, 25 December 1981.

96 Almost all these negative criticisms, however, are contradicted by the enthusiastic reviews. For example, Helmut A. Lange (*Schwäbische Zeitung*, 28 December 1981) wrote: "[Beauvais] nahm das Traumwandlerische und Märchenhafte, das Gefühlsverwirrende und Romantisierende ganz ernst, ohne viel daran herumzudeuteln, und ließ so die dem Stück eigene Märchen- und Wunder-Logik in sich schlüssig und glaubhaft erscheinen, von Kleists poetischer Sprachkraft überstrahlt."

97 gam, *Schwäbisches Tagblatt*, 12 February 1982.

98 Gerhard Jörder, *Badische Zeitung*, 26 April 1982.

99 Gerhard Stadelmaier, *Stuttgarter Zeitung*, 26 April 1982.

100 *Weser-Kurier*, 24 March 1986.

101 Jan Bielicki, *Süddeutsche Zeitung*, 13 November 1986.
102 *Der Bund*, 12 September 1987.
103 *Schwäbische Zeitung*, 17 October 1987.
104 "Mitteilungen aus meinem Tagebuch [Rom, 21 February 1845]: Gedanken beim Wiederlesen des Käthchen von Heilbronn." In Sembdner, *Heinrich von Kleists Nachruhm*, 426.

CHAPTER SIX

1 Fraude, *Kleists "Hermannsschlacht,"* 12.
2 Treitschke, "Heinrich von Kleist," 616–18.
3 Feodor Wehl, quoted in Kühn, *Kleist*, 93.
4 Fraude, *Kleists "Hermannsschlacht,"* 23. Fraude is my main source for descriptions of nineteenth-century adaptations.
5 Eduard Devrient, quoted in Fraude, *Kleists "Hermannsschlacht,"* 24.
6 Many have assumed incorrectly – cf *Kindlers Literatur-Lexikon*, 4378, or *Encyclopedia of World Drama*, 481 – that the Detmolder Hoftheater in Pyrmont and Münster offered the *première* in 1839. However, according to Sembdner, the play here produced, although having the identical title, was a "geschichtliche[s] Schauspiel" by Johanna Franul von Weißenthurn (Kleist, *Sämtliche Werke*, 1: 942).
7 Quoted in Fraude, *Kleists "Hermannsschlacht,"* 25. Subsequent reviews of the *première* are also cited from Fraude.
8 Bogumil Dawison, quoted in Fraude, *Kleists "Hermannsschlacht,"* 34.
9 Fraude, *Kleists "Hermannsschlacht,"* 34.
10 Ibid., 35.
11 Quoted in Fraude, *Kleists "Hermannsschlacht,"* 45.
12 Quoted from Fontane's review of Hein's production for the Berlin Schauspielhaus of 19 January 1875. *Sämtliche Werke: Aufsätze*, 2: 200–4.
13 This reference and the three following are taken from theatre reviews kindly provided by the Schiller-Nationalmuseum Deutsches Literaturarchiv, Marbach a.N. Unfortunately, the newspapers' names and dates have been lost.
14 Reichsamtsleiter Stang, *Königsberger Allgemeine Zeitung*, 2 December 1934.
15 Hans Frank, *Kleist. Ein vaterländisches Spiel*, quoted in Busch, *Imperialistische ... Rezeption*, 80.
16 *Stuttgarter Tageblatt*, 6 November 1933.
17 Faßbinder, *Heinrich von Kleist*, 40f.
18 Hoppe, "Die Staatsauffassung," 52.
19 Cf Atkins, *German Literature*, 55.
20 Quirin Engasser, *Völkischer Beobachter*, 30 January 1935.

21 Cf "Seitdem die Hitlerfaschisten in gleicher Weise verfahren sind, um ihrem Eroberungskrieg einen Vorwand zu schaffen, seit dem Fall Gleiwitz und der Bombardierung von Freiburg im Breisgau durch deutsche Flugzeuge sind derartige Handlungen [Hermann's tactic of having his own men dressed as Romans plunder German villages] selbst als poetische Möglichkeiten unerträglich geworden" (Streller, *Das dramatische Werk*, 183).

22 *Völkischer Beobachter*, quoted in Rühle, *Theater für die Republik*, 823. All subsequent references to this production are drawn from this review.

23 Carl Weichardt, *Berliner Morgen Post*, 25 October 1934. The following quotations referring to this staging are from this review.

24 *Nachtausgabe*, 24 October 1934.

25 Victor Weimer, *Sonntag* (Wochenzeitung für Kultur, Politik und Unterhaltung), 11 August 1957. Unless I have indicated otherwise, additional references are also taken from this article.

26 Quoted in a review of the 1982 Bochum production of *Die Hermannsschlacht* by C. Bernd Sucher for the *Süddeutsche Zeitung*, 12 November 1982.

27 Ingeborg Schader, *Stuttgarter Nachrichten*, 12 November 1982.

28 Hellmuth Karasek, *Der Spiegel*, 15 November 1982. This would appear to be the official political tag applied to Peymann since it appears in only a slightly modified form in Hannes Schmidt's review for the *Rhein-Neckar-Zeitung* of 20/21 November 1982: "Claus Peymann, der engagierteste linke Flügelmann unter den westdeutschen Regisseuren."

29 Hannes Schmidt, *Rhein-Neckar-Zeitung*, 20/21 November 1982.

30 Jochen Schmitt-Sasse, *die tat*, 21 January 1983. According to Walter Schulze-Reimpell (*Rheinischer Merkur*, 19 November 1982): "Ähnlich wie in seiner *Tasso*-Inszenierung nimmt Peymann die Dialoge vom klassischen Kothurn einer gesteigerten Kunstsprache und läßt sie in alltäglichem Parlando pointieren."

31 Quoted in an article by Matthias Matussek from the magazine *Stern*, 4 November 1982.

32 Georg Hensel, *Frankfurter Allgemeine Zeitung*, 12 November 1982.

33 Schmitt-Sasse. Günter Grack also refers to "einem kämpferischen Antikolonialismus unserer Tage" in his review for the *Tagesspiegel* (12 November 1982).

34 Cf "Wohl verlockt Peymanns Inszenierung zu zeitgenössischen Assoziationen – aber sie verfällt ihnen nicht" (Benjamin Heinrichs, *Die Zeit*, 19 November 1982).

35 Peter Iden, *Frankfurter Rundschau*, 16 November 1982.

36 Quoted in Kleist, *Sämtliche Werke*, 1: 943–4.

37 I have dealt with this aspect in greater detail in *In Pursuit*, 23–111.

38 One reviewer, Heinz Klunker, was reminded of *"Slow-motion-Sequenzen aus japanischen Samurai-Filmen"* (*Deutsches Allgemeines Sonntagsblatt*, 21 November 1982).

39 Cf also Roesner.

40 *Badische Zeitung*, 19 November 1982. This was the only decidedly negative review of Peymann's production.

41 Jürgen Beckelmann, *Stuttgarter Zeitung*, 25 May 1983.

42 Günter Engler provided these summaries in his article for the *Mannheimer Morgen*, 9 November 1983.

43 *Budapester Rundschau*, 13 February 1984. The phrase "die deutsche Misere" the reviewer also borrowed from Brecht, specifically from his adaptation of J.M.R. Lenz's *Der Hofmeister* in which he attacked the ethical and social wretchedness of Germany's past. Pierre Marcabru (*Le Figaro*, 1 March 1984) also attributes a Brechtian influence to Peymann in that he demonstrates "l'envers de l'idéalisme et la dérision qui s'y cache."

44 Rüdiger Krohn, *Badische Neueste Nachrichten*, 21 March 1985.

45 After the success of the Bochum production, Voss was voted actor of the year for his portrayal of Hermann and, according to Karin Kathrein, he subsequently became "[die] bejubelt[e] Super-Nova des Burgtheaters," a status again in part attributable to his interpretation of the "Fürst der Cherusker."

46 Sammons, "Rethinking Kleist's *Hermannsschlacht*."

47 Wickert, *Das verlorene heroische Zeitalter*; Loose, *Kleists "Hermannsschlacht"*; Reeve, *In Pursuit*.

48 Kittler, *Die Geburt des Partisanen*, 15. If one were to examine the numerous reviews of Peymann's production, one could easily arrive at Kittler's concluding statement: "Dieses Stück, von dem Kleist selbst sagte, er habe es für den Augenblick geschrieben, beschreibt zum ersten Mal die Gestalt des Partisanen, der in der Grenzzone zwischen Krieg und Frieden operiert und der in unseren Tagen anstelle der alten Helden im Schatten des drohenden Völkermords erscheint. Es ist die eine Seite dessen, was Krieg im 20. Jahrhundert heißt. Die andere ist der berechenbare Tod" (404).

## CHAPTER SEVEN

1 For a revealing study of *Prinz Friedrich von Homburg* as a stageworthy masterpiece, see Silz, *Heinrich von Kleist*, chapter VII ("Stagecraft in *Prinz Friedrich von Homburg*"): "From its first line to its last, *Prinz Friedrich von Homburg* is stage drama of the highest order" (223).

2 Ludwig Tieck, "Vorrede zu Kleists *Hinterlassenen Schriften*," quoted in Goldammer, *Schriftsteller über Kleist*, 503.

3 Zimmermann, quoted in Ziegelski, "Kleist im Spiegel," 204.

4 Kleist, *Sämtliche Werke*, 2: 833.

5 Ibid., 2: 871.

6 Quoted in Albrecht, "Kleists *Prinz Friedrich*," 16.

7 Franz Grillparzer, quoted in Kühn, *Kleist und das deutsche Theater*, 72.

8 *Dresdner Abendzeitung*, 4 December 1821.

9 Quoted in Albrecht, "Kleists *Prinz Friedrich*," 16.

10 Ibid., 24.

11 Ibid., 25.

12 Catholy, "Der preußische Hoftheater-Stil," 82.

13 *Vossische Zeitung*, 4 August 1828.

14 Catholy, "Der preußische Hoftheater-Stil," 87.

15 Quoted in Fischer, "Heinrich von Kleist," 460.

16 Quoted in Albrecht, "Kleists *Prinz Friedrich*," 69.

17 Ibid., 71.

18 Ibid., 72.

19 Ibid., 76

20 Cf Catholy, "Der preußische Hoftheater-Stil," 89; Albrecht, "Kleists *Prinz Friedrich*," 83.

21 Albrecht, "Kleists *Prinz Friedrich*," 85.

22 Catholy, "Der preußische Hoftheater-Stil," 89.

23 Fontane, *Sämtliche Werke. Causerien*, 648. In an earlier review of a performance in the Königliches Schauspielhaus (10 October 1876) for the *Vossische Zeitung*, Fontane characterized *Prinz Friedrich* as "das schönste und vollendetste Stück, das uns der unglückliche, an der Zeiten Mißgunst gescheiterte Dichter hinterlassen hat" (*Sämtliche Werke. Aufsätze*, 2: 250–1).

24 Cf Catholy, "Der preußische Hoftheater-Stil," 88.

25 Albrecht, "Kleists *Prinz Friedrich*," 90.

26 Ibid., 93.

27 Norbert Falk in a review reprinted in Rühle, *Theater für die Republik*, 615–16.

28 Siegfried Jacobsohn in a review reprinted in Rühle, 617.

29 Kurt Gerlach in *Nationalsozialistische Erziehung*, 1937, quoted in Wulf, *Theater und Film*, 186.

30 Jean de Rigault, *L'Observateur*, quoted in Richardson, 140.

31 *Femina Théâtre. Supplément du nouveau femina*, November 1955.

32 Richardson, *Kleist in France*, 145.

33 Cf Reeve, *Georg Büchner*, 73–4.

34 René Drommert, *Hamburger Anzeiger*, 16 June 1953.

35  Klarmann, "Kleist und die Gegenwart," 230.
36  *Stuttgarter Zeitung*, 15 November 1960.
37  *Stuttgarter Nachrichten*, 4 April 1961.
38  *Stuttgarter Nachrichten*, 19 September 1966.
39  E. Hennemann-Bayer, *Schwarzwälder Bote*, 21 September 1966.
40  Richard Biedrzynski, *Stuttgarter Zeitung*, 19 September 1966.
41  Kurt Honolka, *Stuttgarter Nachrichten*, 19 September 1966.
42  Reported in *Die Welt*, 11 September 1969.
43  Quoted in *Ludwigsburger Kreiszeitung*, 10 February 1971, from the *NVA Wochenzeitung*.
44  Wilhelm Ringelband, *Stuttgarter Nachrichten*, 5 November 1971.
45  Crosby, "Regie as Interpretation," 245.
46  Roland H. Wiegenstein, *Frankfurter Rundschau*, 11 September 1972.
47  Wiegenstein, "Der Widerspruch," 71.
48  Crosby, "Regie as Interpretation," 246.
49  Gunter Grack, *Der Tagesspiegel*, 22 May 1975.
50  Sibylle Wirsing, *Frankfurter Allgemeine Zeitung*, 5 June 1975.
51  Carl J. Becher, *Neue Zürcher Zeitung*, 14/15 March 1976.
52  Mel Gussow, *New York Times*, 1 November 1976.
53  Cf "Indeed, after an adaptation of this production [Chelsea Theater Center staging] was carried over the Public Television Network in April of 1977, an audience for Kleist's final play was created which – at least in theory – probably outnumbered the cumulative total of 'live' spectators who have viewed the play in the theater during the last century!" (Crosby, "Regie as Interpretation," 244).
54  Cf Brecht, "Über Kleists Stück," 612–3.
55  Günter Zehm, *Die Welt*, 8 March 1978: "Es soll wohl eine Anspielung auf die norddeutschen Kartoffelsteppen sein, aber der Witz bleibt dunkel, wie so vieles bei Karge/Langhoff."
56  Dietmar N. Schmidt, *Schwäbisches Tagblatt*, 11 March 1978.
57  Gunter Zehm, *Die Welt*, 8 March 1978.
58  Karin Kathrein, *Die Presse*, 30 May 1978.
59  Karin Kathrein, *Die Presse*, 8 May 1978. All subsequent references will be drawn from this review.
60  *Kronenzeitung* as quoted in *Neues Deutschland*, 9 May 1978.
61  Karin Kathrein, *Die Presse*, 8 May 1978.
62  Ibid.
63  Hannelore Kubelka, *Neues Deutschland*, 9 May 1978.
64  Further evidence of the great variety of interpretations inspired by *Prinz Friedrich* was provided in January of the same year when Dietrich Taube staged a production for Mainz, "die in sparsamster Dekoration nur auf das Wort gestellt ist," but which alluded to the *fall* of the Third Reich: "Doch der Adler [a stone eagle on stage for the first

scene] vor weißem Feld auf der im übrigen in strengem Schwarz ausgehängten Bühne ... ist beschädigt, eine Flügelspitze hängt angebrochen herab, nicht Sieg, sondern ein letztlich böses Ende, Untergang verheißend, das Anno 1947 auch formal eintrat" (*Frankfurter Rundschau*, 23 January 1979).

65 Pierre Marcabru, *Le Figaro*, 16 July 1979.

66 Bruno Villien, *Le Nouvel Observateur*, 23 July 1979.

67 Le Monde, 19 July 1979: "[Bozonnet] était tellement meilleur que cela devait même pour lui en être gênant ... Et cette disparité a fait boiter tout le spectacle."

68 Villien.

69 Ursula Bunk, *Weser-Kurier*, 14 March 1980.

70 Andreas Roßmann, *Der Tagesspiegel*, 16 March 1980.

71 Roßmann. The next quotation is also taken from this review.

72 Agnes Tasnadi, *Budapester Rundschau*, May 1980.

73 Michel Cournot, *Le Monde*, 30 March 1982.

74 Julian Exner, *Der Tagesspiegel*, 5 May 1982.

75 *New Statesman*, 30 April 1982.

76 Irving Wardle, *The Times*, 23 April 1982.

77 *Times Literary Supplement*, 14 May 1982. Cf also: "In London wird jetzt bloß der klassische Fall der preußischen Militärtradition im Dafür und Dawider noch einmal durchgespielt" (Karl Heinz Bohrer, *Frankfurter Allgemeine Zeitung*, 13 May 1982).

78 Stephen Spender, *Times Literary Supplement*, 14 May 1982. The next two quotations are also taken from this review.

79 *Corriere della Sera*, 14 November 1982. In this article, both Walter Pagliaro and Gabriele Lavia were given the opportunity to defend their respective interpretations of *Prinz Friedrich*.

80 Roberto De Monticelli, *Corriere della Sera*, 20 October 1982.

81 From an article written by Walter Pagliaro for the *Corriere della Sera*, 14 November 1982.

82 *Corriere della Sera*, 14 November 1982.

83 Hans-Klaus Jungheinrich, *Frankfurter Rundschau*, 7 September 1982. Jungheinrich summarized Henze's own interpretation of *Prinz von Homburg* in an essay written in 1960 for *Blätter und Bilder*.

84 Gerhard R. Koch, *Frankfurter Allgemeine Zeitung*, 7 September 1982.

85 Jungheinrich. The next quotation has also been taken from this article.

86 Johannes Breckner, *Mannheimer Morgen*, 10 September 1982.

87 Rainer Kerndl, *Neues Deutschland*, 18/19 September 1982. All quotations referring to the Potsdam production are drawn from this review.

88 Reinhard Hübsch, *Badische Zeitung*, 24 September 1982.

89 Gerhard Jörder, *Badische Zeitung*, 27 September 1982.
90 Karin Kathrein, *Die Presse*, 9 August 1983. In her very sarcastic review, Kathrein characterizes Werner's theatrical parody as "das schlechteste Theater, das man sich vorstellen kann."
91 Rudolf Krämer-Badoni, *Die Welt*, 3 December 1983.
92 Michael Skasa, *Süddeutsche Zeitung*, 24/25/26 December 1983.
93 Krämer-Badoni.
94 Hannelore Schlaffer, *Badische Zeitung*, Christmas edition, 1983.
95 *Frankfurter Rundschau*, Christmas, 1983.
96 Cf "Heyme hat sich … bemüht, sich völlig auf die 'sehr klare und als solche ungemein spannende Handlung dieser Kleist-Fabel' zu konzentrieren" (*Stuttgarter Zeitung*, 21 December 1983).
97 Skasa. Similarly, Wolfgang Ignée poses the rhetorical question: "War's die Unerfahrenheit mit Kleist, der Respekt vor bekannten Vorbildern oder die Furcht vor der eigenen Zukunft, daß es im Stuttgarter *Homburg* nicht zur polemischen Auseinandersetzung mit dem Text, weder zu einer großen Sicht auf ihn und nicht zu seiner Vergegenwärtigung kommt?" (*Stuttgarter Zeitung*, 24 December 1983).
98 Jürgen Holwein, *Stuttgarter Nachrichten*, 24 December 1983.
99 *Stuttgarter Nachrichten*, 22 December 1983.
100 *Neue Zürcher Zeitung*, 29 December 1983.
101 Reinhard Stumm, *Basler Zeitung*, 24 December 1983.
102 Holwein.
103 Schlaffer.
104 When asked by Collette Godard if the TNP version was different from the German, Langhoff responded: " – Complètement. D'abord il y a le temps, six ans ont passé. Le pays, les références. La langue. En allemand, le texte est très simple, les acteurs ont à jouer les mots sans avoir besoin de rien souligner. Les attitudes romantiques viennent naturellement. Les acteurs français ont un chemin à trouver" (*Le Monde*, 10 May 1984).
105 Brigitte Salino, *Les Nouvelles*, 21–27 June 1984.
106 Collette Godard, *Le Monde*, 8 June 1984.
107 Monique Le Roux, *La Quinzaine Littéraire*, 15 July 1984.
108 Godard.
109 Guy Dumur, *Le Nouvel Observateur*, June, 1984.
110 Peter Iden, *Frankfurter Rundschau*, 30 October 1986.
111 Gerhard Ebert, *Neues Deutschland*, 22 April 1987.
112 In contrast, Michael Stone, writing for *Der Tagesspiegel* (25 April 1987), was favourably impressed: "Ein vertracktes Stück, das aber selten so klar, so eindeutig und darum so verständlich in Szene gesetzt wird."
113 Rolf Lehnhardt, *Schwäbische Zeitung*, 2 October 1987.

CHAPTER EIGHT

1 I have described this development in *Georg Büchner*.
2 Claus Peymann and Joachim Kreutzer, "Streitgespräch über Kleists *Hermannsschlacht*," 77–97.
3 Ibid., 93. I used this same dialogue to conclude a short article entitled "The Lion That Squeaked?: Kleist's *Hermannsschlacht* on Stage," 268.

# Works Cited

Albrecht, Egon-Erich. "Heinrich von Kleists *Prinz Friedrich von Homburg* auf der deutschen Bühne." Dissertation, Kiel 1921.

Atkins, H.S. *German Literature through Nazi Eyes.* London: Methuen 1941.

Bab, Julius. *Über den Tag hinaus: Kritische Betrachtungen.* Heidelberg/Darmstadt: Lambert Schneider 1960.

Bentley, Eric. *The Fall of the Amazons.* Newark, Delaware: Proscenium Press 1982.

Brahms, Otto. *Theater, Dramatiker, Schauspieler.* Berlin: Henschel 1961.

Brecht, Berthold. "Über Kleists Stück *Der Prinz von Homburg.*" *Gesammelte Werke in 20 Bänden.* Vol. 9. 612–3. Frankfurt a.M.: Suhrkamp 1968.

Buchtenkirch, Gustav. *Kleists Lustspiel "Der zerbrochene Krug" auf der Bühne.* Heidelberg: Carl Winter 1914.

Busch, Rolf. *Imperialistische und faschistische Kleist-Rezeption 1890–1945.* Frankfurt a.M.: Akademische Verlagsgesellschaft 1974.

Catholy, Eckehard. "Der preußische Hoftheater-Stil und seine Auswirkungen auf die Bühnen-Rezeption von Kleists Schauspiel *Prinz Friedrich von Homburg.*" In *Kleist und die Gesellschaft,* ed. Walter Müller-Seidel, 75–94. Berlin: Erich Schmidt 1965.

Crosby, Donald H. "Regie as Interpretation–Kleist's *Homburg* and *Käthchen* on the Current West German Stage." In *Heinrich von Kleist-Studien,* ed. Alexej Ugrinsky, 243–50. Berlin: Erich Schmidt 1980.

David, Claude. *Kleist und Frankreich.* Berlin: Erich Schmidt 1969.

*Deutsches Bühnen-Jahrbuch: Theatergeschichtliches Jahr- und Adressenbuch.* 1915ff.

Dorr, Rüdiger. *Heinrich von Kleist's [sic] Amphitryon. Deutung und Bühnenschicksal.* Oldenburg: Schulzesche Verlagsbuchhandlung Rudolf Schwartz 1931.

Eisenberg, Ludwig Julius. *Großes biographisches Lexikon der deutschen Bühne im 19. Jahrhundert.* Leipzig: P. List 1903

*Encyclopedia of World Drama.* Vol.2. New York: McGraw-Hill 1972.

Faßbinder, Joseph. *Heinrich von Kleist. Die Hermannsschlacht*. Paderborn: Schöningh/Wien: Beck 1941.

Federn, Karl. *Das Leben Heinrich von Kleists*. Berlin: Brückenverlag 1929.

Fischer, Ernst. "Heinrich von Kleist." In *Heinrich von Kleist. Aufsätze und Essays*, ed. Walter Müller-Seidel, 459–552. Darmstadt: Wissenschaftliche Buchgesellschaft 1967. First appeared in *Sinn und Form* 13 (1961): 759–844.

Fontane, Theodor. *Sämtliche Werke. Causerien über Theater*. Munich: Nymphenburger Verlagshandlung 1964.

– *Sämtliche Werke: Aufsätze. Kritiken. Erinnerungen*. Vol. 2. Munich: Hanser 1969.

Fraude, Otto. *Heinrich von Kleists "Hermannsschlacht" auf der deutschen Bühne*. Leipzig: Spamersche Buchdruckerei 1919.

Goethe, Johann Wolfgang von. *Goethes Briefe*, ed. Bodo Morawe. Vol. 3. Hamburg: Christian Wegener 1965.

Goldammer, Peter, ed. *Schriftsteller über Kleist*. Berlin/Weimar: Aufbau 1976.

Grathoff, Dirk. *Erläuterungen und Dokumente. Heinrich von Kleist: Das Käthchen von Heilbronn*. Stuttgart: Reclam 1977.

Harden, Maximilian. "The Genius of Max Reinhardt." In *Max Reinhardt and his Theater*, ed. Oliver M. Sayer, 209–48. New York: Brentano's 1926.

Hensel, Georg. *Kritiken. Ein Jahrzehnt Sellner-Theater in Darmstadt*. Darmstadt: Reba 1962.

Hilpert, Heinz. *Gedanken zum Theater*. Göttingen: Hainbund 1951.

– *Liebe zum Theater*. Stuttgart: Ernst Battenberg 1965.

Hoppe, Alfred. "Die Staatsauffassung Heinrich von Kleists." Dissertation Bonn 1938.

Jacobsohn, Siegfried. *Jahre der Bühne*. Reinbek b. Hamburg: Rowohlt 1965.

*Kindlers Literatur-Lexikon*. Ed. Wolfgang von Einsiedler. Vol. 5. Zürich: Kindler 1970.

Kirchbach, Wolfgang. *Bühne und Welt*. 1 December edition, 1899. Quoted in Rüdiger Dorr. *Heinrich von Kleist's "Amphitryon". Deutung und Bühnengeschichte*. Oldenburg: Schulzesche Verlagsbuchhandlung Rudolf Schwartz 1931.

Kittler, Wolf. *Die Geburt des Partisanen aus dem Geist der Poesie*. Freiburg: Rombach 1987.

Klarmann, Adolf D. "Kleist und die Gegenwart." In *Festschrift für Detlev W. Schumann*, ed. Albert R. Schmitt, 230–45. Munich: Delp 1970.

Kleist, Heinrich von. *Sämtliche Werke und Briefe*, ed. Helmut Sembdner. 2 vols. Munich: Hanser 1984.

Kosch, Wilhelm. *Deutsches Theater-Lexikon: Biographisches und bibliographisches Handbuch*. Halle: Niemeyer 1927ff.

Kühn. W. *Kleist und das deutsche Theater*. Munich: Hans Sachs 1912.

*Kurschners Biographisches Theater-Handbuch: Schauspiel, Oper, Film, Rundfunk, Deutschland; Österreich*. Berlin: de Gruyter 1956.

Loose, Hans-Dieter. *Kleists Hermannsschlacht*. Karlsruhe: von Loeper 1984.

Lowien, Kurt. "Die Bühnengeschichte von Kleists *Penthesilea*." Dissertation Kiel 1923.

Luft, Friedrich. *Berliner Theater 1945–1961*. Hannover: E. Friedrich 1961.

Mann, Thomas. *"Amphitryon* – Eine Wiedereroberung." Reprinted in *Heinrich von Kleist. Aufsätze und Essays*, ed. Walter Müller-Seidel, 51–88. Darmstadt: Wissenschaftliche Buchgesellschaft 1967.

Michaelis, Rolf. *Heinrich von Kleist.* Friedrichs Dramatiker des Welttheaters. Velber bei Hannover: Friedrich 1965.

Müller-Seidel, Walter, ed. *Heinrich von Kleist. Aufsätze und Essays*. Darmstadt: Wissenschaftliche Buchgesellschaft 1967.

– *Versehen und Erkennen. Eine Studie über Heinrich von Kleist*. Cologne: Böhlau 1961.

*Neuer Theater-Almanach: Theatergeschichtliches Jahr- und Adressenbuch.* 1890–1914. (continued as *Deutsches Bühnen-Jahrbuch* from 1915)

Peymann, Claus & Kreutzer, Joachim. "Streitgespräch über Kleists *Hermannsschlacht*." *Kleist-Jahrbuch 1984*. Berlin: Erich Schmidt 1984: 77–97.

Reeve, William C. *Georg Büchner*. New York: Ungar 1979.

– *In Pursuit of Power: Heinrich von Kleist's Machiavellian Protagonists*. Toronto: University of Toronto Press 1987.

– "The Lion That Squeaked?: Kleist's *Hermannsschlacht* on Stage." *Seminar* 23 (1987): 265–69.

Richardson, F.C. *Kleist in France*. Chapel Hill: University of North Carolina Press 1962.

Rühle, Günther. *Theater für die Republik*. Frankfurt a.M.: Fischer 1967.

Ruppel, K.H. *Großes Berliner Theater*. Hannover: Erhard Friedrich 1962.

Sammons, Jeffrey L. "Rethinking Kleist's *Hermannsschlacht*." In *Heinrich von Kleist-Studien*, ed. Alexij Urginsky, 33–40. Berlin: Erich Schmidt 1981.

Sauer, Kurt. "Heinrich von Kleists *Familie Schroffenstein* auf der deutschen Bühne." Dissertation Munich 1925.

Schmidinger, Liselotte. "Kleist und das Burgtheater." Dissertation Munich 1945.

Scheider, Irmela. "Aktualität im historischen Gewand. Zu Filmen nach Werken von Heinrich von Kleist." In *Literaturverfilmungen*, ed. Franz-Josef Albermeier and Volker Roloff, 99–121. Frankfurt am Main: Suhrkamp 1989.

Sembdner, Helmut. "Der *zerbrochene Krug* in Goethes Inszenierung." In *In Sachen Kleist*, ed. Helmut Sembdner, 57–67. Munich: Hanser 1974.

– *Heinrich von Kleists Nachruhm*. Vol. 2. Frankfurt a.M.: Insel 1984.

Silz, Walter. *Heinrich von Kleist*. Philadelphia: University of Philadelphia Press 1961.

Stolze, Reinhold. *Kleists "Käthchen von Heilbronn" auf der deutschen Bühne*. Berlin 1923 and Nendeln/Lichtenstein: Kraus Reprint 1967.

Streller, Siegfried. *Das dramatische Werk Heinrich von Kleists*. Berlin: Rütten & Loening 1966.

Syberberg, Hans Jürgen. *Kleist. Penthesilea*. Berlin: Edition Hentrick 1988.

Treitschke, Heinrich von. "Heinrich von Kleist." *Preußische Jahrbücher* 2 (1858): 616–8.

Wickert, Gabriele M. *Das verlorene heroische Zeitalter*. Bern/Frankfurt a.M./ New York: Lang 1983.

Wiegenstein, Roland H. "Der Widerspruch des *Prinzen von Homburg*. Zu zwei Berliner Inszenierungen." *Merkur* 27 (1973): 63–72.

Wittkowski, Wolfgang. "The New Prometheus: Molière's and Kleist's *Amphitryon*." *Comparative Literature Studies* 8 (1971): 109–24.

Wulf, Joseph. *Theater und Film im Dritten Reich*. Gütersloh: Sigbert Mohn 1964.

Ziegelski, H. "Kleist im Spiegel der Theater-Kritik des 19. Jahrhunderts bis zu den Aufführungen der Meininger." Dissertation Erlangen 1932.

# Newspapers and
# Magazines Cited

Abend Zeitung
Allgemeine Deutsche Theater Zeitung
Allgemeine Preußische Zeitung
Allgemeine Theater Chronik (Leipzig)
Allgemeine Zeitung (Munich)
Badische Neueste Nachrichten
Badische Zeitung
Basler Zeitung
Bayern Kurier
Berliner Börsen Courier
Berliner Morgenblatt, Das
Berliner Morgen Post
Berliner Rundschau
Berliner Tageblatt
Breslauer Theater-Nachrichten
Budapester Rundschau
Buffalo Courier-Express
Bund, Der
Corriere della Sera
Daily Telegraph
Deutsche Illustrierte Zeitung
Deutsches Allgemeines Sonntagsblatt
Deutsche Theater Zeitung
Deutsche Volkszeitung/die tat
Deutsche Wochen-Zeitung
Deutsche Zeitung
Dresdner Abendzeitung
Dresdner Neueste Nachrichten
Femina Théâtre

Figaro, Le
France observateur
Frankfurter Allgemeine Zeitung
Frankfurter Rundschau
Furche, Die
Gießener Allgemeine
Grätzer Zeitung
Grenzbote
Hamburger Anzeiger
Journal de Paris
Journal des débats
Junge Welt
Kieler Nachrichten
kleine Bund, Der
Kölnische Zeitung
Königsberger Allgemeine Zeitung
Kreuz Zeitung
Kronenzeitung
Leipziger Tageblatt und Anzeiger
Ludwigsburger Kreiszeitung
Manchester Guardian
Mannheimer Morgen
Mecklenburger Tageblatt
Meininger Tageblatt
Monde, Le
Morgenblatt, Das
Münchener Neueste Nachrichten
Münchener Theater-Journal
Münchner Zeitung

Nachtausgabe
National Zeitung
Neue Freie Presse
Neue Preußische Zeitung
Neues Deutschland
Neue Zürcher Zeitung
New Statesman
New York Times
Nordwest Zeitung
Nouvelles, Les
Nouvelles Littéraires, Les
Nouvel Observateur, Le
Österreichische Annalen der Literatur
   und Kunst des In- und Auslandes
Österreichische Beobachter, Der
Prager Presse
Prager Tageblatt
Presse, Die
Privilegierte, wöchentliche,
gemeinnützige Nachrichten von und
für Hamburg
Quinzaine Littéraire, La
Repubblica, La
Rheinischer Merkur
Rheinisch-Westphälische Anzeiger, Der
Rhein-Neckar-Zeitung
Rheinpfalz, Die
Saarbrücker Zeitung
Sammler, Der
Schlesische Zeitung
Schwäbisches Tagblatt
Schwäbische Zeitung
Schwarzwälder Bote

Sonntag
Spiegel, Der
Stampa, La
Stern
Stuttgarter Morgenblatt
Stuttgarter Nachrichten
Stuttgarter Tageblatt
Stuttgarter Zeitung
Süddeutsche Zeitung
Südwest Kreiszeitung
Sunday Times, The
Tagesspiegel, Der
Tägliche Rundschau
tat, die
Theater Nachrichten
Theaterzeitung
Times Literary Supplement, The
Times, The
Unsere Zeit
Völkische Beobachter, Der
Volkszeitung
Vorwärts
Vossische Zeitung
Weimarische Zeitung
Welt, Die
Weltwoche, Die
Weser-Kurier
Wiener Allgemeine Theaterzeitung
Wiener Zeitung
Wilhelmshavener Zeitung
Zeit, Die
Zeitmagazin
Zeitung für die elegante Welt

# Audio-Visual Material

For a listing of filmed versions of Kleist's plays (and other works), consult:
Klaus Kanzog, "Heinrich von Kleist und der Film. Eine Bibliographie," in
*Erzählstrukturen – Filmstrukturen. Erzählungen Heinrich von Kleists und ihre filmische Realisation*, ed. Klaus Kanzog (Berlin: Erich Schmidt 1981) 142–172.
For cinematic interpretations of the eighties see:
Irmela Schneider, "Aktualität im historischen Gewand. Zu Filmen nach
Werken von Heinrich von Kleist," in *Literaturverfilmungen*, ed. Franz-Josef
Albersmeier and Volker Roloff (Frankfurt a.M.: Suhrkamp 1989) 99–121.

### A SELECT BIBLIOGRAPHY OF VIDEO CASSETTES OF KLEIST'S DRAMAS

*Amphitryon*
– Regie: Reinhold Schünzel. Ein deutsches 'Musical' (Spielfilm nach dem
gleichnamigen Lustspiel). Duisburg: Atlas Videothek o.J. (Die großen
Klassiker des deutschen Films). VHS. 22125. 104 Min. s/w.

*Die Familie Schroffenstein*
– Buch und Regie: Hans Neuenfels. Fernsehspiel nach dem Trauerspiel
von Heinrich von Kleist. (Die aktuelle Inszenierung) VHS. ZDF 29.5.1984.
130 Min.

*Die Hermannsschlacht*
– Bearbeitung und Regie: Claus Peymann. Aufführung aus dem Schauspielhaus Bochum (Die aktuelle Inszenierung). VHS. ZDF 15.5.1984. 135 Min.

*Das Käthchen von Heilbronn*
– Regie: Peter Beauvais. Fernsehspiel nach Heinrich von Kleist. VHS.
25.12.1981. 118 Min.
– Inszenierung: Fritz Bennewitz. Eine Aufführung des National-Theaters
Weimar. o.O.: Toppic o.J. VHS. 96702. 93 Min. Farbe.

- Regie: Jürgen Flimm. Fernsehaufzeichnung einer Aufführung des Schauspielhauses Köln. VCR–L. ZDF 16.11.1980. 155 Min.
- Regie: Cesare Lievi. Eine Aufführung des Theater Basel. (Schauspiel im ZDF.) VHS. ZDF 15.5.1990. 160 Min.
- Die deutsche Theaterlandschaft und Versuche, sie zu verändern. Klassiker sind nicht heilig. Claus Peymann spricht über seine Inszenierung des *Käthchens von Heilbronn*; Peter Stein kommentiert seine Interpretation des *Prinzen von Homburg*; mit zahlreichen Szenen aus beiden Inszenierungen. VCR–L. S3 (NDR) 16.8.1979. 50 Min.

*Penthesilea*
- Buch und Regie: Hans Neuenfels. Heinrich Penthesilea von Kleist. Träumerien über eine Inszenierung. VHS. ZDF 9.10.1984. 140 Min.

*Prinz Friedrich von Homburg*
- Regie: Fritz Bornemann. Fernsehinszenierung aus der DDR. VHS. S3 (SDR) 12.2.1990. 110 Min.
- Regie: Jaroslav Chundela. Hessisches Staatstheater Wiesbaden. Held und Antiheld. Einblick in zwei Inszenierungen (Goethes *Egmont*, Schauspiel, Frankfurt 1986) Theatertreff im ZDF. VHS. ZDF 20.1.1988. 125 Min.
- Regie: Peter Stein. Eine Aufführung der Schaubühne am Halleschen Ufer, Berlin. Prod.: SFB/ORF VHS. 27.7.1991. 140 Min.
- Über Peter Steins *Prinz Friedrich von Homburg*. Schaubühne am Halleschen Ufer, Berlin. Theater von heute. 1. Regie-Ideen, Regie Stile. VHS. 420069. 26 Min. Farbe.
- Die deutsche Theaterlandschaft und Versuche, sie zu verändern. Klassiker sind nicht heilig. Peter Stein kommentiert seine Interpretation des *Prinzen von Homburg*; Claus Peymann spricht über seine Inszenierung des *Käthchens von Heilbronn*; mit zahlreichen Szenen aus beiden Inszenierungen. VCR–L. S3(NDR) 16.8.1979. 50 Min.

*Der zerbrochene Krug*
- Regie: Hans Lietzau. Eine Aufführung des Schloßpark-Theaters in Berlin. VCR-L. DFS (SFB) 6.9.1980. 105 Min.
- Regie: Heinz Schirk. Fernsehbearbeitung. VHS. EDF(HR) 6.1.1991. 120 Min.
- Regie: Gustav Ucicky. Spielfilm nach der gleichnamigen Komödie. Duisburg: Atlas Videothek o.J. (Die großen Klassiker des deutschen Films). VHS. 22128. 85 Min. s/w
- Inter Nationes Videokassette, forthcoming.

A SELECT BIBLIOGRAPHY OF
SOUND RECORDINGS OF
KLEIST'S DRAMAS

Deutsches Theater. Höhepunkte der Schauspielkunst. Königsdorf: Delta Music 1984

3 Schallplatten/Kassette C 50075 (contains material featuring Paul Wegener and Friedrich Kayßler from *Prinz Friedrich von Homburg* and Emil Jannings and Max Gülstorff from *Der zerbrochene Krug*).

"Ist es ein Traum? Ein Traum, was sonst?" Szenen aus *Amphitryon, Prinz Friedrich von Homburg, Das Käthchen von Heilbronn*. Regie: Ernst Ginsberg. Interpr.: Thomas Holtzmann, Liselotte Rau etc. Hamburg: Deutsche Grammophon/Polydor 1966, 1980. Kassetten-Tonband (Compact) 3321 108. 51 Min.

Von Kainz bis Heinz. 100 Jahre Deutsches Theater Berlin. Berlin: VEB Deutsche Schallplatten o.J. 4 Schallplatten/Kassetten 860 338–341. (contains material featuring Emil Jannings and Max Gülstorff from *Der zerbrochene Krug* and Paul Wegener and Friedrich Kayßler from *Prinz Friedrich von Homburg*).

*Amphitryon*
– Teil I and II, Deutsche Literatur, "Die große Szene" 1/1–412/76/546301 Inter Nationes (reel to reel).

*Das Käthchen von Heilbronn*
– Hans Pfitzner, Musik zu Heinrich von Kleists *Käthchen von Heilbronn* für Orchester. Op. 17. Wiener Philharmoniker: Dir. Hans Pfitzner. Urania, URLP 7050.

*Penthesilea*
– Deutsche Literatur: "Die große Szene", Bestell-Nr. 32279. Inter Nationes (cassette).
– Othmar Schoeck, Oper in 1. Aufzug nach Kleist
  (i) Kölnisches Radio-Symphonie Orchester, Dir. Zdenek, BASF harmonia mundi 1975: 49–22485–6.
  (ii) O.R.F. Chor und Orchester, Dir. Gerd Albrecht, Pädagog Verl. Schwann Düsseldorf, 95102 (2 LPS).
– Hugo Wolf, Symphonische Dichtung für großes Orchester nach dem gleichnamigen Trauerspiel Heinrich von Kleists komponiert.
  (i) Wiener Philharmoniker: Dir. Otto Gerdes, DG 2726067.
  (ii) Orchestre de la Suisse Romande: dir. Horst Stein, Teldec SXL 6985 AW.

*Prinz Friedrich von Homburg*
– Aussschnitte. Deutsche Literatur, "Die große Szene", Inter Nationes, 1/2–431/71/5300/1 (reel to reel)
– Regie und Aufnahmeleitung: Peter Stein. Aufnahme der Aufführung der Berliner Schaubühne, November 1972. Interpr.: Peter Lühr, Katharina Tüschen etc. Deutsche Grammophon/Polydor Kassette mit 3 Platten. 2750005.
– Hans Werner Henze, Oper in 3 Akten nach dem Schauspiel von Heinrich von Kleist, für Musik eingerichtet von Ingeborg Bachmann, Norddeutscher Rundfunk, Hamburg. Bandaufnahme.

*Der zerbrochene Krug*
- Regie: Lina Carstens. Ausschnitte/Szenen. Ariola-Eurodisc 26345 W.
- Regie: Heinz Schimmelpfennig, Interpr.: Lina Carstens, Eva-Ingeborg Scholz, Kurt Ehrhardt, Walter Richter, Günther Lüders. Athena 51003x 1977. Also available on Eurodisc/Wort 89140xDW or Ariola-Eurodisc xD89140w 2 Schallplatten/Kassette.
- Interview mit Berthold Viertel über die Inszenierung *Der zerbrochene Krug* von Heinrich von Kleist in Salzburg. Sprecher: Werner Hinz. München: Sellmaier o.J. Schallplatte.
- Große deutsche Schauspieler. Szenen und Monologe. München: Ariola-Eurodisc o.J. 3 Schallplatten/Kassette 26345 XFW.
  contains material featuring Günther Lüders, Walter Richter and Lina Carstens from *Der zerbrochene Krug*).
- Zbyněk Vostřák, Oper nach dem gleichnamigen Lustspiel von Heinrich von Kleist. L.P. Supraphon 92002.

# Index

238    Index

## DATE DUE

| | | | |
|---|---|---|---|
| | | | |
| | | | |
| | | | |
| | | | |
| | | | |
| | | | |
| | | | |
| | | | |
| | | | |
| | | | |
| | | | |
| | | | |
| | | | |
| | | | |
| | | | |
| | | | |
| | | | |
| | | | |
| | | | |
| | | | |
| | | | |
| | | | |

GAYLORD | | | PRINTED IN U.S.A.